MEN WHO SHAPE BELIEF

MEN WHO
SHAPE BELIEF

Major Voices in American Theology

Volume II

DAVID WESLEY SOPER

KENNIKAT PRESS/PORT WASHINGTON, N. Y.

MEN WHO SHAPE BELIEF

Manufactured by Taylor Publishing Company   Dallas, Texas

ESSAY AND GENERAL LITERATURE INDEX REPRINT SERIES

To Marjorie

Fellow journeyer
Fellow sufferer
Friend
"Marriage is one soul in two bodies"

FOREWORD

At the invitation of Principal John Marsh, the substance of these lectures was given on the Oxford University Faculty of Theology — at Mansfield College, during Trinity term, 1954. My admiration and affection are beyond measure for Dr. and Mrs. John Marsh, Dr. and Mrs. Horton Davies, Dr. and Mrs. Eric Routley, and Dr. and Mrs. Will Cadmon, for the stimulating fellowship of the Mansfield Junior Common Room, and for Mr. Buckingham and his staff.

DAVID WESLEY SOPER

CONTENTS

7

INTRODUCTION

*I*t *is important* that the purpose of the following studies be clearly understood. In the book *Major Voices in American Theology* (The Westminster Press, 1953), it was my purpose to present and explain the life and thought of six contemporary leaders. In this volume somewhat briefer accounts of the life and thought of eleven additional "major voices" are given. I have attempted, as honestly and sympathetically as I can, to think *with* each theologian studied, to outline his life, and to listen patiently and thoroughly to his message — to understand him as he understands himself. For this enterprise I have examined with care and love the primary sources only, and in particular the full-length books in which, under a theologian's exclusive authorship, he has presented his thought. Periodical literature, consulted exhaustively, is treated directly in this volume only where an author's book output does not present the full range of his characteristic ideas.

As you read the following pages, one external limitation must in fairness be borne in mind. Since it was our purpose to focus careful attention upon eleven contemporary Americans, available space in a volume of predetermined length required that we include here a meaningful survey of each theologian's life and book production, enriched with an analysis of central ideas, but not an exhaustive summary of his arguments. Since only six men were presented in *Major Voices in American Theology,* a fuller treatment of each man's structure of ideas could be given. It is obvious that ten or twelve volumes would be necessary to give similarly full treatment to sixty or more important theologians now at work in America.

The belief seems justifiable that American students and laymen will read two books rather than ten. The following studies could therefore be little more than half the length of the *Major Voices* presentations. Hence, these treatments are introductions, descriptions of basic directions, outlines of central ideas, not exhaustive summaries — and as such designed to whet the reader's appetite for fuller study. These presentations are neither synthetic nor superficial, but their true character and purpose cannot in fairness be understood unless it is realized that they are, by necessity, synoptic rather than exhaustive. Each study is bifocal: that is, roughly fifty per cent of the space is devoted to the over-all view of a man's life and work; then, in a concluding section, the remaining space examines at closer range the strength of central ideas.

The question will be asked, Why these eleven? In preparing *Major Voices in American Theology* the writer conducted an informal poll among seminary leaders and churchmen about the country from many denominational backgrounds. Twenty-four " major voices " were recommended. The eleven studies in this volume continue the presentation of America's major theologians begun in the preceding book. These thinkers are not " minor prophets." Each name stands in this list because a solid block of contemporary seminary leaders consider him important in his own right and truly representative of a living school of thought, an authentic strand in the present theological tapestry.

The reader will find himself quite out of agreement with some of these contemporaries; they may prove the more stimulating to him on that account. Similarly the reader will not always find himself in sympathy with my interpretations and occasional criticisms of these leaders. It is well to remember that these studies are presented as they appear, after sustained reading and reflection, to one man only. The reader is not only invited, but urged, to enter the conversation as he reads, and to interpret these voices as he must from his own point of view.

It will be noticed that five themes recur again and again in the body of this book: epistemology (in particular, the relation between revelation and reason), the nature and purpose of God, the nature and dilemma of man, the character and goal of the Church, and the structure and *telos* of the world. These themes are treated as they rise in each theologian's sequence of books; not systematically presented (that is, not under headings one, two, three, and four), they are nonetheless always present with varying degrees of emphasis, depending upon each author's particular interests.

The two volumes together neither cover nor uncover contemporary American theology. They do, however, introduce the subject, and attempt to assess, and advance, the unfinished theological conversation in our time.

A CENTRAL TREND:
    GOD, THE LORD OF HISTORY

James Luther Adams

A THEOLOGY OF HISTORY AND HOPE

Theology is constantly filled with surprises, particularly modern American theology. On the one hand it is nothing less than astounding that people who believe in a robust Deity often have no confidence in the success of his enterprise in and with history. On the other hand it is equally astounding that the people who believe strongly in the success of the enterprise often have little confidence in a God big enough for the task he has undertaken. These are inexplicabilities.

I must now record a new surprise — that a liberal theologian is interested not alone in time and history, as you would expect, but also in a God whose purpose and power are sufficient for the success of the undertaking. I find in James Luther Adams a mature and creative theology, which neither dissolves into utopian optimism on the one hand nor evaporates into otherworldliness on the other.

First a look at his life, then at three accents in his theology: Two Necessities — Skepticism and Faith; Time and History Are to Be Taken Seriously; and Fulfillment Is Divine Promise.

UP FROM FUNDAMENTALISM

Theodore Parker once said that the Egyptians required seventy days to make a mummy of a dead man, but Harvard Divinity School could make a mummy of a living man in three years, and Chicago's Meadville Theological Seminary could do it in less.

Whatever the truth of Parker's statement, James Luther Adams is busy making men out of mummies. He is professor of religious ethics on the Federated Theological Faculty of the University of Chicago and at the Meadville Theological School. He is not an embalmer of the living.

Adams was born in 1902, the son of a premillenarian Baptist preacher, otherworldly in theology and not less so in life. One of Adams' earliest memories is family prayer in the midst of a death-dealing dust storm. The father was a circuit-riding evangelist, announcing the imminent Second Coming of Christ; young James often went along with his violin to help with the hymn-singing. At eleven James knew, and accepted, the plan of salvation according to the Scofield Bible. He entered college an enthusiast for religion, and left an enthusiast against it. So ardent was his interest in religion, whether for or against, that it was obvious to all that he was going to be a minister.

He has an A.B. from Minnesota, an S.T.B. and an A.M. from Harvard, and a Ph.D. from Chicago. He studied in Germany and France in 1927, in 1936 and 1938 at Heidelberg, Marburg, Strasbourg, and Paris.

He was minister first at Wellesley, then at Salem, Massachusetts. For a time, as he contemplated leaving the ministry, he was instructor in English at Boston University.

He has been editor of *The Christian Register* and an editor of *The Journal of Liberal Religion*. He has been secretary of the American Theological Society (Midwest branch), chairman of the Independent Voters of Illinois, a member of the Unitarian Commission on Planning and Review, an instructor in the Y.M.C.A.'s Presidents' School at the University of Chicago, and an instructor in the Federal Council's Chicago School on the Church and Economic Life.

He is now vice-president of the Independent Voters of Illinois. He believes every worker in the gospel should at the same time labor in some social organization to create one sane world out of our insane fragments. He is a member of the advisory board of the American Civil Liberties Union (Chicago chapter), a member, along with G. Bromley Oxnam, of the National Advisory Council of Protestants and Other Americans United for the Separation of Church and State, editor of the Phoenix volumes on theology and philosophy of religion, coeditor of *The Journal of Religion,* and participant in the University of Chicago Round Table.

In 1936 and 1938, Adams was in Germany observing the underground movements, interviewing Nazi and anti-Nazi leaders; for a time the Gestapo imprisoned him and withheld his passport. He is genuinely preoccupied with history as God's serious enterprise; continually therefore he has studied at close range the relation between religion and Fascism and the more creative relation between religion and democracy. In 1952, as a member of a study tour of the Middle East (sponsored by the American Christian Palestine Committee), he visited Egypt, Israel, Cyprus, and Greece. During the summer of the same year he was visiting lecturer at Oxford, Cambridge, and Manchester Universities in England, and the new Albert Schweitzer College in Switzerland.

His theme is the application of religion to social life; for this reason he is author or translator of innumerable articles on social ethics, race relations, and the relation of the Church to society. He is best known for his translation of Paul Tillich's *The Protestant Era.* The Tillich point of view, with some important differences, has become his own. He has contributed chapters to many books, but is the author of only one monograph: *The Changing Reputation of Human Nature* (reprinted in slightly revised form from *The Journal of Liberal Religion,* autumn, 1942, and winter, 1943. 5701 Woodlawn Avenue, Chicago). I am deeply indebted to him for his kindness in sending along mimeographed copies of his chapters in books under other editors. What he has to say needs hearing. Excessive humility keeps him grinding out translations of meaningful but esoteric offerings from Europe and elsewhere, rather than speaking from his own mind to ours as one who has authority, and not as the scribes. I hereby petition him and his publishers to set his candle on a candlestick.

His 1953 William Belden Noble Lectures at Harvard will presently be available for all to read. With Hans Gerth and Philip Rieff, he is now editing a series of volumes on the Sociology of Religion and Politics. None has yet appeared, but three or four are in process. In his introduction to Henry Nelson Wieman's *Directive in His-*

tory, Adams rightly classified Wieman's work as social psychology
sicklied over with a pale overcast of theology, but important and
valuable nonetheless for its stress on the reality of process. Wieman's
Directive in History was the first volume in the Phoenix series,
followed by Wilhelm Pauck's *Heritage of the Reformation* and
Charles Hartshorne's *Reality as Social Process*. The fourth volume
in this series, by Fritz Buri, the liberal theologian at Basel, will accent Schweitzer's eschatologism and Tillich's dialectical theory.

He is a young man as theological graybeards go; we should hear
much from him in years to come. The influences in his life in the
order of their appearance are revealing: from the Scofield Bible he
leaped to the scientific humanism of John Dietrich and the anti-
Rotarianism of H. L. Mencken, thence to Irving Babbitt and Paul
Elmer More, and onward through Bach, Von Hügel, Rudolf Otto,
Francis de Sales, Karl Marx, Reinhold Niebuhr, Walter M. Horton,
John C. Bennett, and a Parisian Benedictine monastery, to Tillich.
From inherited and exclusive otherworldliness his pilgrimage has
led him to the reality of the historical process and the creative Power
which directs it.

TWO NECESSITIES: SKEPTICISM AND FAITH

Orthodoxy has always accented faith; liberalism has always accented skepticism. That we ever allowed the two to drift apart is
evidence of our startling irrationality. The idea that either could do
business without the other created fanaticism on the one hand and
futility on the other.

To begin with, orthodoxy (whether " neo " or not so " neo ") is
not primarily a content; it is rather an epistemological method.
Similarly, liberalism is not so much a content; it is rather a method
as well. The method of orthodoxy is faith — in a tradition believed
to embody direct and infallible divine revelation. The method of
liberalism is skepticism — free inquiry, rejection of fiat authority,
a real question and answer (dialectic), a shaking of all foundations
till the truth appears. Either method without the other is sterile;
together both are fruitful. Truth exempt from criticism is in *rigor*

mortis. Criticism alien to affirmation is paralysis. For what reason does skepticism separate wheat from chaff if not that faith may make wheat into bread?

James Luther Adams, a liberal Christian, insists upon both faith and skepticism, with neither undernourished. He is as thoroughgoing a critic of the old liberalism as any man now writing, and for one simple reason: the old liberalism made an infallible dogma out of disbelief; it was allergic to all positive content, all conviction. He is as serious a critic of faith without criticism as of criticism without faith.

In his little book *The Changing Reputation of Human Nature,* Adams has given a careful account of the use and abuse of liberalism in the history of thought — with particular attention to its view of man. Few things in history are fixed, least of all reputations. There is a perennial dissatisfaction with established views, whether orthodox or liberal; a perpetual demand for novelty, though change is not always progress. The generalizations of one period have only a restricted validity in another.

The current revolt against the older liberal estimate of man is partially due to the fact that the so-called Age of Liberalism has reached a terrifying crisis. In every established movement there is resistance to movement; even in liberalism there develops a stultifying conservatism, a resistance to change, a belief in its own infallibility. Too many liberals offer only a static defense of liberalism as the truth once for all delivered to the saints; they have forgotten the meaning of liberalism, dynamic movement — the incompleteness of all things human, liberalism included. On the other hand liberalism's freedom of inquiry and freedom of conscience are permanent necessities — safeguards against fanaticism, obscurantism, and authoritarianism. The older liberalism was skeptical about God but insufficiently skeptical about man. The doctrine of inherent goodness cannot survive the facts of life. The God of older liberalism was exclusively immanent; there was no transcendence, no basis of criticism, no adequate awareness of sin. Where orthodoxy made too much of sin, liberalism made too little.

Adams outlines three rival conceptions of man — two from the

Greek tradition, and one Judaeo-Christian. In Greek thought Apollonian rationalism accented " nothing to excess," the dominion of reason, of form and harmony, the classical spirit; but Dionysian dynamism, also Greek, stressed vitality, movement both creative and destructive, the nonrational, today called the voluntaristic, recognizing tragedy, struggle, contradiction. Thus in Greek thought (also examined with insight in Adams' analysis of the law of nature, *The Journal of Religion,* Vol. XXV, No. 2, April, 1945), reason and process each claimed exclusive hegemony over the life of the world and man. The Judaeo-Christian view was like and unlike both Greek conceptions: it accented forward movement in history against the cyclical view of the Apollonians, but also the tragic sense of life of the Dionysians (the Fall, universal guilt, human rebellion against God, etc.). In Christian thought, tragedy is transcended by a good God and a good creation; in Dionysian thought, tragedy was never transcended; fate was merciless. Judaeo-Christianity held a common love of reason with Greek rationalism; it opposed Dionysian irrationalism and amoralism. In the Middle Ages, Christian thought developed a static rationalism called Thomism, but in modern times has moved beyond it to dynamic rationalism with Tillich.

Modern voluntarism senses keenly the embarrassments of existence, understands the necessity of the existential attitude of decision and commitment. In theology, voluntarism produced the idea of arbitrary divine sovereignty, and in secular affairs, the arbitrary sovereignty of a particular tradition, race, or class. Modern intellectualism (that is, liberalism) arose in reaction to these voluntarist extremes. The Renaissance was antiobscurantist and antiauthoritarian, against both Lutheran and Calvinist excess. Modern liberalism thus developed its two values — freedom of mind and freedom of conscience, a revolt against the Protestant dogma of total depravity, against voluntarism gone to seed. Unitarianism arose in New England where Calvinism was in full dominion, a necessary revolt against Reformation pessimism about man. Unitarianism emphasized a doctrine generic to Christianity but lost in the Reformation, man's reason as a child of God, and the Church as a means, not of exclusion, but of salvation. Indeed, contemporary Protestantism owes primarily to religious liberalism its social emphasis. In time, the prophetic power and purpose of Unitarianism was lost, became static, cognitive, theoretical, neglected emotion and the necessity of decision; this is the meaning of liberalism's decay. The so-called objective scientific method (skepticism) left modern man subjectively decisionless (without faith). Middle-class liberalism simply became accommodation to the world; the necessity of conversion (decision) was replaced by character-building. The whole personality acting for or against God's will was replaced by an exclusive emphasis upon reason. Unitarianism depreciated affective experience, frowned on the use of emotive symbols. Religious liberalism in the name of intellectual integrity neglected deeper levels of human consciousness and of reality itself, and came thus to paralysis — asceticism toward the imagination, indifference to all gripping loyalties. Not to have loyalties was to be a Unitarian. The objective was poise, life at low temperature, bourgeois common sense. Liberalism of mood became liberalism of metaphysic — a new idea of the universe and of man in relation to it. Against this self-sufficient finitude antiliberalism has reacted. Yet antiliberalism is not intended as in any sense a repudiation of human liberation from economic, social, and ecclesiastical tyrannies. "We liberals," says Adams, "are largely an uncommitted and therefore a self-frustrating people" (P. 48). Our task, and the task of the Creator, is not mere enlightenment but also raised affections — vitality and reason together. The creative, redemptive Power is not easily domesticated within present culture, whether orthodox or liberal. All human systems, considered as final, are doomed to be broken open by God. We must preach both the judgment and the love of God, and realize that it is not our wills alone that have acted. The function of a Church is to bring men into communion with a group who are experiencing the divine power of transformation in ethics and in life. Without commitment, enlightenment becomes enfeeblement; without criticism, commitment becomes catastrophe. The constant Creator and Re-creator now broods over the deep, now brings forth new life. Good will is no substitute for intelligent problem-solving, yet man is what he loves.

TIME AND HISTORY ARE TO BE TAKEN SERIOUSLY

Adams believes three movements have characterized his mental and spiritual pilgrimage since graduate school: slow deprovincialization, rapport with the catholic tradition in Christianity, and continuity of interest in the historical process.

In his youth he felt himself a stranger in time, a pilgrim on a foreign strand. More recently, under the influence of Dewey, Whitehead, Tillich, and the Bible, time has become for him the basic reality to God and man. Formerly he thought of salvation as an escape from time; he now envisages salvation as a divine action in and upon time and community, whether here or hereafter. He found in Irving Babbitt and literary humanism a living tradition of spiritual and intellectual heroism, but no historical dynamism — an individual self-culture neglecting the social order, and with little grasp of sin and grace. Slowly Adams moved beyond both scientific and literary humanism; he experienced an increasing desire not alone for ethical standards but also for metaphysical meaning, together with a historical purpose which would involve them both. He began to see religious liberalism as a cultural lag, the vestigial remains of nineteenth century laissez-faire atomistic individualism. He eventually joined the Greenfield critics of liberalism, a group that attempted together to hammer out a Church theology that would take contemporary history seriously — to unite Francis de Sales and Karl Marx. The modern world, he discovered in Nazi Germany, faces decisive options — paganism or Christianity; America now confronts nationalism or Christ. Rudolf Otto taught him that Jesus took time seriously. Tillich destroyed heteronomy (a sacred-secular split) in his mind, and led him from empty autonomy (mere secularism) toward theonomy (one world under one God); Tillich taught him to take history seriously. As he sees it, the big question now confronting Christendom is this: Can the Churches learn to take time seriously? Can they forego the salvation of a doctrine or a sect long enough to save the world?

In Adams' chapter "The Religious Problem," in *New Perspectives on Peace* (Edited by George B. de Huszar. University of

Chicago Press, 1944), he emphasizes the historical task of the Church — in and for itself, in and for the world. Religion exalts peace, but is itself caught in the toils. It offers peace only as the reward of struggle and suffering. Conflict, as he sees it, is the essence of life. Without conflict neither individuality nor social change is possible. Conflict is an inextricable aspect of religion. Return to religion is not a return to peace; it is rather a return to creative conflict. The modern world, says Adams, is not secular, but simply non-ecclesiastically religious. Religion, as he defines it, is orientation to whatever is regarded as worthy of serious and ultimate concern. There are two types of orientation — sacramental and prophetic; either without the other is death. In all groups are to be found people who want peace without sacrifice, and people who want peace. World peace is not only a spiritual problem; it is also political and racial and economic. Unity is not identity. Progress will be made, but slowly, and only through struggle and sacrifice.

In 1945, Adams analyzed the history of Meadville Theological School in terms of its presidents' views. Clearly there had been a progressive grasp of the historical process as God's serious enterprise. Adams believes there is no automatic progress; there is moral deterioration as well as growth; truth is always dearer than triumph. In Adams' view, Unitarianism as the democracy of Christianity has asserted a basic cosmic principle: truth can come only through the conflict of free inquiry. The world is a dynamic process. God is at work through freedom, reason, and humanity. Eschatology returns to its own — not the static legerdemain of the past, but a grasp of God's serious action in, through, and upon history. The optative mood — the mood of choice and decision — joins Unitarianism to Judaeo-Christianity. The final issue is the answer to the question, Does history have a meaning and a demanded direction?

In his article on "Freud, Mannheim, and the Liberal Doctrine of Man" (*Journal of Liberal Religion,* winter, 1941), Adams asserted three essentials: first, human nature must be interpreted dialectically — that is, peace and truth can come only through conflict; secondly, the bonds of society are nonrational and imaginative as well as rational — unconscious as well as conscious; and thirdly, there are

irrational elements in human nature that respond to the pressures
of social structure. God's creative enterprise in and with history offers no escape from conflict.

Indeed, there is no such thing as neutrality. This Adams discovered existentially in Nazi Germany; he was told that one agrees
with the Nazis or gets his head bashed in. Long before Pearl Harbor, Adams learned that Nazism had to be abolished for the survival
of the spirit of man. Commitment to another and a better philosophy than Nazism is not a luxury, but a necessity. Adams returns
to this theme in his 1950 analysis of our current American nationalism, our mood of inquisition. The article " Love and Law and the
' Good Old Cause ' " (*The Divinity School News,* August 1, 1950)
should be read everywhere. Adams defines a subversive as anyone
who does not identify the will of God with the will of the men
who hold the reins of power — from Jeremiah onward. In every
age sheer power wages war against principle, hysteria against freedom. In the Bible, in Russia, and in the *Congressional Record* innocent victims are offered on inquisitors' altars. The good old cause
is the dignity of every child of God versus every effort to destroy the
justice which guarantees his right to think and speak. The good
old cause is Christian love, love that cherishes law and justice as
well as charity and meekness.

Education itself is a central arena of God's historical enterprise.
In his article " Religion in Higher Education " (*Journal of Bible
and Religion,* November, 1945) Adams defines liberal education, not
as an end in itself, but as a means to produce men and women
capable of freedom. Not all forms of religion have a place in higher
education — neither imperialistic religions nor religions hostile to
free inquiry. Only free religion is compatible with higher education;
only free religion can encourage the creative spirit of man to be
creative Heteronomy (religious tyranny) in education is or ought
to be finished; but the choice now before public education is meaninglessness or meaning, autonomy (secularism) or theonomy (a
sacred view of all life), a spiritual vacuum or recognition of a
sovereign, creative meaning-reality, the Lord of history. He concludes:

" No kind of religion has a place in higher education. Rather, higher education must find its place in the religion that liberates man from slavery to man-made gods, in the religion that elicits commitment to the creative principle that fulfills the meaning of all human thinking, valuing, and doing " (P. 192).

Fulfillment Is Divine Promise

Always James Luther Adams is interested in time and history, but the whole enterprise is meaningful to him precisely because it is the theater of divine action. Through the process God, the Lord of history, is now *at work* — creating man and the world. And God is big enough for the job he has undertaken, not in escape from freedom but through and for freedom; not in escape from tragedy but through and beyond the ministry of tragedy; not in escape from history but through history.

In 1952, at Manchester College, Oxford, Adams addressed the Fourteenth Congress of the International Association for Liberal Christianity and Religious Freedom. His theme, "Our Responsibility in Society," is the continuing emphasis in all he has written. He asks, What does liberalism stand for? The answer is, The authority of the free spirit, the necessity of education through and for freedom; his accent, however, is not primarily on what man is doing, but rather on what God is doing. Man's action is response to God's creative initiative. " I will pour out my spirit on all flesh " — this, says Adams, is not a promise we make to ourselves; we receive it in faith from the Lord of history. Its fulfillment, however, is contingent upon our response in responsibility. The Christian's responsibility in society issues from concern for something more reliable than the desire for personal success. Social responsibility issues from the Christian demand for community — a response to God's Deed " in the beginning," God's Deed of Agape in Christ, and God's Deed of community-forming power, the Holy Spirit. Early Christianity, dominated by Agape, was community-forming, but in subsequent centuries Christians have created pneumatocracy, theocracy, absolute monarchy, constitutional monarchy, sectarian

communism, constitutional democracy, and democratic religious socialism. Skepticism can never relax its guard, lest faith disintegrate
into folly. Our responsibility is to maintain the heritage that is
ours, the heritage of response to the community-forming Power that
we confront in the gospel and in the Church of the Spirit. This
community-forming Power calls us to preach and to practice the
abundant Love which is not ultimately in our *possession*; it is a
holy gift. Agape is the ground and goal of our vocation.

Liberal religion has fostered three principles which must be
kept in mind: the fact that nothing human is complete or perfect,
hence nothing is exempt from criticism; the dignity of human nature and the principle of mutual consent; and finally, the principle
of community — " co-operate or die." To avoid the pseudo spirituality of lethargic liberalism, there must be personal decision, a new
commitment to the Church of the Spirit.

It is God who is at work among us; we are not alone. In Adams'
words:

> " In our time of troubles the problems are vast in their dimensions.
> But they were vast also in the birth period of the primitive Church and
> in the birth period of our free churches. To cringe in despair of our-
> selves is to despair of the divine promise. It is to forget that responsibility
> is response to a Spirit that is *given* to us — to the light that has shone
> and that still shines in the darkness" (P. 62).

The only reliable object of faith and devotion is Agape, the power
of God which reconciles and reunites those who are separated.
Natural religion is necessary but inadequate. Neither the Enlightenment, with its accent on reason and creation, nor the Reformation,
with its stress on sin and redemption, is adequate alone. A new age
of grace and power is upon us. The eternal gospel, which still belongs to the future, commands and compels our finest response.
The Enlightenment alone offered no mystery, no intimacy, no
awareness of the beyond; it was nonhistorical, a religion of personal
success, overlooking social tragedy.

As Adams puts it:

" The idea of a mythless man is itself a chimera, a dream, an absurdity. Man, even the enlightened man, is by nature a myth-bearing creature. He lives by faith. . . .

" A myth is a symbolic means whereby a culture or an epoch, confronting the demands, the threats, the possibilities of existence, dramatizes its decisive insights and its strongest inclinations.

" There is no such thing as a mythless age " (" Natural Religion and the Myth of the Eighteenth Century," the Dudleian Lecture for 1949–1950 at Harvard University, Andover Chapel, April 18, 1950).

The positive value of the Enlightenment was its desire for autonomy (rational integrity); its guide was reason, meaningful reason, structural alike to man and God. But intellectual integrity must transcend itself and become spiritual integrity, for God is the Lord of history. God's grace is both prevenient and actual, that is, both transcendent over the process and immanent within it.

No historical optimism suffices for Adams. In his view, the simple doctrine of gradualistic progress represented a grossly inadequate conception of human nature. Nonetheless, crisis is a stage in process; hence, the Protestant confidence in the growth of civilization was and is justified, for it is based upon the sovereign power of the Lord of history. God is creating two things: material satisfaction and spontaneous co-operation. Both are growing, and will grow — for God is God.

'Way back in 1939, Adams asserted that the resources (human and divine) available for the achievement of meaningful change justify ultimate hope. As he put it: " The divine element in reality both demands and *supports* mutuality. Thus the ground of hope is in the prevenient and the actual grace of God " (" Why Liberal? " in *The Journal of Liberal Religion,* autumn, 1939, p. 3).

Adams' four theological bases for social action underscore his confidence in the Lord of history. The Power that is worthy of confidence is the Creator of the world and of man; the Power worthy of confidence has a world-historical purpose; the Power worthy of confidence places upon us the obligation to righteousness; and the

Power worthy of confidence is the basis of a fellowship of persons. Power expresses God's law and God's love, and power is the meaning of man's freedom exercised in response to divine Law and Love. In Jewish and Christian prophetism Adams finds the permanent demand for responsible, communal fellowship issuing from loving obedience to the divine Power, the Lord of history and of the soul of man — not the power of tribalism, mana, which is its own law, but New Testament dynamis, forgiving, healing love (*Journal of Religious Thought,* autumn–winter, 1950–1951).

Adams learned from Von Hügel that the essential task is to make spirituality civilized, and civilization spiritualized. Through our commitment to the Other and the More, what now is, in individuality, in history, and in society, can and will become what ultimately is — for God is (*The Christian Register,* October 11, 1934).

Modern man cannot be content with skepticism only. He must choose meaning or nonmeaning for the total process and for each individual person. Adams urges us to ask ourselves the question, How do you distinguish between yourself and a Nazi? Faith is simply a living option. The question is not, Shall I be a man of faith? That question was settled for us when we joined the human race. The only proper question is, What faith is mine? Faith is a matter of life or death. Nobody is through with religion; he only changes his religion. The free man is not bound to the faith once for all delivered; the free man cannot live by an unexamined faith. Skepticism is not a blasphemy; it is a duty. History is meaningful. The achievement of freedom in community requires the power of organization and the organization of power.

Finally, sin and salvation are realities. Sin is a wrong relationship, both ethical and theological, rising from the tension between the power to exist and the necessity of mutuality. Man exercises his freedom for or against the creative process; he cannot evade the decision one way or the other. Original sin means that man is in a situation that is not yet what it ought to be and he has a responsible relation to it. Salvation is vision and commitment. The idea of self-salvation is idolatry. Always Adams would have us bear in mind that the potentiality of existence is a *divine promise,* not merely a human possibility. We cannot escape a growing, critical awareness of man's dependence upon the divine creative reality for both the actuality of the good and the possibility of the new good. Salvation is transformation — the total process of God's activity in history, our share in the process through co-operative fellowship with God and man. God creates through, and not in escape from, conflict. Our freedom is our privilege, our responsibility, to live in conformity with the divine promise of human fulfillment. It is our glory that we may become self-surpassing channels of grace.

In conclusion, Adams' specific contribution is this: God is the Lord, and the Life, of the world. God is not indifferent to time and history; it is precisely in, and upon, time and history that God is at work to accomplish his purpose. On the other hand, history is not God; rather it is God's unfinished enterprise. The dilemma confronting every nation, every century, and every soul is a decision — to seek escape from the common task through idolatry (exalting race or class or cult to the place of ultimate loyalty), or to walk and work humbly in this world with God the Almighty, whose will is always other than and better than our own, whose strength is our hope.

Douglas V. Steere

A THEOLOGY OF PRACTICAL MYSTICISM

R *eligion* without a taproot in the soul exists only in libraries and
archives. It is a mummy, an embalmed memory. If religion is
devoted living, and Christianity is living devoted to God's will for
the total process, God's will made flesh in Jesus Christ, neither religion nor Christianity exists except in *devoted* persons. Prayer is
therefore inescapably central. There is no Christianity without it.
It is possible, even in Christianity, perhaps peculiarly in Christianity,
for prayer to become a personal escape from history, from creative
activity, a self-centered pursuit of personal salvation or personal success. Yet escape from history is specifically contrary to the genius of
Christianity. The cross translated Agape into history. Hence, Christianity is a historical religion, filled with drive and hope for all generations. Christian prayer is an attempt, not to direct God, but to be
directed by him; a report for duty; a communion with the Source
of renewing power and creating love; and an intercession for persons and process. Only false prayer is an escape from the historical
process. True prayer is *for* the world. Through prayer God releases
his Agape into history, and hope (*elpis*) replaces fear (*phobos*) and
anxiety (*merimna*). Prayer is power for progress in process — God's
power taking possession of human flesh, and moving creatively
through the world.

Personal religion is not the whole of religion. Personal prayer,
unaware of its involvement with history, becomes personal escape
from history. But personal prayer, realizing its historical function,
puts soul and body to work for historical achievement, for social
justice and individual dignity, with neither watered down. What

God is doing *now* in and for the historical process, he is doing *now* also in and for the individual person — as rapidly as mind and heart and will are open to his creative enterprise; he is also at work with or without human consent in levels below Agape. What God is now doing in the macrocosm, the total process, he is also doing in the microcosm — the individual person. The total process is, and will become more consciously, a prayer; hence prayer cannot be eliminated from the process-in-miniature, the individual person. A person *is* a prayer; to pray consciously is to be a cocreator with God. One world at prayer is the objective of divine creation, of sufficient grace and power; one person at prayer is irrevocably relevant to one world-in-process, and a picture of its future. Christianity is social justice and individual dignity conscious of present incompleteness before one God; that is, the total community and the solitary person are of equal and ultimate importance. God is not more interested in the total process than the individual person; the individual *is* the process written small. God is not more interested in the individual person than in the total process; the total process *is* the person written large. But there is one difference: the total process is, or appears to be, harder to convert, to transform, than the individual person. Only God can accomplish this impossibility. It is God alone, working with and in and upon the process, who will bring his will to pass — through, because of, and *for* freedom, and in spite of freedom's abuse, our pursuit of self, of the past, of the part.

Personal prayer is not all the truth, but it is not a half-truth. It is a whole truth, with its own right to exist. There are simply other truths as well in the total cluster.

Douglas V. Steere accents historical prayer — practical mysticism, functional worship, with a God who *is* God and not a deity demoted. Let us take a quick look at his life, then examine his central message. Humility is a rarity in theology, as in life, yet Steere, a Quaker, is willing for other theologians to examine and develop other aspects of Christian truth and practice. His own speciality is prayer.

DEVOTED LIVING

Douglas Van Steere was born at Harbor Beach, Michigan, August 31, 1901, the son of Edward Morris and Edith Ruby (Monroe) Steere. He has earned three degrees in America, and one in England. He received the Bachelor of Science in Agriculture at Michigan State College (1923), the A.M. and the Ph.D. at Harvard in 1925 and 1931. As a Rhodes Scholar, he received the B.A. at Oxford University (1927). He intended to be a man of the soil but became instead a man of the soul.

He married Dorothy Lou MacEachron, June 12, 1929, and there are two children: Helen Weaver and Anne.

Douglas V. Steere was a high school teacher at Onaway, Michigan, 1921–1922. After graduate work, he became assistant professor of philosophy at Haverford College, Pennsylvania, 1928–1931; associate professor, 1931–1941; and professor, since 1941. From 1943 to 1945 he was also director of the Graduate Reconstruction and Relief Training program of the Society of Friends — a necessary work in wartime for conscientious objectors.

Steere was Reinicker lecturer at Episcopal Theological Seminary (1938), Ingersoll lecturer at Harvard (1942), William Belden Noble lecturer (1943), Alden Tuthill lecturer at Chicago Theological Seminary (1943), Carew lecturer at Hartford Theological Seminary (1945), and Hoyt lecturer at Union Theological Seminary in New York (1947).

A member of the board of directors of Pendle Hill School of Religion and Social Studies since 1930, he was director of its summer school for five summers. This wedding of religion and sociology, against the disappearance of either in the other, offers profound hope.

He was visiting lecturer at Union Theological Seminary in New York for the summer session (1947). He is a member of the American Philosophical Association, the Association of Rhodes Scholars, and the American Theological Society (he was secretary, 1935–1942; vice-president, 1944–1945; and president, 1945–1946). He is a member of the American Association of University Professors, vice-president of the Fellowship of Reconciliation, and a Phi Beta Kappa.

As a member of the Society of Friends, he has played an active role (he is as much an activist as a Methodist) in Quaker missions to disturbed and despairing Europe: to Scandinavia and Germany (1937); to Germany and Finland (1940–1941, on the eve of America's entry into World War II); to Finland, Norway, and Poland (1945); to Scandinavia and Germany (1947 and 1948, and 1950). He participated in the Federal Council's Commission on the Relation of the Church to the War (1944–1945) — which declared that the Church was both the servant and conscience within, and an ecumenical fellowship beyond, each competing sovereignty. He labored also with the Commission on Atomic Warfare in the Light of the Christian Faith (1945–1946). He has been chairman of the board of trustees of the John Woolman Memorial since 1936.

Action within the drama of history, and direct communion with God, are one in him.

WITHOUT VISION THE PEOPLE PERISH

Christianity is a lot of things — more than you can count in a pleasant afternoon. For this reason, there is often loss of Christian simplicity, essential Godward and worldward movement. God is all-important. The historical process is his enterprise, hence its seriousness. The problem is to keep God and his creative enterprise together in the minds and hearts of the people. Prayer is one way to keep God and his world together. In true prayer the barricade between man and God is broken; in true prayer the barricade between man and man is shattered; in true prayer the barricade between the present and the future is destroyed.

All this, and more, is the meaning of Douglas V. Steere's permanently valuable book *On Beginning from Within* (Harper & Brothers, 1943). Mankind is always busy with scheme-making, with the plans of so-called experts (ignoramuses away from home with brief cases and on expense accounts), adjusting and readjusting the maladjustments, drafting blueprints for tomorrow's brave new world. Man must plan, whether wisely or foolishly. And man will plan. To stop planning is to stop hoping. To stop planning is to stop being a man. A planned economy, like a planned life, is a fallible but human necessity. Nonetheless, exclusive *social* efforts to reorganize the universe to brain-trust specifications often, if not always, overlook, ridicule, and neglect a simple and obvious fact: enduring change that takes place in no actual individual takes place nowhere — is paper work only. To place needed new blueprints on the nation's statute books is a Christian necessity, but if blueprint never becomes blood print, the enterprise is more grandiose than grand. Of what value, of what interest, is a perfectly organized society with no people in it? Plans, without persons, offer only a ho-hum appeal.

Steere perhaps underestimates the *two* foci of Christian action — macrocosm *and* microcosm. As he sees it, accenting one half of the truth, enduring reform must come from within individuals. With this theme in mind, he examines the contributions of the saints — Roman Catholic and catholic alike. In his view, to separate saint and society is to make both uncreative. He defends no heteronomy, no schizophrenic world. The saint may leave society to receive his vision, as Toynbee has emphasized, but if saint and society are not reunited in holy wedlock, there is no vision and the people perish. Steere examines the authority of the saint — not external sacrosanctity, not the alleged " divine right " of kings and popes, but the self-evident authority of the Holy Spirit, the self-authenticating presence of the Inner Light. He re-emphasizes Loyola's exercises of self-examination, discusses the relation between devotion and theology. Theology is not Love but Love's logic. In conclusion, Steere discusses death's illumination of life. To him, personal immortality is not escape from history but the light of history. If we live beyond death, we live for the sake of God's creative enterprise, not in escape from it. Death itself, a contributor to forward movement, is not an enemy but an ally.

This book is excellent Lenten reading, and more. It is basic Christianity in America or in Timbuctoo. Get hold of it, or better still, let it get hold of you, and your community — in Lent, in Advent, all the time. Steere combines the personal devotion of the mystic with the zeal of the missionary. The book meets the real test of greatness — it makes the reader search his own soul; it makes him *want* to pray.

As Steere sees it, the Church and the world must be freshly concerned with Christian nurture — must freshly offset the mass shallowness of our collectivist age. Communism is simply mass spiritual emptiness, a mechanized vacuum. Capitalism is too Communistic at this point; it asserts the spirituality of man in theory but the exclusive drive of economic hunger in practice. And Communism is obviously too capitalistic in its wholehearted pursuit of Mammon. Both forms of materialism, Communism *and* capitalism, lose sight of the individual — his ability to obstruct or assist spiritual and social advance. The massive problems of our age cannot be solved by prayer alone; but without prayer they cannot be solved at all.

In Steere's view, the trouble with collectivists, whether sociological or theological, is this: they begin from without. We need saints, now underproduced in our society, as well as critics and workers. Indeed, true saintliness is a form of work, perhaps the hardest form; further, it is work not in escape from the world, but strictly *for* the world. Steere mentions no modern saints, though there must be some, else the light has gone out. Still, who would be bold enough to scoop God in announcing them? The book is good for beginners — especially for the modern religious first-graders, the college professors. It is also good for travelers farther along the Christian road. The book will disturb the complacency of the average Rotarian; he may doubt his own righteousness, even his historical usefulness. The book is a single-minded plea for the pursuit of Christian perfection. The true Christian is not a perfect man, but a man who is not content to be less. The only sorrow is not to be a saint. The only sorrow of the world is to be less than universal prayer, universal love, universal freedom in fellowship. Life is lent to be spent — for God and his creative enterprise upon and within the process.

Not the least of Steere's insights is the realization that sainthood is not for the favored few (the Roman idea). Sainthood is precisely from God, but in and for history — *now*. Sainthood is to be appropriated by all as a present realization in process and person. The idea is blasphemous that saints are limited to New Testament times and churches, to medieval cloisters, ritualistic denominations, or sheltered situations. In the struggle *of* the world, at the center of storm and stress, saints are needed and found. Steere defines a saint simply as a Christian in full degree. As Jacopone da Todi understood, the saint is one in whom Christ is felt to live again. In both definitions you have Paul's idea: " It is no longer I who live, but Christ who lives in me " (*Gal. 2:20*).

Some saints get top billing, and reach the headlines. These saints with better publicity directors are a light to the rest of us, but the nameless saints, sweating and praying amidst the joy and despair of life, are the strength and salt of the earth. Now and then in Korea, or on other battlefields, an individual hero received a good press; but the life and light of the total war for freedom are the " little deaths " of heroes unsung; to them death is the " finis " but not the " telos " of their lives. The individuality of their lives has ended in time; the sociality of their lives has no end.

In the practice of prayer Steere urges a new self-discipline, as necessary among the armed forces of the Spirit as among the armed forces of the State, a new creative obedience. The two words (creative and obedience) are necessary. Obedience alone is a static idea; it tends to look and move backward, to the less rather than the more, to the minimum that kills rather than the maximum that makes alive. Mere creativity without obedience is change without progress.

Meditation and prayer are islands of silence in a world of noise; on these islands creative obedience is born, and movement receives meaning. After a night of prayer, Jesus went to the cross, and turned prayer into historical progress. The cross turned theory into history, vision into creation, eternity into time — for the healing of the world.

Prayer needs no apology. To whom must one apologize for prayer? In 1948, Douglas V. Steere opened five neglected *Doors Into Life* (Harper & Brothers). The book contained introductions to five devotional classics, and better ones could hardly be found: Thomas a Kempis' *Imitation of Christ;* Francis de Sales' *Introduc-*

tion to the Devout Life, The Journal of John Woolman, Sören Kierkegaard's *Purity of Heart* (to will one thing); and selected letters of Friedrich von Hügel. Steere provides the background, and an interpretation of the meaning of each work. Four of the chapters were given as lectures at theological seminaries. These productive classics are not regarded as a new canon, a second New Testament (though they might well be added to the first). Nonetheless, "they rise above their centuries and above their confessions in the universal authority with which they speak to our condition today" (P. 12). As T. S. Eliot put it, "We may find companions in men of other centuries who are nearer to us than most of our own contemporaries" (*Ibid.*). Each man will cherish his own aids to prayer — Jakob Böhme, Meister Eckhart, Fénelon, Brother Lawrence, Francis of Assisi, Pascal, and in our own time Thomas Kelly, Thomas Kepler, and Nels F. S. Ferré.

THE NEED FOR BEATITUDINARIANS

The need of our time, and of every time, as Rendell Harris put it, is not latitudinarians nor attitudinarians nor platitudinarians, but beatitudinarians. In his excellent book *Time to Spare* (Harper & Brothers, 1949), based upon the familiar line in Kempis, "Blessed are those who are glad to have time to spare for God," Steere urges the Church to become, not a debating society, but a society of saints. If, on Toynbee's terms, we must return to the world to bless it, we must first withdraw to receive a blessing. The world in which we are living, as Steere understands it, is slowly suffocating. To prevent this spiritual suffocation, Christians must be deeply and costingly involved in the life of their time. Steere provides a full account of the content and method of religious retreats, two- or three-day laboratories of the Holy Spirit, and lists a dozen or more now going on. The Third Order of Saint Francis is available, in substance, to us all. A primary need is to develop through these periodic occasions of withdrawal a widely diffused stream of quickened and committed men and women who will plant themselves, thousands deep, at every strategic center of contemporary life: in homes, in government, in churches, among sharecroppers and among the poorly clothed and fed and housed of the great cities, in factories and mines, in schools and colleges, in the quiet rooms where books are written or pictures painted, or in the noisy workshops of artisans and craftsmen.

Christianity is not, in Steere's view, primarily a philosophy, nor is it a code of morals, nor a nursing home for psychoneurotics; it is the power of God here among men, forgiving, reconciling, harmonizing, vitalizing.

" If the history of religious practice is any guide, it affirms that it is only those Christians who have had a firsthand experience of the new divine community which they would draw men to, by association with intimate and costly Christian fellowships where they are continually renewed in this life of God, who are able to resist being transformed by society instead of transforming it " (P. 29).

Steere quotes John Chapman: " The less I pray, the worse it goes " (P. 181). This common experience of the devout is our continual call to prayer.

In 1938, Steere translated Sören Kierkegaard's *Purity of Heart* (Harper & Brothers), and added an appreciative introduction. He regarded the work as the best devotional classic produced in the nineteenth century, emphasizing the individual's solitary responsibility before the living God, and therefore to some extent alien to modern collective thinking, collective action, and collective salvation. As Steere sees it, the mass flatters, the mass excuses, the mass condemns, the mass counts heads, the mass pronounces on truth, and in all these things the mass is both false and debasing. To speak of social salvation, or salvation by group, by tribe, by race, by class, by nation, is an act of spiritual betrayal. Steere and Kierkegaard together strike a universal note of the inward life of man — " a note that even this age will be compelled to learn again when its present grim honeymoon with collective salvation has spent itself " (P. 26).

In the book *Doors Into Life,* Steere found special value in John Woolman's *Journal;* it united the life of prayer and worship with the life of social concern, and endlessly renewed the faith that Jesus meant us to take literally the words of the Lord's Prayer: "Thy kingdom come. Thy will be done on earth as it is in heaven."

In Steere's view, no day ought to pass without the reading of a major devotional classic, especially in our current wave of secularism. "In times such as these, God can use as his servants only men and women who can be trusted to be loyal to the core to him and his cause. This is the kind of loyalty no Congressional committee can even ascertain" (*Doors Into Life,* p. 18). In the spirit of Saint Francis, Steere continually calls, "Come now, let us begin to be Christians." Spiritual depth is not an accident; it requires continual nurturing, continual cultivation, continual renewal, continual beginning again, if it is to prepare us for the tasks this generation requires. "In the life of devotion, there are no vacations either here or hereafter" (*Ibid.,* p. 189).

No part of Steere's thought advocates blindness to the painful tragedies of our time. Christian love means responsibility, total responsibility. His article "As Germans See Us," in *The Christian Century* (May 16, 1951), illustrates his complete concern for the realistic problems of contemporary Europeans. He is deeply embarrassed as an American at the sheer opportunism, the military expediency alone, that characterizes our call for West German rearmament. Yesterday we told the Germans that militarization was evil; today we ask them to remilitarize. The Germans themselves wonder at our duplicity. Schumacher and Niemöller see the remilitarization of West Germany as an incitement to Russia to move, not as a threat that will stop her. What, asks Steere, is America trying to export? The American still thinks that armament is a possible method of avoiding war; the European is convinced that armament inevitably means war. It is the task of the Church, in Steere's view, to keep open the avenues of reconciliation and understanding, and to strengthen men's sense of unlimited liability for each other on both sides of the ideological conflicts that threaten to destroy us all. In his words:

"In an America that is dropping back to wartime oversimplifications, we need a rekindling of the imagination that will permit us to see beyond 'our view' and 'their view' to a view that is neither ours nor

theirs but is prepared to go on expanding areas of agreement and re-
moving major causes of disastrous disagreement. We need an inner
solvent for our mental hardening of the categories " (P. 610).

Steere's practical mysticism recognizes that the Christian's stance
in history is between realization and expectance. In his meaningful
article " The Hope of Glory and This Present Life " (*Theology
Today*, October, 1953), he considers hope the fruit of the action of
the Holy Spirit. A Christian, in his view, does not begin by hoping
or by accepting the Christian hope; he begins by a personal living
encounter with the redemptive love of God in Christ that sweeps
away his alienation and gives him an overwhelming awareness of
the infinite transforming caring love of One that gathers up his life
and the world's life and draws them both within its redemptive
field of healing. The Christian who has been baptized into this hope
is prepared to accept a share in the historical decisions of his hour
and day and to confront them with a radical ethic of love.

The Christian needs to bear in mind, especially today, that the
" givenness " of God, as Von Hügel described it, is greater than the
" givenness " of evil. In Steere's words:

" A redemptive power . . . is connected both Creator-wise and Re-
deemer-wise with the whole cosmos. This redemptive power is focused
through a Person and is intensely concerned for man. This redemptive
power has entered into this life, identified itself with the body of man
which is cheek and jowl joined to the cosmos and to all of nature, and
has already triumphed over illness, sin, and death. It has witnessed to its
power to transmute each of them. But it has also declared its power to
transmute societies and even nature including the earth and the heavens.

" If this power exists and its reign has begun, then the *ultimate*
triumph of illness and sin and death and the flourishing of evil societies
and of the harsh and alien orders of nature has been forever denied.
This I take to be the essential substance of the good news of Christian
hope. This is what I take Scripture to be saying " (P. 368).

In conclusion: Steere, like Socrates, is always talking about the
same thing; even more, he is always saying the same thing about it.
A meaningful prayer life releases Agape into history. Deep Chris-

tian experience always begins in a personal Pentecost, to accompany the historical one — always begins *from within.* Steere combines three necessities too often separate in our pietist Protestantism: social action, intellectual vigor, and spiritual vitality.

Prayer which seeks personal or ecclesiastical escape from the historical process is A.W.O.L. from its function. Men who seek to remake the world without prayer have forgotten the Power and the Purpose. Steere insists that true prayer play its indispensable part in the divine-human enterprise of man-and-world making.

John A. Mackay

AN ECUMENICAL THEOLOGY

M*ackay* has a word or two to say about professional conferencegoers, who consider active religion a matter of committees,
paper crusades, and resolutions. Nonetheless, he is himself a man of
action, with the difference that he also is a man of thought. His
theme in deed and word is the growing Community of Christ across
all barriers of time and culture. His books and articles describe: the
Road to Nowhere, the Road to Somewhere, Problems on the Way
and the Power Not Our Own; and present an important insight:
The Church Is Not the End but the Means.

MAN OF ACTION

Mackay is an American, but the fact that his roots are in Scotland
may account for his sense of continuity with the wide world, his
lack of provincialism. He was born in Inverness, Scotland, May 17,
1889, the son of Duncan and Isabella (Macdonald) Mackay. His
degrees are legion: an A.M. with first class honors in philosophy
from the University of Aberdeen (1912), and a D.D. from the same
institution (1939); a B.D. from Princeton (1915); a Litt.D. from the
University of Lima, Peru (1918); another from the University of
Bonn in Germany (1930); a D.D. from Princeton and an LL.D.
from Ohio Wesleyan (both 1937); an LL.D. from Albright College
(1938); a D.D. from Debrecen University in Hungary (1939); a
D.D. from Presbyterian College, Montreal (1942); an L.H.D. from
Boston University (1939) and another the same year from Lafayette
College. He studied at the University of Madrid in 1915–1916. In
1941 he was made an honorary Fellow of Stanford University.

August 16, 1916, he married Jane Logan Wells, and there are three daughters and a son.

His positions have been numerous. He was principal of Anglo-Peruvian College in Lima, 1916–1925, and during the last year professor of philosophy at the National University of Peru. From 1926 to 1932 he was a lecturer and writer under the South American Federation of Young Men's Christian Associations, residing first at Montevideo and then at Mexico City. He was secretary of the Presbyterian Board of Foreign Missions from 1932 to 1936, and from then until now has been president of Princeton Theological Seminary and professor of ecumenics.

He has given the Merrick Lectures at Ohio Wesleyan (1932); the Sprunt Lectures at Union Seminary, Richmond, Virginia (1940); the Lyman Coleman Lectures at Lafayette College (1941); the Otis Lectures at Davidson College (1942); the Chancellor's Lectures at Queen's University (1945); the Charles Deems Lectures at New York University (1946); the Moore Lectures at San Francisco Theological Seminary (1946); the N. A. Powell Lectures at the Canadian School of Missions (1946); the Croall Lectures at New College, Edinburgh (1948); the Gary Lectures at Southern Baptist Theological Seminary in Louisville (1948); and the Fondren Lectures at Southern Methodist University (1949).

Since 1941 he has served on the advisory council of the Princeton Department of Philosophy. He was president of the board of trustees of Mackenzie College, São Paulo, Brazil, 1948–1950. He is a trustee of Waynesburg College. A member of the American Association of Theological Schools, he was president from 1948 to 1950. He is an honorary foreign member of the British and Foreign Bible Society. He is a member of the American Theological Society. Since 1948, as a member of its central committee, he has helped to guide the World Council of Churches. He has been chairman of the International Missionary Council since 1947, president of the Presbyterian Board of Foreign Missions (1945–1951), and was formerly chairman of the Council on Theological Education of the Presbyterian Church in the U.S.A. In 1937 he was chairman of the Commission on the Universal Church and the World of Nations at the

Oxford Conference on Church, Community, and State. He is editor of the *Quarterly Review;* was editor of the pithy journal *Theology Today* from 1944 to 1951, and is now chairman of its editorial council. He is a member of Princeton's Nassau Club.

These activities are two-worldly in many directions: they unite Scotland with America, Spain with South America, the past with the future, and the broad earth with a heaven that is Presbyterian — and more.

THE ROAD TO NOWHERE

In 1933 came Mackay's important contribution to the understanding of Latin America: *The Other Spanish Christ,* A Study in the Spiritual History of Spain and South America (The Macmillan Company). The volume, like all Gaul, is divided into three parts: a study of the Ibernian soul and the background of Roman Catholicism in South America, an analysis of Spanish Roman Catholicism as a religious system, and a presentation of spiritual movements outside the Roman Catholic Church that have influenced South American religious thought. The book contains little criticism of Protestant shortcomings and a long and sad list of Roman miscarriages. It should of course be obvious that a Protestant, who is one in fact as well as in name, can hardly look out upon the world as a defender of Roman Catholicism. For American Protestant and Roman Catholic alike, the book sheds needed light on a dark continent.

In reading the volume the impression grows that Roman Catholicism is always and everywhere unethical, unspiritual, irreligious, and socially and politically reactionary, while Protestantism is always and everywhere a force for progress. This is probably overstating both cases, yet there is important truth in the characterizations. The London *Times* found little knowledge of traditional Spain in the book, and considered many of its statements fantastic.

The road to nowhere is precisely the strange mixture of pious profession with impious greed from the conquistadors onward. The official Spanish motive for "the last of the crusades" was the spread of religion, but the worship of Mammon was as evident as the worship of God. And the religion of South America, which has developed its own peculiarities, emphasizes magic rather than meaning. With Miguel de Unamuno, Mackay is convinced that the Christ evolved in South America is a dead Christ, with little interest in daily affairs and with no transforming power. The pious South American finds his consolation, not in Christ, but in the Virgin and the saints. In Mackay's view, South American Roman Catholicism lacks two Christian essentials: spiritual vitality and ethical seriousness. Alongside Unamuno, Ricardo Rojas, Julio Navarro Monzo, and Gabriela Mistral, Mackay seeks for South America a better Spanish Christ, a living Lord, and finds him already present, and growing, among Protestant minorities. All in all, the religion of South America seems predominantly static, more of a burden than a blessing, a backward-looking miscarriage. The meaning of Christian dogma is revolution; the worship of dogma is reaction. Nonetheless, there are signs of hope, faint streaks of dawn. In *That Other America* (Missionary Education Movement, 1935), Mackay described more fully present-day Spanish American religion, but added little to his first analysis.

THE ROAD TO SOMEWHERE

Mackay is less a flaming evangel of the future than a wholesome apostle to the present. Every word he has written contains balance, constructiveness, and maturity; he continually persuades to fuller truth and seasoned judgment. In *A Preface to Christian Theology* (The Macmillan Company, 1941), Mackay asked American leaders to consider with seriousness the immediate agenda of a living theology. The book in substance was given as a series of lectures at Union Seminary in Richmond (February, 1940). It is not a formal introduction to theology; it is not a theological primer; it simply analyzes the contemporary culture to which alert theology must speak.

Our Western world, in Mackay's view, is in part a directionless relativism, an empty, secular autonomy. We have lost the authority of ultimates. With Presbyterian charity he welcomes Neo-Thomism, a spiritually reinvigorated Orthodoxy, and Barthianism as three concrete efforts to reduce relativism and restore the fixed stars. Our Western incoherence, our amorphous culture, our corrosive nihilism, our lack of a sense of purpose — these form *our* road to nowhere.

The road to somewhere is precisely a road, not a balcony. Mackay, who has learned much from Kierkegaard, finds four types of modern dilettantes, well-meaning dwellers in an unreal world: those who glorify knowledge at the expense of ethical action, apocalypticists coldly indifferent to today's struggling world, religious aestheticians who cater to sentimental religion, and the professional conferencegoers who place their confidence in one more committee, one more resolution. Mackay must have seen a multitude of messianic committee members in his time.

Salvation lies in the conversion of history. Mackay preaches no escapism, rather an endless relevance to the actual problems of our day-to-day world, an individual experience of reality, an existential seriousness, a complete identification with the Eternal in the midst of time, a genuine concern and commitment. He knows no other avenue to the authority of ultimates. Yet in nature and culture also Mackay finds the footprints of God. Especially in the newly liberated Bible is help available. God is the solution, not the problem, and he is never an intellectual formula; to talk about a God of abstractions is not to talk about God. Truth is personal. Mackay sees with Kierkegaard that " only the truth that edifies is truth for thee."

Truth is not a formula but an event, an experience, a personal encounter with God, a disturbing impact, a whole response to the divine initiative. The God-man, Jesus Christ, is to Mackay, and to us, the personal and absolute key to all that God is, to all that man may become.

There is hope in the realization that God is at work among us, that he is moving faster than we are ready to travel toward the fulfillment of his historical purpose. Precisely this awareness finds clear and vigorous expression in Mackay's rejection of the cyclical view of history. Not biological birth and death, but dialectics and dramatics describe historical movement.

With keen insight Mackay perceives that the real issue of our time is whether or not history has religious significance. With all Christians who take history seriously, Mackay believes in the historical unfolding of the divine purpose — not in a denial of freedom and its cost but through and for freedom. Brotherhood is both a natural heritage and a human achievement, but even more, the embrace of the human spirit by the Holy Spirit, the encounter of mankind with Jesus Christ. The task of the Church is to lead the way; the Church has therefore three functions: prophetic, regenerative, and communal. It must be the conscience of the world, the critic of every human claim of finality; it must call men effectually from darkness to light; and it must practice the fellowship it preaches. The Church can perform its task only when it abandons its Babylonian captivity to secondary cultural and social movements, its capitulation to capitalism, nationalism, sectionalism, and racialism. Within the Church, Mackay believes, the foremost need is the restoration of living theology, the rediscovery of the past and its meaning, the understanding of the present and its alternatives, the consciousness of the summons to somewhere.

In *Heritage and Destiny* (The Macmillan Company, 1943) Mackay emphasized that creative acceptance of the call to the future requires a discerning appropriation of the vital and permanent in the past. To move forward without wisdom is to move forward without hope; to find the meaning of yesterday is to find the direction for tomorrow. God lives in the eternal present and his purpose is ahead of us, not behind us, but his direct dealing with historical men and movements constitutes our living heritage, provides the basis of our sense of destiny. In a profounder understanding of what God has done with man and community is our clearest grasp of what God is doing and will do — our sense of direction. Without the authority of ultimates, movement is a mere groping in the night.

PROBLEMS ON THE WAY AND THE POWER NOT OUR OWN

The journey to somewhere is endangered less by godless ideologies than by Protestant apathies, a preoccupation with secular activities, a first-class allegiance to second-class values, a substitution of means for ends. Mackay's *Christianity on the Frontier* (The Macmillan Company, 1950) seeks to remove these modern barriers to progress. Christianity is always on the frontier, for every human maturity is alarmingly premature. These fourteen essays are occasional pieces written over a span of years — no doubt crowded into spare minutes between Mackay's innumerable committees — yet, like Mackay's life, they possess continuity. The theme, perennial in Mackay and permanent in Protestantism, is the true basis of Christianity — the word and act of God. The power of Christianity to correct its own distortions was the meaning of the Reformation, but a new Reformation is our pressing need, a rediscovery of the needle of creativity in the haystack of activity. Mackay's Protestantism runs true to form: he asserts the dependence of creative Church and civilized State upon religious liberty. The reassertion of religious liberty is a desperate necessity — if freedom of thought and freedom of speech are to survive our era of inquisitions and thought control. Christianity to be Christian must resist the idea regimentation of the State — even for so-called Christian ends. In the chapter "A Theological Meditation on Latin America," Mackay stresses essential Christianity as the word and act of a forward-moving God, the command to correct distortion, the necessity of religious liberty for progress in South America or elsewhere.

To my mind, the best chapter is an unabashed appeal not for uniformity but for Christian unity. The journey to somewhere must increasingly be a community enterprise, a family affair. Evangelical catholicity, in Mackay's view, embraces all who pledge their loyalty to Jesus Christ and manifest the fruits of the Spirit. To refuse to admit to the Lord's Supper anyone who believes in, loves, and follows the Saviour, to deprive any believer of Holy Communion in the name of a secondary principle, is a crime against the body of Christ and a sin against the Holy Spirit. Evangelical catholicity, founded upon and inspired by the gospel, is a unity in Christ transcending the defensive differences the children of God have set up to distinguish them from one another.

With leadership of the Mackay quality, the World Council of Churches will transcend the obstacles in its path — the idolization of ephemeral institutions — and lead our anarchic humanity to the Agape Community.

In Mackay's latest book, *God's Order,* The Ephesian Letter and This Present Time (The Macmillan Company, 1953), two things receive special attention: the Power which bears the human pilgrimage on the road to somewhere, and the problem of delay. The volume makes productive union of theology and homiletics; it points the way to an increase of divinity in the dust of oratory. One hardly thinks of a Presbyterian as ecstatic, yet this book is a song: it is Mackay's own experience as a Christian pilgrim; he shares Paul's confidence in final construction beyond present frustration. In no sense does Mackay underestimate the causes of delay. One, in his view, is the modern loss of belief in a personal power of evil. Behind our current hysteria he sees the cunning of the devil. To disbelieve in a personal power of evil, in his estimation, is philosophically unjustifiable, Biblically unsound, and religiously catastrophic. Yet beyond the power of evil is the greater power of God. Crucifixion, frustration, delay, breakdown — these are not new experiences on the road of history. They merely demonstrate the evil that is stronger than we think, yet not strong enough to defeat God the Almighty — infinitely greater than our small formulas. Beyond all man-made crucifixion is God-made resurrection.

Mackay, both in life and in thought, is a forward-looking Christian. He thinks with the Church of the ages, if only that he may not be caught by the distortions of the age. The Christian faith and fellowship, purged of its secular involvement, provided the creativity of Western civilization; the same faith and fellowship, with the authority of ultimates, is the inevitable corrective of the present and hope of the future. The Church is one throughout the earth and the ages; the Church is the mission of today and the meaning of tomorrow. Within this Church Universal the individual Christian may walk and work with God.

THE CHURCH IS NOT THE END BUT THE MEANS

"The Church can never be an end in itself, however perfectly it may formulate its faith, establish its order, and conduct its worship. The Church, to be truly the Church, must be everlastingly an instrument of God's saving will, fulfilling his missionary designs in human history" ("How My Mind Has Changed," *The Christian Century,* July 27, 1949, p. 889).

There is no idolatry of the Church in Mackay's thought, but rather a continual awareness of the task of the Church — to be an open channel of Grace into history. He acknowledges that he has been gripped, and sometimes overwhelmed, by the realization that eternity is a present-tense demand; that in the here and now of one's life, and the life of the world, the eternal order must become real and potent, that it must shed light and mold living. New meaning has come to him in the words, "Jesus Christ is Lord." Christ's importance for both the historical and the cosmic order has become increasingly luminous. The implications for history in our time, and for the march of Christ through time, of the Lordship of Jesus Christ, have given his spirit a new glow. As he sees it, "Christ is the Lord of all the so-called immanent forces of nature, of life and logic. He is the Lord in particular of that tremendous thing called the 'dialectic of history'" (*Ibid.,* p. 888).

More than ever, Mackay finds abhorrent and anti-Christian the pretense of ecclesiastical functionaries to possess the power to manipulate Jesus Christ. He feels that new dynamism must break forth in and through the Church to combat an emergent Communism, a resurgent Roman Catholicism, and the modern human craving for a short-cut to authority and order. As he sees it, the chief need of the moment is not an emphasis upon revelation, already achieved in European theology, but new dynamism among those who hear God's Word and obey it — against the dynamism of other crusading faiths. In his view, the vitality that comes from the mystic collectivism of Communism and the mystic institutionalism of Roman Catholicism can be met only by the dynamism of the new man in Christ, and of the community which is the organ of Christ's will. In his words:

" Our supreme need . . . is a theology of life, and not merely a theology of light. Where both Barth and Niebuhr fall short is in that neither has taken seriously enough the new man in Christ and what God can do through him. Both have been too much afraid of subjectivity and of anything that might appear to savor of mysticism " (*Ibid.*, p. 889).

The Church, to be the Church, must be missionary as well as worshiping. Even the achievement of ecclesiastical unity is not an end in itself. Spiritual health in the Church is not primarily for exhibition or exultation, but for use. Evangelical catholicity must transcend the ecumenical/confessional conflict. There must be a fresh awareness that membership in the body of Christ is on an individual basis. We do not belong to Christ and to his Church upon a denominational or confessional basis. We do not create the body of Christ by fusing churches together. Always the question must be asked, What do the churches contribute to perfecting the saints for the work of ministering?

The Church is the universal community designed by God to transcend and embrace all differences of race, station, and sex that divide mankind. It constitutes the pattern for all true community; hence the surest way to achieve harmony in the secular order is to extend the bounds of the Christian community throughout the world. It is in the measure in which men are reconciled to God, practice the worship of God, seek the Kingdom of God, and live with one another in peace as Christian brethren, that society shall be influenced, directly and indirectly, to seek peace and concord. Christian instruction must seek to guide all thinking into the obedience of Christ, to bring every sphere under the law of Christ. Hence, in the Christian Church, structure is essentially functional. Institutional order is not an end in itself. In Mackay's view, the moment the Bible is made a substitute for Christ it becomes an idol. " So, too, whenever the Church, instead of Christ the Church's Head, becomes the supreme object of devotion, an equal act of idolatry takes place " (" Church Order: Its Meaning and Implications," in *Theology Today*, January, 1953, p. 466).

As Toynbee has pointed out, the Church is to become the inheritor of all religions and all cultural achievements. Hence, asserts

Mackay, all human knowledge and culture must be brought under the light and influence of Christ and be allowed to make their distinctive contribution toward the promotion of the cause of Christ. In this way alone shall Christians come to prize that which is true in their own religious heritage and that which is true in the religious heritage of fellow Christians. What is purely conditioned by time will then begin to disappear; the pure gold will be brought into the Christian treasure house. It will be Christ himself, rather than any lesser object, who shall become more and more the supreme center of devotion.

Mackay gives the word "ecumenical" a new depth and breadth of meaning. He thus demonstrates the functional purpose of the Church — to be an avenue of God's creative action in and upon history.

"In a sense and to a degree not true of any previous epoch in history, our age is ecumenical in character. The world of today is an ecumenical world. To employ the term 'ecumenical' in this purely secular sense may sound strange, but it is a legitimate use of the term. For, linguistically, 'ecumenical' means simply 'that which affects men everywhere throughout the globe.' Every major occurrence tends to have world-wide repercussions or relations and so to become ecumenical in this basic sense. Potent forces in our time affect the inhabited earth, the *oikoumene,* and make the world one, whether for weal or for woe" (Editorial in *Theology Today,* April, 1952, p. 1).

Evangelical catholicity, the essential nature of Christianity, is that world-wide expression of the Christian religion which is centered in Jesus Christ and the gospel and not in any particular organizational or institutional structure of Church life. It recovers for our time the meaning of that adage of the Early Christian Church, "Where Christ is, there is the Church." In Mackay's view, evangelical catholicity stands in this respect in sharp antithesis to the Roman Catholic or institutional conception of the Church and of Christian unity. Ecumenical Christians do not regard the Roman Catholic pattern as the true pattern of Christian community or as the ideal pattern for Church unity. Evangelical catholicity, the catholicity of early Christianity and of the ecumenical era, involves a basic affirmation that unity in Christ and its fullest expression in thought and life and ecclesiastical relations do not involve the Romanization of non-Roman Christianity.

Rather, the Ecumenical Movement today means both the missionary movement of the Church to occupy the *oikoumene* in the name of Christ, and the ecclesiastical movement to unify the forces of occupation. Corresponding to these two objectives there are two organizations, equally ecumenical in character. They are the parent ecumenical body, the International Missionary Council, and the more recent ecumenical body, the World Council of Churches. While the International Missionary Council has traditionally represented the mission of the Church, it is equally interested in the unity of the Church. While the World Council of Churches was created to seek the unity of the Church, it becomes, to an increasing extent, interested in the mission of the Church.

Mackay offers a challenge and a warning to ecumenical enthusiasm:

"In the spiritual order mere structural bigness need not necessarily engender greater prophetic insight, greater redemptive action, greater organizational efficiency, or greater human harmony. The two bodies which constitute the organizational foci of the Ecumenical Movement must grow together on the road of loyal devotion to the Church's mission" (*Ibid.,* p. 6).

Theology must recognize its own ecumenical task. To Mackay, theology is that understanding of God which comes from communion with God and leads to the contemplation and discussion of all things human and divine in the light of God. In Mackay's words, "Christian theology is an intellectual effort to interpret the meaning and apply the implications of God's self-disclosure of himself in history" ("Theology in Education," in *The Christian Century,* April 25, 1951, p. 521). However, theological education is interested not only in the knowledge of God and its relevancy to the human situation but also in the service of God. Its supreme objective, as Mackay understands it, is to prepare servants of God genuinely concerned for broken minds as well as broken bodies. Kindly leadership in devotion to the Church Universal and its ecumenical task must characterize the men trained in our seminaries.

Mackay's book *A Preface to Christian Theology* emphasizes that Christian theology today has a missionary role to fulfill, of a kind that has not been required since the early Christian thinkers outthought the pagan world. Once both thought and action in secular society were basically determined by Christian conceptions. When that was so, theology could follow, without loss to life, a purely technical, scholastic, sectarian course. However, when things, taken for granted for centuries, are called in question, when total disintegration threatens, when secular theologies emerge, Christian theology "is invested with a new missionary role. 'Today,' as F. R. Barry says, 'the intellectual initiative is passing back to Christian theology.' But if this initiative is to be worthily taken, theology must abandon its isolation; it must also rise above the issues born of family strife" (*Ibid.*, p. 25). The two types of American seminaries, vertical and horizontal, must allow their interests to intersect in a prophetic approach to the world of our time; the eternal must challenge the temporal.

But theology, conscious of its modern task, must also be aware of its taskmaster. As Mackay sees it, knowledge of things divine can be obtained only by those people in whom personal concern has been born and an absolute commitment produced. We cannot insist too strongly that no true knowledge of God is possible where concern and commitment are absent — a concern about righteousness and a commitment to righteousness. Truth is thus an existential pilgrimage, aware that God both individualizes and universalizes. Faith is not, however, an immanental process as such, but in God who moves within and upon it. In Mackay's words, " The Kingdom will come by an overwhelming manifestation of divine power, not by the development of immanent processes already at work in human society " (*Ibid.*, p. 102). The Church grows in the faith that the things for which it stands are the only things that have a future; that history and the gospel, the human heart and the cross of Christ, were made for each other. True life for man is the life in which the old self dies. The spirit of the life of Christ is normative for all Christian life in every age. Thus, " it is in the measure in which the reality of the Holy Catholic Church is present in the churches that true churchly reality can be theirs. . . . The supranational can only be achieved through the supernatural " (*Ibid.*, pp. 163, 182).

In Mackay's view, both civilization and religion stand under the divine judgment, that is, both have a functional role to play in openness to divine action. While the process of soul-making contributes more than anything else to social improvement, not such improvement, but rather souls, is the ultimate function and test of both civilization and religion. Souls hold the key to every form of human welfare. Four views of man have alike overlooked man in personal relations with God and the fellowship: the naturalistic, the economic, the humanist or rational, and the voluntarist. In the Christian view, man was made for responsible relations in love, for fellowship with God and man. True community can be achieved only when men meet the Everlasting Other, the eternal Thou, and become related to him. To Mackay, only when man meets God and responds to him does he become truly man. Only when men meet one another in the love of God does true community become possible. In Mackay's words: " The encounter between the human spirit and the divine is the source of renewal. The cure for emptiness is the incoming of God into life. The cure for fear is to be swept along in the mighty current of God's redemptive purpose for mankind " (*Heritage and Destiny*, p. 64). God, the ancient heritage of Israel, the transforming patrimony of the soul, and the everlasting wellspring of culture, must become the chosen heritage of this and every nation, if human destiny is to be worthily fulfilled within a world framework. " The most creative and steadying word in human speech is the word ' remember ' " (*Ibid.*, p. 78).

In our day when Church and State are again in conflict, Mackay bids us re-examine their respective roles. As he sees it, religion is concerned with the ultimate relationship of man to God and with the duties and responsibilities which that relationship determines for human life, both in the religious and the secular order. Government

is concerned with the common good of citizens and with the main-
tenance of order and the promotion of justice in all the relations
between individuals, groups, and institutions in the national society and between one nation and another. The area of reciprocal
responsibilities is harder to define. Always, however, it is the responsibility of religion to proclaim the spiritual bases of government — of all public administration, whether local, national, or international. Not the secular State, not the totalitarian State, not the
clerical State, but the lay State, conducted by men and women conscious of the Lordship of Christ, is the Christian objective. It is the
pursuit of righteousness and not of security that must be the supreme law of nations. No absolute security is possible or desirable.
When a nation feels that it has achieved security, it stands in deadly
peril. "Inexorable gravitational forces which operate in history will
demolish every structure of man-made security" ("Religion and
Government," in *Theology Today*, July, 1952, p. 207).

Mackay insists that it is the responsibility of government to recognize the importance of religion as a determining force in human
society which molds the thought, the character, and the attitudes of
people. There is no escaping the fact that American democracy is
the child of religious influences. Education, therefore, that is non-
religious is alien to American history. To Mackay, an educational
system inspired by a philosophy of secularism, which is something
quite different from religious neutrality, must never be allowed to
have complete control. But freedom of thought and speech is also a
central Christian requirement. In Mackay's words:

"In granting freedom to religion, the State must grant equal freedom
to those who criticize and attack religion. The interests of truth, in the
widest and deepest sense, are dependent upon freedom to discuss the
most crucial matters, and to express and propagate ideas of all kinds,
provided that those ideas are not subversive of public morals and do not
advocate the violent overthrow of government.

"It is only through the toleration of ideas that we can look forward
to increased truth and to the preparation of robust and stalwart representatives of truth. It is in fact good for truth to have to struggle with
error. Nothing . . . can be more fatal to truth and to the welfare of

society than to try to suppress by force so-called ideological errors. . . . Error must be met by truth in free and open encounter and not by a sword or a fagot, not by a boycott or an Index" (*Ibid.*, p. 212).

Mackay defines the seat of trouble in the relation between religion and government. In his view, it is the lesson of history that whenever a given religion has demanded and secured for itself a preferred status in government, on such terms as to affect the civil rights and the religious freedom of those who do not profess that religion, the most devastating consequences have inexorably followed. As Mackay expresses it: " It is a violation of basic principles and is contrary to the best interests of religion and government in the United States, and to the peace of American society in general, that any religious organization as such should be given preferential status or be granted a unique distinction or receive special privileges in the national life or in international relations" (*Ibid.*, p. 216). For this reason Mackay is opposed to the appointment of an American ambassador to the Vatican. To him, what is at stake is whether the American State shall symbolically recognize that there is one Church above all others which, by its nature, has a claim to special honor and consideration by the American Government. Similarly, Mackay opposes special privilege or special aid to parochial schools.

In particular, in the light of current American hysterias, Mackay believes that the Roman Catholic Church, according to the testimony of history, has had more natural affinity with Fascism than with democracy. Both in theory and in practice, he sees a great threat to American freedom in the Roman Catholic support of anti-Communist crusades. In his penetrating words:

" When a Church believes and teaches that it alone, in its organized, institutional form, is the true Church; that its hierarchy belongs to the Church in a sense that the laity do not; that the will of God in new situations is revealed to the hierarchy alone, and not in free discussion between clergy and laity in the light of God's revelation and under the guidance of his Spirit; and, most important of all, when it believes that the hierarchy, identifying its own will with the will of God, and the interests of the Church with the interests of society and the State, should feel a God-given compulsion, when circumstances are favorable, to make the State and its agencies subservient to its will, then a sinister phenomenon eventually emerges " (*Ibid.*, p. 219).

Both Spain and Latin America have demonstrated Christopher Dawson's word that the God-State is the greatest enemy of God.

Similarly, when Americanism considers itself the end rather than the means, a new idolatry is formed. Mackay is very much aware of the emergence of this foe in contemporary American life. In his words:

" A new form of idolatry, a religious devotion to something other than God and his Kingdom, is gripping the popular mind in our country. Detestation of Communism is producing in certain circles a religious fervor, and this fervor is creating a substitute religion. A passionate, unreflective opposition to the Communist demon is coming to be regarded as the one and only true expression of Americanism and even of Christianity " ("The New Idolatry," in *Theology Today*, October, 1953, p. 382).

Idolatry engenders fanaticism and stifles thought. Even more, it is perilous, in Mackay's view, for any human being to live by negation. We must be increasingly aware of the danger of accepting Fascist partners in the anti-Communist crusade. A Fascist victory would be as bad as a Communist one. In any form of fanaticism, freedoms to which a person is entitled as a human being are disregarded. Investigation becomes inquisition. When fear dominates the popular mind, as it does today, the tendency arises to choose a private deity for one's personal devotion. A profound shift occurs from " My nation under God " to " My nation, thou art my God." In Mackay's words: " Jesus Christ is Lord — he alone, and the Kingdom which he came to establish, constitutes for Americans, as for all humans, the one and only object of absolute allegiance " (*Ibid.*, p. 383).

The Christian Church is called upon to reassume its prophetic role in our time, to indicate where and why false absolutes are false, and to summon nation and person alike to serve the living God.

But Mackay's thought everywhere breathes the validity of hope. Evil is not more real than God. As he puts it:

" While Christians may accept as completely as do Marxists that there are in history inexorable forces of a dialectical character, they proclaim that Jesus Christ is Lord over human nature in the depths of its depravity and the range of its influence. They affirm also that all human logic and dialectic, together with every force, historical or cosmic, which controls human existence, has been transcended and can be overcome by the ' Living One who was dead and is alive forever more ' " (Editorial, *Theology Today*, January, 1951, p. 436).

As Mackay sees it, the Church knows that in God's world might will not permanently triumph. It knows that Jesus Christ is Lord and that a will to fellowship, and not a will to power, will ultimately prevail. To make that will prevail, the life and thought of the Christian Church are dedicated.

This hope is not vaporous and distant; it is the offer of divine grace to America today. Mackay believes that it is not necessary that a nation that has access to the full light of the Christian revelation for its political direction, and which is seriously convinced that a nation primarily exists to serve God, shall pass irrevocably away. It is not inevitable therefore that the American nation, if loyal to its heritage, shall suffer decay. There is power in the God who comes to us in the Hebrew-Christian tradition, which is our heritage, to pilot us through the darkness and neutralize all our natural tendencies to impotence and dissolution.

Mackay asserts the reality of hope, not alone in his theology, but also in his personal faith. In his words:

" I believe in the Lordship of the living Christ in the Church and in secular society, and over all the events, processes, and forces of human history. I take my stand in this regard upon the earliest and most basic Christian creed: ' Jesus Christ is Lord ' " (*Religion and Government*, p. 205).

Walter M. Horton

A THEOLOGY OF LIBERAL CLASSICISM

A *clear* voice announcing the gospel, the hope greater than our hopelessness, with an unmistakable call to the forward look, is Walter Marshall Horton. Four developments in his intellectual career are evident: a break with humanism, a break with mere liberalism, a growing appreciation of European *depth* and British *balance* in theology, and a discerning emphasis upon historical eschatology. His thought, from first to last, perceives the goodness and greatness of God.

MAN OF GROWTH

Congregationalists are sometimes made, not born. Walter Marshall Horton, now a Congregationalist, was born a Baptist in Somerville, Massachusetts, April 7, 1895, the son of Walter Emery and Clara Powers (Marshall) Horton. He was educated at Harvard (A.B., 1917), at Union Theological Seminary in New York (B.D., 1920, and S.T.M., 1923), at Columbia University (M.A., 1920, and Ph.D., 1926), and at the universities of Paris, Strasbourg, and Marburg. He was ordained a Baptist minister in 1919; the same year, May 20, he married Lidie Loring Chick.

Horton was instructor in philosophy of religion and systematic theology at Union Theological Seminary from 1922 to 1925. He became associate professor of systematic theology at Oberlin Graduate School of Theology (1925), and has been Fairchild Professor of Theology since 1926. He is a member of the American Theological Society, Phi Beta Kappa, the Cosmos Club, and Oberlin's Social Science Club.

He has contributed important chapters to innumerable symposia, but his own volumes are a major contribution.

The Break with Humanism

The distinction between nontheistic humanism and Christian theism is the point in Horton's important book *Theism and the Modern Mood* (Harper & Brothers, 1930). Few attempts have better analyzed the self-defeating effort of humanism to deny ultimate meaning with one voice, and with another to assert the reality of human values. All men to some extent assert in practice what they deny in theory, or vice versa, but the nontheistic humanists have abused the privilege; they occupy a nebulous middle ground between proud self-sufficiency and cosmic nostalgia.

Back of the humanism of the American twenties, as Horton views it, lay the classical humanism of the sixteenth century, the naturalism of the seventeenth, the humanitarianism of the eighteenth, and the positivism of the nineteenth. And one might add — the common tendency from the Stone Age onward to distrust divine and human reason working together, to trust instead man's own strength of mind working alone. One feels some sympathy for the humanists of the twenties; the first World War was not a tea party; the one-sided myth of a gentle God, meek and mild, seemed, and was, premature. And humanism has always been a necessary corrective to authoritarian religion.

In spite of the humanists' unsolvable problem, to maintain meaningful life in a meaningless universe, Horton sees in them a deep yearning for the abundant life for all men, a genuine movement toward "the more beyond," and therefore an authentic Christian hope, a healthy breaking away from premature finalities; their weakness lies in the belief that no reality corresponds to the stubborn hopefulness of man. To Bertrand Russell, lately in closer rapport with the saints, man was a victim in fact, but might be a conqueror in value. Man was therefore both vermin and royalty. The Christian view of man similarly accents both finiteness and freedom, but stresses the fact that man may have made himself

vermin, but was not vermin to begin with, and is not hopelessly vermin at any time, for God is at work with and within him. Humanism, to gain self-consistency, must accept the full implications of a
meaningless world and thereby destroy all faith in man, or it must
affirm the meaningful reality behind all human values and thereby
become theistic.

One camp within humanism was represented (in 1930) by the
scientific naturalists: Dietrich, Reese, and Krutch; to them science
was the new Moses; they endeavored futilely to maintain human
values in a world valueless by definition. In the second camp Walter
Lippmann believed that God was dead and Whirl was king, or thus
expressed the sentiment of his day, but sought nonetheless to summon mankind to disinterestedness, the mortification of selfishness,
the recovery of the king in man.

Against muddled humanism, Horton described the God of human experience, of the upward quest, with Wieman, Lyman, and
Hocking around Tolstoi's dictum: " God is he without whom one
cannot live." At this point Horton's own theism seemed apologetic.
He defined God as man's own better self, as the best in our human
heritage, as the cosmic drift (or drive?) toward harmony. He was
himself close enough to Lippmann, and the upward-looking humanists, to appreciate them — or was deliberately presenting an
irreducible minimum lest the humanists be frightened away. Yet
he insisted that Christianity added something to the God of human
aspiration, namely greatness and goodness. Evolution is dominated
by divine greatness, and salvation by divine goodness — made flesh
in Jesus Christ. Horton challenged the lethargic humanists, feeble
in the will to believe, to take the gambler's chance on the goodness
of God. He saw no reason to pity Jesus, the supreme lover and sufferer of the human race, for the faith in God that led him to his
death — and our life.

THE BREAK WITH MERE LIBERALISM

In 1934, Walter Horton's lectures at Andover Newton Theological
School were published under the title *Realistic Theology* (Harper &

Brothers). He announced to a world of liberals that liberalism was dead — not as a method but as a metaphysic. Many liberals responded, with Harris Franklin Rall, that Horton himself was an incorrigible liberal, that the reports of liberalism's death, as in the case of Mark Twain, were greatly exaggerated. Horton's point was nonetheless important; he was a true herald of the dawn after a night of doubt. Horton had discovered Tillich's "belief-ful realism," the attempt to look at things as they are (autonomy), yet to see them also as enclosed within God's world of meaning (theonomy) — the attempt to destroy religion divorced from life on the one hand and life divorced from religion on the other, to make one world of sacred and secular spheres under one forward-moving God.

This movement in Horton's mind meant one thing — his dynamic rediscovery of the Christian religion as more than man's wishful thinking. With Tillich, Horton began to move toward the political left and the theological right. What H. Richard Niebuhr calls "accommodationism" and Karl Barth calls "culture-Protestantism" — the identification of Christ with culture — breaks open in Horton's Christian realism. Horizontal, immanental religion meets vertical, transcendent religion, and a two-way God/world dimension, a creative tension, is born. It is possible that Horton condemned more in liberalism than he meant to: he was violent against the religiosity of Schleiermacher, the ethicism of Ritschl, and the speculative abstractionism of the Hegelians. He found liberalism politically inept, sociologically shallow, and psychologically stupid. Liberalism overemphasized immanence and continuity, bowed down uncritically before the Baal of scientism, tossed basic Christian truths away as impossible absolutes, placed its faith in reason without revelation, substituted ignorance for sin, education for salvation, and romantic optimism for painful growth.

It all depends, of course, on what liberalism is. If liberalism worships human reason alone, it is idolatry. If liberalism places intellectual integrity in the service of God, it is Christianity. Horton was all for the liberal attitude — love of truth, appeal to experience, readiness to accept new knowledge. He was against tradition *as* tradition, against sacrosanct authority (heteronomy); he was strongly in favor of realism, sound method, and the pursuit of truth wherever it leads.

Horton's political left did not go as far as Reinhold Niebuhr's necessity of coercion against the holders of power; his theological right did not go as far as Barth's Neo-Calvinism. Horton's position was and remains essentially " free catholicism " or liberal evangelicalism, placing its faith in a personal and transcendent God, in religion as redemption, as creation.

Rapport with Europe and England

In 1936 and 1938 appeared Walter M. Horton's selective, if not wholly comprehensive, studies of theology abroad: *Contemporary English Theology* and *Contemporary Continental Theology* (both Harper & Brothers).

These two studies were particularly meaningful then, and remain useful now. American theologians had only begun to look abroad. English theology, as Horton experienced it, possessed sanity, balance, and comprehensiveness. European theology was rather preoccupied with tragic depth and transcendent hope. The European study is the more thoroughgoing of the two; through both analyses American theology is summoned to venture beyond its traditional isolationism.

English theology had already passed the crisis of liberalism; Horton hoped his report from England would help to rid America of the blight of relativism. Horton described the main British movements in the preceding thirty years. American theologians did not see the value of the book, being excessively anxious that American theology be recognized in its own right; Anglicans regarded the book with interest plus exasperation, feeling that Horton had failed to genuflect three times toward the apostolic succession. The book was of basic value nonetheless; it preached continuity with the total Christian Community. Americans resented the implication that culture is " the Europeanization of the mind," but needed, and received in Horton's study, a new awareness of tradition as a fellowship of free minds — a transmillennial dialectic. Horton presented three distinct traditions — Catholicism, Protestantism, and Liberalism. His liberals were L. P. Jacks, Dean Inge, F. R. Tennant, and the then younger prophets — Streeter, Raven, and Macmurray. Catholicism and Protestantism were presented in one insufficient chapter — " Essays Catholic and Critical " for the one and " John Oman " for the other. Cadoux, Reckitt, and Peck were omitted or relegated to footnotes. In William Temple, Archbishop of York, Horton found a leader he could accept, and recommend to Americans. This was significant, for Temple was filled with hope — for one world, filled with one Spirit, under one God. As a comprehensive study, the book was less than satisfactory; nonetheless its plea for balance and perspective, for Christian continuity, for one-world fellowship is permanently valid.

On the continent, as Horton saw it, Berdyaev and Bulgakov (after Dostoevsky) represented Orthodox thought; both stressed the tragedy of man's existence and the hope of man's redemption. Horton's Romanists were Maritain and Przywara. Maritain mediated between Barthian pessimism and discredited liberal optimism. Przywara emphasized man's freedom in and before the immanent and transcendent God. In Germany, Horton found Barthianism and Aryanism, two extreme reactions against effeminate liberalism. Horton considered the John Huss Faculty at Prague the final outpost of liberalism. He doubted the American willingness to follow Dostoevsky, Bloy, Kierkegaard, and Barth to the neglect of Masaryk. Horton considered European theology deductive, Anglo-Saxon theology inductive. To the Europeans, God was an eschatological promise; to the Anglo-Saxons, God was an ontological presence. The Europeans, in Horton's view, made up in depth for what they lacked in breadth and balance — depth in the Bible (Barth), depth in the relation between God and the world (Barth, Heim, Przywara, and Berdyaev), depth in the human soul (Dostoevsky, Berdyaev, and Brunner), depth in the mystery of iniquity (Heim's personal devil), depth in the work of Christ (Aulén, Althaus, and Heim), depth in Church and State (Maritain, Bulgakov, and Brunner), and depth in the mystery of the future (Althaus, Berdyaev, and Holmstrom).

Horton acknowledged common ground with European liberals. In his words:

"The truth of liberal Protestantism is much better conserved by Berdyaev and Maritain than by Barth and Heim. . . . As a believer in the need of a transformed, reinvigorated liberal Protestantism, I am therefore led to declare myself a liberal Catholic. . . ."

He did not leave the subject without an appreciative glance at America's home-grown dynamism:

"Truncated as their religious philosophies may seem from the European point of view, Ames and Wieman are nevertheless truly religious and genuinely inspiring in their certitude that God lives and works to-day and tomorrow, and his handiwork is recognizable in fresh creative activity, transforming the world before our eyes" (*Contemporary Continental Theology,* pp. 228, 233).

Horton asks American theologians to think more recklessly than the British and more cautiously than the Europeans; for all theology he stresses the necessity of the forward look. Our half-finished world and our half-finished souls exist to be converted, transformed, created.

THE BEGINNINGS OF HOPE

Every work of Horton's is important; his 1926 *The Philosophy of the Abbé Boutain* accented the Pascalian "reason of the heart" above the "reason of the head"—love above knowledge. His 1931 *A Psychological Approach to Theology* built a needed bridge between theology and psychiatry. Creative, digestive, it predated many a lesser work on the relation between the mechanism and meaning of personality. Horton's *Theism and the Scientific Spirit* (the Ayer Lectures for 1932–1933 at Colgate-Rochester Divinity School) traced the survival of the God-dimension through Copernican, Newtonian, Kantian, and Darwinian revolutions. His 1942 *Our Eternal Contemporary* presented the classical view of Christ in a liberal vocabulary. His 1949 *Toward a Reborn Church* (a book for specialists) champions the ecumenical movement and mentality. In each Horton book the realization grows that Christianity is not only faith, looking toward the past, not only love, which holds the present in its arms; but hope, which *moves forward* to embrace the purpose of God.

Horton's prophetic *Can Christianity Save Civilization?* (Harper & Brothers, 1940) grasps the reality of hope. The title is awkward (titles always are!); more accurately the title should read, *Can Christianity Create Civilization?*, for that is the underlying question. Christian redemption is not the restoration of the good, but the creation of the better, God's future for this world, the future that was made flesh in Jesus, the future that invaded the hearts of the disciples at Pentecost, and now invades the world to create it. To Horton, the present crisis in parochical cultures is not an end but a beginning; the door is open to the building of a universal culture, a world community. Christianity, contrary to its genius, has sometimes idolized ephemeral institutions, has too often placed a pious strait jacket upon progress, has worshiped the *status quo*; yet, in Horton's view, Christianity has often rescued and reconstructed dying civilizations. With Spengler and Schweitzer (Toynbee had not yet made his full impact) Horton believed (1940) that the present form of culture was on its last legs, yet beyond all tragedy loomed a new world, already present in creative insight. Christianity is, and must ever be, a drive to cosmic community. Evangelism means nothing less. In this book Horton fashions anthropological and philosophical supports for the coming Kingdom. Horton is not for the fearful; he offers only doom to present self-sufficiency. Yet he offers also the prophet's certain hope: God *is* God and God *is* Love; God has no permanent problem world; God's grace, greater than man's waywardness, will yet bring the total process to fulfillment. That fufillment will not be a static society of nice people, a stately minuet, but a wild dance of freedom in fellowship. Our world is challenged, and may be destroyed. Horton sees beyond destruction "the resurrection of the body social," the *kairos* — the union of logos and chronos, of meaning and time.

Christianity, not a convention but a creative power, not a letter but a spirit, now confronts our primary problems: the relation of men to machines; the achievement of economic justice; the traffic snarl among individuals, families, and states; the nationalist/internationalist conflict. The world with all its chaos exists within, not outside, the hand of Omnipotence — exists to be created, to be fashioned into the *imago Dei*. Within Christianity itself, the ecumenical movement must increase, and narrow defensiveness decrease. The Christian world community must grow — must provide the nucleus or chrysalis of Christian world civilization. A short vision sees the present as disaster; the long view sees the dawn beyond the dark. This is not "automatic progress," not the theme, "Glory to man in the highest." This is the sober realization that history moves irreversibly toward its purpose. Because man is man and mostly self-love, tragedy is possible and probable. Because God is God and God is Love, increasing triumph is inevitable.

THE GOODNESS AND GREATNESS OF GOD

In Horton's view, the God of human experience, substituted by liberalism for the God of Christian faith, lacked three essentials: personality, infinitude, and omnipotence. The God who is God was surrendered to the God who is less than God. Yet to affirm faith in the God of Christian faith inevitably involves a paradox. Nonetheless, better a vague and inconsistent idea of God which embodies some real insight into the meaning of Christianity, than a neat well-trimmed idea of God which fails to allow for the element of mystery. The paradoxical ways of systematic theologians may provoke laughter, for they love to affirm, at one and the same moment, both free will and predestination, omnipotence and moral perfection. Yet Horton ventures to assert that it is precisely in these shocking paradoxes, rather than in the neat, self-consistent systems of the philosophers, that we come closest to the truth. In any case, and in every case, serious religion is a forced option.

Among the profound paradoxes of faith, Horton finds one of supreme importance for our time. One side of the paradox is represented by Baron von Hügel, who accented divine transcendence, the divine aggression, the eternity and self-sufficiency of God; that

God is realized perfection, from whom all beauty, goodness, and truth are derived; that God is a living unity, by whom and in whom all things are constituted and sustained. Von Hügel pushed the search for a perfect object of devotion beyond the evolutionary process itself to an absolute Source and Ground. His thought included all that is found in the empirical quest, but refused to stop there.

The other side of the paradox is represented by Studdert-Kennedy, who found God a creative warrior, eternally laboring and eternally suffering. Nonetheless, both Von Hügel and Studdert-Kennedy found God best revealed in the cross of Christ. One found the greatness of absolute being; the other, the goodness of holy will. How, then, shall these two testimonies be reconciled? In Horton's words, " The best way to hit the bull's-eye of theological truth is by affirming both sides of a paradox that stretches halfway across the center of the target — not by yielding to the pull which either end of the paradox exerts " (*Theism and the Modern Mood,* p. 107).

We thus arrive at the paradoxical nature of the God of Christian faith — a Being both transcendent and immanent, active and at rest, suffering and at peace, personal will and impersonal cosmic energy, born once upon a time in a Palestinian stable and nevertheless without either beginning or ending. " Yet this tissue of logical inconsistencies is rooted in our highest human experience " (*Ibid.,* p. 108). On the one hand, Horton asserts the divine greatness, the transcendence, prior initiative, and self-sufficiency of God; on the other, the divine goodness, the creative good will, the Christlike character of God. To lose either of these emphases is to dissolve the process into the purpose, or the purpose into the process.

To Horton, the modern trend to theological realism has its dangers, but provides the needed next step beyond liberalism. In his words:

" Liberalism *as a system of theology* has collapsed and must be replaced, but it stood and still stands for precious truths and values which must not be allowed to die. I sense a great ground swell of new life in the general ' realistic ' tendency of our times, which I believe is capable of furnishing the guiding principles of the new theology that is required. . . . In what Paul Tillich calls a ' belief-ful realism ' I see hope of a new statement of Christian faith, in which former conservatives and former liberals may find they have more in common than they used to suppose " (*Realistic Theology*, p. ix).

In the new realism Horton finds simultaneous relations of sympathy with Christian orthodoxy on the one hand and with social radicalism on the other. Humanism has stressed the human predicament — individually as the enemy within, socially as the enemy around, and cosmically as the enemy beyond. Barthianism has stressed divine providence in law and grace as a prior consideration. The two together form the content of Christian realism.

Examining the work of Christ from the realistic standpoint, Horton finds that three things were accomplished: (1) A permanent change took place in the relations between God and man; God got inside humanity as never before. (2) A power was permanently released, and henceforth available, whereby individual human souls might conquer their sinful propensities and rise above the fear of suffering and death; this power simply was not released before. (3) A new social organism, the Church, was created, through which God's Spirit and Power have ever since been mediated to human souls in a definitely new way, and in which the powers of darkness which still largely control our social life have found their deadliest enemy — " a kind of benign cancer, which eats destructively into the vitals of evil institutions " (*Ibid.*, p. 137); this social organism was not here before.

Horton does not mean to suggest that the Christian Church is the only channel through which the grace of God is flowing. As he sees it, the life of God impinges universally upon human life, and every human institution — secular and religious — that survives at all survives because a spark of the life of God is in it. In his view, if the Kingdom of God should ever come completely on earth, it would not simply be a magnified Church, but a cluster of glorified institutions — states, families, trade guilds, religious orders, and the like — of which the Church would be simply the vitalizing center and organizing entelechy. It is the function of the Christian Church to bring out the divine spark in other institutions, other movements, and other religions, by entering into commerce with them all, opposing their sins and arrogances, helping them to define their true functions, communicating to them the breath of the Spirit which is needed to fan into flame the spark of God which is in them. In Horton's words: " What an amazing burst of flame has the Spirit of Christ brought up out of the spark of God in Hinduism, in modern times! What a burst of flame might come from Nationalism and atheistic Communism if the Christian Church dared to go to Calvary in their midst! " (*Ibid.*, p. 151). But today, in its corrupt condition, as Horton sees it, the Christian Church is not fit to shoulder the cross, not fit to be the savior of the world. It must and will undergo judgment and purging to fit it for its task.

Realism must always guard against the scaling down of earthly hopes to opportunist proportions, yet guard as well against mere otherworldliness. Realistic theology, in Horton's view, tends to revert to a traditional conception of the Kingdom of God, to regard it as God's Kingdom, not man's, governed by an often inscrutable Providence whose workings man must humbly seek to discern, if his small efforts are to count at all; and it tends to doubt whether the perfect consummation of the will of God is ever going to come to pass within the sphere of earthly human life. As Horton puts it, " To acknowledge the reality of God's transcendent activity in providential judgment and redeeming grace, and then refuse to ' hope in God,' is self-contradictory " (*Ibid.*, pp. 115–116).

The Christian's hope, from Horton's standpoint, focuses on personal immortality, yet the Church seeks the transformation of history through five activities: by individual transformation, by preaching, by fellowship, by charities and missions, and by changing the public mind and will and the social policy. In and for the world, it is the task of the Christian Church, on Horton's terms, to prepare and announce the coming — by shreds and patches, no doubt — of a communal world civilization of which God's relation to his true sons is the best pattern: a civilization to which existing nations, races, and classes are capable of making distinctive contributions, as is every individual and every group, but which will not be under the egoistic domination of any. History has taught us that this ideal, grounded as it is in the structure of reality, is nevertheless not capable of sudden and total realization, as the early Christians supposed. Neither is it realizable through any ecclesiastical theocracy, as the Roman Catholics and the Puritans supposed. It demands for its realization a common consent on the part of all the fundamental human collectives — states, families, trades and professions, etc. — which is infinitely hard to obtain. Yet to resist the encroachments of concrete private and sectional interests against the universal interests of the invisible Kingdom, to collaborate with every agency that makes for the common weal, and to help individuals and small groups to live even now as if the Kingdom had already come, is infinitely worth-while, and this is the task of the Church.

The method of advance is clear in Horton's realistic words:

" It was the glory of the scientific age which lies just behind us that it learned how to chart the vast resources of nature, discern the lines of connection that link us with these resources, and then build connecting channels through which nature's abundance flowed out to meet our need. I cannot believe that the social problems of the age that lies ahead of us are to be solved in any other way. They will not solve themselves if we pray to God, beat our breasts, and let things drift as they have been going. They cannot be solved by human cunning and human willpower alone, though these must play their part. We shall be delivered from our social ills only if we first learn how to discern behind the surface of human events the constant action of divine Providence, and then learn how to align ourselves with the great thrust of that holy Will, and serve as instruments in that mighty Hand " (*Ibid.*, pp. 195–196).

In short, the Church must learn, at one and the same time, to strengthen its own contribution, and to allow science to do likewise, as an ally, not an enemy. In Horton's excellent chapter " Science and Theology " (pp. 91–107 in *The Church Through Half a Century,* essays by former students in honor of William Adams Brown, Scribner's, 1936) he has outlined the recent history of conflict, of efforts at restatement of the Christian understanding of immanence, and the realistic hope of better things to come.

The Darwin earthquake resulted in a new approach to the Bible, as a source not of scientific fact but of religious and moral truth.

The view that theology must square with science was expressed by the Manchester trilogy in 1887 and by the *Lux Mundi* in 1889. A new awareness of immanence as against mere deist transcendence was apparent. The evolutionary reconstruction in theology, which Horton dates from 1889 to 1914, applied Darwin's genetic method to the Bible. The problems raised by evolution and higher criticism were in dispute longer in America than in England. However, William Newton Clarke, of Colgate; Henry Churchill King, of Oberlin; and William Adams Brown, of Union, accomplished for our century exactly what Aquinas accomplished in his synthesis of Aristotle and Augustine for the thirteenth. The inerrancy of the Scriptures was given up, and an attempt was made to restate the doctrine of God and the world. The idea of continuous creation, of God's work in natural law, was developed. Traditional ideas of man, sin, and salvation were revised. If there was no Adam, there was no Fall, rather the beginning of a long ascent. Yet the idea of original sin was not wholly lost, for every man was seen to be two men, both continuous and discontinuous with the past. Salvation was seen to be, not restoration, but the next step in man's development, a transition from man to superman.

Since the First World War new tension has arisen between science and theology. The synthesis of the earlier period has partially broken up. Yet one idea has emerged to stay: the immanence of God in the whole unfolding process of cosmic and social evolution. Evil is viewed as a means to a greater good, not as an independent reality. The First World War, however, exploded the idea of a dramatic whole. One trend has therefore abandoned the infinity of God, and another exalted transcendence above the struggle. Liberalism in particular sacrificed to continuity the idea of discontinuity between God and the world. Since the First World War, the science of psychology offered new challenge to religion. In Horton's words, " Wags remarked that psychology, having long since lost its soul and its mind, was now about to lose consciousness " (P. 103). Freudian theory regarded religion as an escape mechanism, an infantile regression, an illusory father-image, yet Freudian practice in time proved an ally in its discovery of depth in man, of human sin and human need. The new physics, popularized by Sir Arthur Eddington, Sir James Jeans, and A. N. Whitehead, broke with materialistic mechanism, considered science itself a partial and symbolic account of reality.

Today the prospects for friendship between science and religion are immeasurably improved. Lloyd Morgan's emergent evolution inserted discontinuity into the evolutionary process. Wieman's description of God as " growing good " surrenders transcendence, but asserts the reality of immanence. Nonetheless, a certain inevitable tension between science and religion remains. Science focuses its attention on the world, and religion upon God, as William Temple pointed out. Yet, as Temple also insisted, there need be no final war, since the cause of constancy in nature is itself the cause of variation when that serves the one purpose best. In any case, the religious demand for the priority of God can never be satisfied with any conception of God as merely immanent. The transcendence of God asserts that God is eternally self-identical; the immanence of God explains the principle of variety. As Horton sees it, the independence and supremacy of modern religious interest is far from the anxious conciliation of the eighties, while retaining reverence for scientific truth in its own sphere. It would be fatal for science to become religion, or for religion to become science, yet each has its part to play; both are permanent necessities in one world.

From Horton's standpoint, the great need of the Church in our time is not mere unity, but rather rebirth. At Edinburgh, in 1910, co-operation of the Christian world in evangelism was stressed; at Stockholm, social action was accented. Lausanne attempted to re-think our diverse Church traditions. At Amsterdam, in 1948, the Ecumenical Movement crossed the Jordan. It was not following a mirage in the desert; it had really arrived at the entrance of the Promised Land. The weak things of the world still confound the mighty. But the rebirth of the Church must take precedence over the unity of the Church. " All creeds are testimonies and not tests of faith " (*Toward a Reborn Church,* p. 89).

Since Amsterdam, the Church is experiencing criticism and correction from within and without, but more. The World Council of

Churches is a fellowship of Churches loving and serving the same Lord, learning to love and emulate one another, and growing into a genuine body with many members. In Horton's words:

" The Christian Church in its first great centuries and in several critical times since then, has been a disciplined revolutionary minority — an *ekklesia,* 'called out' of the existing order to live by faith the life of a new order. It is a matter of history that Western civilization has been transfigured and renewed more than once by what Toynbee calls the 'withdrawal and return' of revolutionary Christian minorities. I am convinced now as I was before the war that a reborn Church, refilled with the revolutionary spirit of the first apostles, the missionary monks, and the Protestant Reformers, is the appointed agency through which our dying civilization may be saved, in the only proper meaning of the word 'saved.' Not of course preserved intact — no earthly power could do that now, and no heavenly power would want to — but transfigured, redeemed from its grievous sins, and reoriented to God as its Chief End " (*Ibid.,* p. 108).

From beginning to end, Horton's theology stresses both the greatness and the goodness of God, the divine power and the divine purpose at work within and upon the process. The Christian word " hope " is therefore more than a word to him; it is the structure of reality. As he sees it, both now and for years to come the world's greatest blight is a spirit of hopelessness, leading to meaningless and nerveless inaction. Christ the crucified Lord, who has passed through the blackness of hell into the eternal light, is the One who can exorcise this evil spirit — for the Church clearly and simply, for the world vaguely and confusedly. Two manifestations of the same evil spirit of hopelessness are worldliness on the one hand and isolation from the world on the other. What, then, of the future? In Horton's prophetic words:

"A conflict . . . between emphasis on 'the eschatological future' and on 'the present activity of God in history' must be surmounted. Frankly, I believe that unless faith asserts divine providential control of this present segment of history, and discerns instances of 'overruling for good' here and now, no hope of victory in an eternal world can finally be sustained. We put our final and eternal hope in the One who is our very present help in time of trouble. By thus stressing the 'present activity of God in history,' I mean only to protest against a *purely* futuristic or *purely* eternalistic version of 'the Christian hope.' If the Kingdom of God (including 'the Kingdom of Christ') is the comprehensive expression of the Christian hope, it must always include a present, a future, and an eternal reference, in intimate union with one another. On such a basis, I see a better chance of agreement today between European and American theology than twenty-five years ago, when Americans were more addicted to Utopian optimism, and Europeans to quietistic irresponsibility. Let us try to spell out this agreement " (" Comment on the First Report of the Assembly Commission on the Theme of the Second Assembly," in *The Ecumenical Review*, January, 1952, pp. 162–163).

John C. Bennett

A THEOLOGY OF SOCIAL REVOLUTION

S ome theology seems to have been produced in an air-conditioned ivory tower well away from the struggle of the world. Not so the theology of John C. Bennett; he breathes the air of purpose amidst the dust of process. From first to last, his theology is historical — not an analysis of drive and dry rot in the past, but a realistic grappling with this world, a steadfast refusal of the alternate temptations to capitulation or escape. At times his thought approaches pessimism. Anyone who wrestles with the stubborn stuff of history is bound at times to veer toward hopelessness. Indeed pessimism is more realistic and understandable, even admirable, than blithe optimism in this world as it is; hope lies primarily though not exclusively in the greater world which embraces this one. Bennett never quite breaks forth into song. His eyes are on present social inadequacies more than on the adequacy of God — the God who is going somewhere and is on the way, the God who is Hope. There is little doxology in his books, and there ought to be more. Perhaps he has lived too close to Reinhold Niebuhr. To every Christian-in-the-making, God is more than the frustrating present, and herein is joy.

Hope may or may not be fully formed in Bennett, but it is there, and there is clearly more hope in his this-worldly grappling than in any view that ignores either the difficulties or God.

Let us look a moment at his life, then examine four aspects of one movement in his mind: The Salvation of History; Christianity Is Self-criticism; Christianity Rejects Communism as Insufficiently Revolutionary; and The Call to the More and the Better.

ONE FOOT ON EARTH

John Coleman Bennett is a Canadian contribution to Congregational and world Christianity. He was born in Kingston, Ontario,
July 22, 1902, the son of United States citizens William Russell and
Charlotte (Coleman) Bennett. He received his preparatory education
at Phillips Exeter Academy (1918-1920); the A.B. at Williams College (1924); the B.A. and the M.A. at Mansfield College, Oxford
(1926 and 1930); the B.D. and S.T.M. at Union Theological Seminary in New York (1927 and 1929). He holds an honorary D.D.
from the Church Divinity School of the Pacific (1940), another
from the Pacific School of Religion (1943), and a third from Williams College (1947).

He married Anne L. McGrew, October 30, 1931, and there are
three children: Elizabeth McGrew, John McGrew, and William
McGrew.

He was instructor in theology at Union Theological Seminary
(1930-1931), assistant professor of Christian theology at Auburn
Theological Seminary (1931-1935), then associate professor (1935-
1938). From 1938-1943 he was professor of Christian theology and
philosophy of religion at the Pacific School of Religion, Berkeley,
California. Since 1943 he has been professor of Christian theology
and ethics at Union Theological Seminary. He was ordained to the
Congregational ministry in 1939.

He has given foundation lectures at Queens Theological College
(1938), Chicago Theological Seminary (1939), Yale University
(1941), Grinnell College (1942), Lancaster Theological Seminary
(1944), Bangor Theological Seminary (1945), the University of Virginia (1945), Hartford Theological Seminary (1946), Eden Theological Seminary (1947), and Colgate-Rochester Divinity School
(1950).

He was secretary of the section on the Church and the Economic
Order at the Oxford Conference on Life and Work, 1937, and chairman of the committee of the World Council of Churches that produced the report on Capitalism and Communism. He is a member
of the American Theological Society and of Phi Beta Kappa. He is

a member also of the editorial committee of *Christianity and Crisis*. He is author of innumerable articles and essays, and contributor to many valuable symposia. Always and everywhere, his thought unites theology and history in productive union.

THE SALVATION OF HISTORY

All five of Bennett's books are written on this theme, and the same title could be given to them all. The first three, however, are specially fruitful in understanding the structure of his thought. *Social Salvation* (Charles Scribner's Sons, 1935) offered a religious approach to the problems of social change; Bennett analyzed with care the fundamental theological questions underlying social Christianity, in particular the relation between personal sin and social evil in the light of God's purpose and man's freedom. The book is not a veneer, but a solid probing of the problem. Genuine hope is in it, for it offers the therapeutic of a gospel. It does not underestimate the seriousness and despair which must attend the mind's love of God. There is no easy road to social and personal victory. Creation, which is the meaning of history, is costly and at times painful.

The book moves beyond the war of attrition between liberals and conservatives. Indeed, the distinction is, or ought to be, obsolete in the serious work of theology. If the terms are kept at all, their meaning will have to be changed. The present war of contrition is between Christian hope and its rivals — automatic progress and a meaningless view of history. The man-centered optimists are all for growth of process, yet they operate with insufficient capital — with a helpless deity or none, and with a naïve view of human nature as unable to crucify good. The otherworldly thinkers are helpful in their assertion of a robust deity, yet their chief interest lies not at all in history, but rather in personal immortality or a posthistorical millennium. There are strange bedfellows among the otherworldly, yet to all alike history is maya (illusion); all subscribe to what Sorokin calls the ideational mentality, to what Tillich calls heteronomy. Bennett is neither optimist nor pessimist; he believes that in and beyond present process is the power and purpose of God.

Bennett begins with the fact of sin, and distinguishes, perhaps prematurely, between personal sin and social evil. Personal sin is deliberate wrongdoing together with a realization of the true standard and the capacity to obey it. Social evil, when it is not misfortune, is more than personal sin: for example, exploitation and war are more diabolical than the evil desires of single persons, though without individual and social consent they could not be. Bennett agrees with Reinhold Niebuhr that social evil is harder to overcome than personal sin; a different method is therefore required. Personal sin can be overcome by inner change through repentance and moral conversion. Evil not deliberately chosen cannot be thus overcome. Many means are needed: knowledge of cause and effect, large-scale changes in institutions and external circumstances through social and political action.

In this writer's view Bennett's distinction is real as a division of labor, but not more. A social group obviously reacts more slowly, more stubbornly, than an individual, yet experiences through criticism of false objectives and the acceptance of new directions exactly in macrocosm what the soul experiences in microcosm — inner change, repentance, and moral conversion. Nonetheless, Bennett's distinction is useful and helpful. Sinclair Lewis' Babbitt, now more than ever in control of American life and considering his creed exempt from criticism, is visible on every page of this book.

Bennett describes also the interaction between personal and social conversion: social change is both the condition and the fruit of individual salvation. The Christian's integrity is measured by what he does about the injustices that are maintained by his privileges, about social conduct controlled by the public opinion of which his opinion is a part. The Christian's social conduct is as much his personal conduct as his private vices and virtues — themselves public in meaning and value. Social salvation therefore involves individual repentance and new commitment, though it is not identical with it. The group can be saved in principle and increasingly in practice long before every one of its members has adopted the new light. The individual, convinced of his sinful participation in social evil, must and can be brought to repentance and new direction. At the same time, God's creative grace must and does reach the individual through a social medium — whether the Church or the State, though the door of personal prayer is never closed.

History acts upon men, and men act upon history; the new, the creative, does break through; God is *at work* within and upon the process, creating man and the world. He speaks in and to and through both macrocosm and microcosm, in great events and in small crises, in creative minorities and creative personalities. History and the soul are both continuous and discontinuous; hence, to be saved or lost means an affirmative or negative relation to the growth of process toward the will of God. A resident of Dallas recently prayed, " Thy will be done on earth as it is in Texas." The first half of the prayer was fully Christian. The society of which man is a part includes God; hence true inner change is socially induced; true repentance is socially conditioned; true moral conversion is socially orientated. The same machinery works, whether conversion is toward the future or the past, toward the divine will or human self-will.

Every pastor should read this book, and with Christian courage hold the mirror before his congregation. Protestants and Babbitts seem two words for the same thing; good men are often blind to the evils of the system that they adorn, are often worshipers of the *status quo,* paternalists filled with Rotarian confidence in the virtue of the system that makes its victims complacently dependent or violently rebellious. Our churches often produce Babbitts by the score — men personally more or less moral, socially *in absentia.*

Christianity and Our World (Association Press, 1936), a Hazen book on religion, presents Bennett's view of Christianity as world healer — a religious faith against secularism, a way of life for individual and society, a creative and powerful movement in, and beyond, the Church. The Christian faith, in contrast to Hindu and Stoic caste systems, asserts the real equality of all men before God — not in ability, but in the right to opportunity. Christianity therefore requires in our kind of world a substructure of economic justice —

an equal opportunity to earn bread, to maintain health, to gain an education, to improve or overcome environment. Christian love is a mockery when content with anything less. Equality requires loyalty to a universal community excluding racialism and national-ism — our current hysterias. The Christian faith asserts that God is now working in and upon the world to lift the level of human life — to push forward the creation of our half-finished fellowship and our half-finished souls.

Of special value is Bennett's discussion of two Christian graces: humility and commitment (skepticism and faith). Humility is ob-jective honesty about oneself, sensitiveness to the needs of the total family of man; commitment is willingness to pay the price of the cross. "What we mean by Christian love is not any one thing. It in-volves all . . .; and it grows out of that unselfishness and that uni-versalism which belong to the substructure of the Christian life" (P. 31).

The task of the Church is to keep every social achievement under critical surveillance to make growth possible; for this very reason the first task is an inside job — to evoke among its members a new attitude not toward specific party platforms, but for definite social objectives: for freedom of expression for minorities, for freedom of economic groups to organize for their own protection. In 1936, when this book was written, collective bargaining was a major sector in the battle for right; today it is understood that the public must also find common protection against collective bullying. The churches must encourage their members not only to prayer but also to social participation, to enter the struggle to make reason and the will of God prevail.

Bennett examines our current danger of tyranny. In 1936, Hitler was Mr. Tyranny. Mr. Stalin later took over the role. But Bennett is fearful of our American lust for conformity. His words are par-ticularly relevant today:

"We have at hand the materials out of which an exclusive nationalism might well develop. Our provincialism, our habit of self-righteousness toward the rest of the world, the fact that as a nation we are quickly swayed by mass emotion, our susceptibility to demagoguery which has a strong nationalist bias . . . these are only the most important factors which might well arouse in us a dangerous form of nationalism" (P. 52).

The social struggle in America was intense in 1936, but is not ended today. Bennett's healthy fear that the appeal to emergency could at any moment destroy our basic liberties — freedom of thought and freedom of expression — seems an immediate possibility. In times of crisis Christianity keeps alive the standards of truth independent of the wills of men; in every generation the Christian is called to put loyalty to God as revealed in Christ before loyalty to the State or any earthly power. Christianity is a universal religion which must say "No" to racialism and nationalism, to all forms of social infantilism or particularism. Before Christians can participate in war they must inquire: Is it a war to defend the territory of a country against actual invasion? Is it a war to implement decisions of the United Nations, to increase international law over national will?

Missionary theology and method need correction and growth, but the missionary movement itself is no more and no less than an embodiment of the universalism of Christianity. If Christianity is true, it is true for all the world. If it can unify the life of men on a level deeper than our recurrent conflicts, it must not be limited to Europe and America.

Profound hope exists in these words:

"There is an old letter, coming from the second century of the life of the Church, the Epistle to Diognetus. The unknown writer says of the Christians in his time that 'they hold the world together.' To his contemporaries those words must have seemed to be absurd enough, but they have turned out to be true. It was Christianity which did hold the world together during a period of disintegration, and it was Christianity which preserved for the future the best in the civilization which collapsed. In our day, to say that Christianity may hold the world together cannot seem quite so absurd as it did then, but it may be hard enough to believe. Yet, if Christianity is true and if its truth is the correction for the specific perversio..s of our time, it is the most solid hope we have in the world, and from the perspective of a distant future

it may be seen that Christianity has in fact held the world together"
(P. 64).

These words need only a slight correction: Is it not God who has
held the world together, often through but sometimes in spite of
cultural Christianity?

The theme "God the Lord of History" — not merely the Lord
of the Church — underlies the book *Christian Realism* (Charles
Scribner's Sons, 1941). Bennett writes as a liberal who is liberal
enough to learn from Barth, Brunner, and Reinhold Niebuhr — a
neo-orthodox trinity. He writes also as a Congregationalist who believes in the centrality of an ecumenical Church. Bennett wanted to
know (1941) what the events of Europe at war meant to religious
thinking. He examined both the world and theology to find the
answer, and he made no pretense of completeness. He saw the
breakup of the moral unity of the West, and the rise of frankly
pagan ideologies strengthened by a political-military autocracy
equipped with technical science. (They later fell.) He saw also the
inconsistency of our Western democracies — our acceptance of the
fruits of imperialism in contradiction to our avowed principles.
Contempt for reason is an occasional hysteria of neo-orthodoxy, but
there is none in Bennett's treatment, and no final pessimism about
human nature or the historical process. On the other hand there is
none of liberalism's naïve optimism, no overlooking of the dark and
irrational forces at work in the world, the demonic claim of finality
in men, and even more, in their religious and political institutions.
The book emphasizes "the combination of cosmic power and righteousness and mercy in the God who is the Lord of history." Christianity, as he sees it, is precisely the movement of redemption. Always the Bennett theme is salvation — not from but of history.

CHRISTIANITY IS SELF-CRITICISM

In 1946 came the book *Christian Ethics and Social Policy* (Charles
Scribner's Sons), the 1945 Richard Lectures at the University of
Virginia. The volume unites personal and social religion, under-

stands the main contribution of Christian ethics to social policy — the elimination of the idea of finality in any human achievement, the insistence upon self-criticism, upon growth toward Christ in the soul and the universal fellowship in society. The positive side of the Christian revolution is less developed than its "No" to existing partialities and idolatries, yet Christianity's negative criticism of every assumption of finality in human religious or political knowledge, in moral codes, or in institutions, is desperately central; without it faith is dead, and also hope. Essential Christianity is the most revolutionary force on earth, much more revolutionary than Communism; it will endlessly split Communism asunder as it once split the pagan Roman Empire. This positive element, however, is the opposite side of the coin. Our present virtue is incomplete, and hardly distinguishable from vice. Our present knowledge, in science and dogma alike, is a mere beginning. Our present usefulness is child's play. Our present world culture is not more than halfway toward Christ's Kingdom. Most important of all, we are given the power to move and keep moving, no matter how often we fall, toward the future, the better, which is God's will — always other than, and better than, our own.

CHRISTIANITY REJECTS COMMUNISM AS INSUFFICIENTLY REVOLUTIONARY

One basic trouble with Communism is that it cannot criticize itself. Since self-criticism is the meaning of Christianity, the two faiths are not, and cannot be, identical. They share common ground: both are interested in a future classless society, a world of freedom in fellowship. The ground not in common covers more territory. Christianity believes that the God who *is* God is now creating one family of free men against all human delay, and through and in spite of and by means of all human effort.

A fundamental divergence between Christianity and Communism is developed in the book of that title (Association Press, 1948). Communism at the moment is the most self-conscious form of secularism. In Communist orthodoxy, religion is an escape from history. Often enough this has been the case, and Communism, itself a Christian heresy, has risen to fill the vacuum left by posthistorical or suprahistorical hope. God gets his will done by sinners as well as by saints, though sin and holiness are generic opposites. The Communists believe naïvely that the success of the revolution and the complete eradication of capitalist exploitation will mean no further frustration, hence no further need of escape from history. The Communists assume that evil is entirely social, that it has no roots in human egoism.

Christians find deep fallacies in the Communist conception of religion. Religion has at least four roots in addition to economic frustration: joy and gratitude, a response to the moral demands made in every social situation, the discovery that the world is meaningful and not " a tale told by an idiot," the increase of spiritual dignity and material enjoyment for all men. The Communist alternative is the meaningless world described in the creed: " There is no God, and Marx is his Messiah." If the world is really meaningless, what is the meaning of Communism? If there is no meaning anywhere, Communism, along with every other conception of meaning, is nonsense.

Christianity believes that there are other causes of frustration than social maladjustment. Sin and ignorance create evil in any social order. In addition to moral evil, there is also natural evil, especially sickness and death. Frustration is one of the chief safeguards against complacency (the sinking of man to animal or vegetable), against human self-sufficiency blind to man's actual dependence upon all men, past and future, and upon God. The fact of our dependence shatters the Communist illusion of independence.

No growth is possible in Communism, for it regards its truth as infallible, as divine, especially when it does not believe in the divine. Christianity is more realistic than Communism: it insures the existence of a standard which will criticize and judge every society, thereby making growth possible. To believe that the ideal has been attained in any social order is to worship the present, to put a strait jacket on the future. Christianity keeps alive the tension between Purpose and process, the ideal and the actual, the love of God and the present lovelessness of man; out of this tension comes all progress in society and the soul.

Communist errors in large part are due to Christian failures — in particular the failure to understand, and practice, the permanent social and personal revolution that is Christianity, the acceptance of every man and the rejection of every human claim of infallibility. God accepts us; he thus decreases our anxiety and maintains our sanity. God rejects our present achievement as sufficient; he thus decreases our *rigor mortis* and maintains our growth toward Christ in the soul and the universal Agape community.

THE CALL TO THE MORE AND THE BETTER

It goes without saying that any attempt to place a specific theologian within a particular trend involves an omniscience not available to man. In point of fact, John C. Bennett could with equal accuracy be placed among the theistic finitists. Edgar S. Brightman claimed him as a member of the school, and in his own writing evidence abounds of the legitimacy of the claim. The evidence, however, is not all on one side. Now and then there is an observable break-through to a confidence that theistic finitism cannot provide. More than any finitist, Bennett emphasizes the theme: " God, the Lord of History." The main weight of his thought stresses Christianity as a creative revolution acting in and upon history. At times Bennett's hope for God's will upon earth seems negative, almost that of a fideist. He would, I think, classify himself as Christian realist rather than as theistic finitist. Theistic finitism is not his main or central theme. Rather, God, the Lord of history, is his dominant concern, and he is fully aware of the obstacles in society and the soul that exist to be surmounted. In his view, fulfillment cannot occur *in* history; yet the more and the better are always achievable. If the reader feels that Bennett should be placed among the theistic finitists, the writer has no objection, yet insists on one observation: The conviction that God *is,* rather than *would be,* the Lord of history transcends finitism.

Bennett is convinced that true or realistic Christianity avoids the illusions of both the optimists and the pessimists. In his words, "I believe that the liberal optimism of the past generation and the theologians who deduce their view of human possibilities from a dogma of original sin which goes beyond the evidence are both wrong" (*Christian Realism,* p. 12).

As Bennett sees it, those who stress the given aspects of the world are less tempted to explain away anything that they find in the real that is not rational; they can believe more naturally that God is himself confronted by a limitation of given possibilities growing out of the temporal character of the world and out of the fact that history is molded in part by finite wills which God Himself does not coerce; they can more easily find a place for a revelation of God that is given to us in events rather than in the universal principles of reason.

Bennett believes that both strength and weakness are to be found in the current European understanding of faith. From his point of view, though we must not follow blindly the thinkers of Continental Europe, neither must we blindly reject their contribution. They have been wiser than we concerning the depths of sin and tragedy in human life. They have been wiser than we in seeing that we cannot make an easy transition from the assumptions of modern culture to the Christian faith. They have been wiser than we in insisting that we can discover Christian truth only when our minds are formed by response to the Bible and to the Christian tradition. If our minds, our canons of judgment, are formed by nationalism or by popular brands of naturalism, we find Christianity intellectually credible only if we have a conversion at the level of our deepest assumptions. They have been wrong when they have suggested that there is a complete discontinuity between reason and faith, between Christianity and the higher insights of the race known apart from Christian influence. They have been wrong when they have said that we cannot find confirmations of Christian truth in the results of science, in the observation of events, or in the conscience of man.

To Bennett, four basic ideas of God must be held together: (1) God is the Creator; (2) God is the God of righteousness; (3) God is the Lord of history; and (4) God is the Redeemer. History, there-

fore, has specific meaning. In Bennett's words: " By history I mean
the irreversible sequence of events which occur in time and which
are the stuff of our human experience, both private and public. For
mystical and pantheistic religions, history has secondary importance,
but for the Jewish-Christian tradition history is the arena of God's
activity that is most meaningful for human beings. What happens
in history makes a difference to God himself " (*Ibid.*, pp. 46, 47).

From this writer's point of view, Bennett seems strong on our
failure through freedom, weak on God's ultimate success. Yet he
rightly grasps one part, at least, of God's way with our freedom.
The Almighty persuades, and never coerces.

Always Bennett thinks in terms of the immediate options confronting Americans. In his view, not only do Christians have a vital
stake in the survival of democracy, but also the Christian conception of the human situation seems to fit exactly the needs of democracy. On the one hand the Christian has faith in human possibilities,
for he believes that man was made to be responsive to the highest.
Without such faith democracy is impossible. On the other hand the
Christian should know more realistically than the secular humani-
tarian the degree to which men are tempted by power; he can insist
therefore that in every situation provision be made for the criticism,
the checking and displacing, of those who exercise power. If this
balance implicit in the Christian point of view is upset, two roads
to tyranny are opened: the road of cynical pessimism that plans irresponsible power at the center because there is no faith in the people; and the road of careless optimism that trusts without sufficient
reservation those to whom power is given. In Bennett's words: " I
cannot imagine a conception of human nature more completely
relevant to the needs of our time. There is indeed a contradiction
within human life. From this we may learn *realism* and the ground
for *hope*" (*Ibid.*, p. 83).

As Bennett sees it, we can no longer identify the Kingdom of God
or the ideas of a fully Christian society with any social order that
is to be expected in this world — for four weighty reasons: (1) every
generation must face afresh the problem of growing up; (2) the
existence of antisocial groups; (3) the prevalence of human inertia

or evasion; and (4) the fact that groups are more sinful than persons. Nonetheless, we may and must look for a better society in this world. With or without hope of final success, we are responsible.

On Bennett's terms, the Christian can see the whole of history as the arena of God's activity. This is the basis of morale. He can know, however dark the age in which he lives, that the most powerful forces in the world are those that are in line with God's intention. He can also know that when he has done his best there is divine forgiveness for his part in the evil that remains. He can also know that there is an order within the larger order of society and yet not of it, an order of life that has as its structure the Christian Church. To this order he can belong. He can hope to Christianize the Church before it is possible to Christianize the world. Whatever he can do to strengthen the fellowship of the world Church will be the means of keeping alive the forces of redemption through this age into the age that will follow. It is these forces of redemption in which he will put his greatest trust, whatever hard decisions he may make on the political level, and to them he will look for God's new beginning.

Bennett's realism enables him to see what might be called the struggle for existence and the survival of the fittest among competing faiths. God's truth, not our truth, will stand. In his sober words:

"I have no faith in theological or ecclesiastical fences to emphasize the uniqueness or finality of Christianity. The uniqueness of Christianity will stand out whenever it meets other religions and Christianity will not be made more unique by having that uniqueness set up as a dogma to be accepted apart from the evidence. The finality of Christianity will depend upon its surviving the test of honest comparison with all real alternatives, comparison in the extent to which it provides illumination and power for human living under all conditions. I believe that it will survive those tests, but it would be no mistake for me to be a Christian now if at some distant time Christianity should be superseded by a religion which preserves what is valid in Christianity in the same way in which Christianity preserves what is valid in Judaism. I know that Christianity will not be superseded by a religion that places power above love or that exalts a tribal God " (*Ibid.*, pp. 180, 181).

Starting with Jesus, who avoided the extremes of ascetic religion and of this-worldly religion, of Hinduism and Communism, Bennett believes that progress to the more and the better means a combination of growth in moral behavior and growth in human welfare. Always, in his view, one must bear in mind that it is doubtful if human egoism, a chief obstacle to progress, can be bred out of the race, though evil has inevitably a self-defeating character. Bennett finds grounds for the expectation of progress in moral behavior and in human welfare in the present increase of welfare possibilities, in obvious gains in public opinion and in public conscience, in the cumulative influence of persons moved by faith and love, and in the self-destructive character of evil. Civilization has turned its back (perhaps insufficiently) on human sacrifice, on religious persecution, on the subjection of women, on slavery, on punishment without trial (one thinks of Senate inquisitions), on the use of torture by responsible authorities, on dueling to kill, on the uncontrolled exploitation of men, women, and children in industry, on irresponsible government, and on the right of a nation to wage war in the pursuit of any policy without regard to any international sanctions. These things, in any case, demonstrate the reality of social progress. On the other hand, Bennett sees four threats to progress: (1) every advance is accompanied by evil by-products or unsolved problems (for example, the reduction of working hours increases the problem of leisure); (2) the increasing possibilities of centralized power in our technological age; (3) the new powers of destruction in the hands of modern men; and (4) the increasing one-sidedness in the development of civilization. Nonetheless, in Bennett's words, "Progress or no progress, our lives do have significant results" (*Social Salvation,* p. 169).

Bennett seems often trembling on the choice to hope or not to hope. He is not sure about final fulfillment of God's will for history, but regards it "as a legitimate inference from the Christian idea of God" (*Ibid.,* p. 179). From his point of view, we can know that evil as are our times, for sheer cold-blooded destruction of persons, they are surpassed by those early centuries and by as recent a century as the period between the rise of the Reformation and the end of the Thirty Years' War. The persecution of Protestants by Catholics, of dissenting sects by both Protestants and Catholics, and the wars of religion made Europe a hell. An observation like this gives us the perspective which we may desperately need as we face our own trials. If religion on its worst side was responsible for much of the madness and tragedy of those times, it was also religion which made them enJurable.

God, the Lord of history, is limited, in Bennett's view, by (1) the logical structure of reality, (2) his own moral character, (3) the determinateness of his own creation, and (4) human freedom. The reader may rightly object that these limitations are not a denial of divine sovereignty, not even a denial of omnipotence. They simply assert that God is what he is, and not more. In any case, Bennett believes that God works in society through creation, persuasion, judgment, and healing. Two things must therefore be borne in mind: the work of God and the responsibility of man. To quote Bennett directly:

" In the processes by which God works men are necessary instruments. Moreover, they are not mere puppets used by the divine power. They can resist God. . . . There has been a persistent trend throughout the whole of Christian history which has affirmed the freedom of man and the resistibility of grace. . . .

" We can always have the confidence that the ideal and the real are both on the side of a world of peace and justice. But it does depend upon us whether or not that new world is to come soon or late. And it does depend upon us whether or not the persuasive process is powerful enough to prevent the most destructive catastrophes. Catastrophes may be the price of redemption and if they are borne voluntarily by those who see their meaning they have the value of the cross. But they are in fact borne chiefly by helpless victims to whom they have no such meaning. It is the fate of those victims that is at stake when we accept or reject our responsibility in the social process " (*Ibid.*, pp. 214–216).

Bennett finds seven hopeful tendencies in the social thinking of the Church: (1) a clearer perception of the stubbornness of evil, partly influenced by Marxist realism; (2) a clearer recognition of the importance for social change of sub-Christian social and political forces; (3) an increasing radicalism in the estimate of the *status quo;* (4) a conviction that there will be tensions between the Christain ideal and every political program and any social order; (5) fresh emphasis upon the importance of the Church in view of the helplessness of the individual Christian in a pagan society, especially under the threat of a totalitarian state; (6) a new awareness of the need of a gospel for times of social frustration; and (7) a new emphasis upon the work of God in society both in judgment and redemption (Cf. " The Social Interpretation of Christianity," *The Church Through Half a Century,* pp. 111–129. Charles Scribner's Sons, 1936).

Bennett analyzes and rejects four traditional strategies in relating the Christian social imperative to concrete situations: the Roman Catholic, with its two levels, the one for the monk, the other for the citizens; sectarian withdrawal, illustrated by Mennonites and Quakers; identification of Christianity with particular social programs, pacifism or militarism, etc.; and the double standard for personal and social life. In their place, Bennett advocates a fifth strategy which is neither the double standard nor identification with particular programs; it rather emphasizes the relevance together with the transcendence of the Christian ethic and takes account of the universality and persistence of sin and the elements of technical autonomy in social policies. The fifth strategy seeks one world, economic justice, racial equality, democracy both in popular sovereignty and in the protection of dissenting minorities, and individual action with its margin for freedom — action both by persons and by churches. The existence of the Christian Church, in Bennett's view, has this ethical meaning for the Christian: he is at the same time a citizen of two communities — the City of God and the city of man. Further, the Christian Church, with all its shortcomings, is the only school in which we are trained for this dual citizenship, precisely because Christianity is a religion that is concerned with history and Christian ethics are relevant to the whole of life.

Bennett takes a wholesome view of the validity of the moral law independently of revelation. From his standpoint there is a moral order in the world that can be known with varying degrees of

clarity apart from revelation; the knowledge of this moral order is
not as a matter of fact universal, but it has a much broader basis
than the Christian faith; some of the perceptions of moral truth
doubtless depend upon the direct or indirect influence of Christianity, but when once they are seen they can be supported by facts of
experience that can be known apart from the Christian faith; there
is wide approval of the idea of equality of races, of the necessity of
free criticism, and of honesty, beyond as well as within the Church;
these moral insights are, as they have always been, strengthened by
Christianity; but a perpetual limitation must be borne in mind —
moral law as such, whether within or outside revelation, offers no
clear guidance on concrete issues. All law has to be applied by men
in the maelstrom of existence.

The Church must freshly assume its teaching responsibility in the
field of social ethics. In Bennett's words:

" The point where concentration is needed is direct teaching on the
meaning of Christian faith and ethics for social policy within the
Church so that its members in their vocations and as citizens may be
changed, actually converted, in conviction and purpose. In so far as our
conviction and purpose are changed, the completely indirect influence of
the Church . . . will be greatly enhanced and it will be freed from some
of the ambiguities that now cancel much of the good in it. The Christian, trained within the Christian Church, must make his own choices in
the world, and the possibilities between which he must choose should
have more promise because the Christian Church is in the world"
(*Christian Ethics and Social Policy*, p. 115).

The call of God to the more and the better, as Bennett sees it, has
come to modern men afresh in the conflict between East and West.
He is specially interested in the attitude of the American Churches
toward the present stalemate. From his viewpoint, there is recognition that Communist power must be resisted but there is also a
tendency to warn against the public hysteria about Communism.
To Bennett, there is a great difference between the mood of Protestantism and the mood of Roman Catholicism in regard to Communism: Roman Catholicism on the whole feeds the spirit of blind
hostility to Communism, whereas Protestants usually recognize

that the appeal of Communism to the world's neglected and exploited peoples is a judgment upon the Church, that a purely negative attitude toward Communism is sterile. Most American churchmen, in common with other Americans, believe in capitalism for America and are quite conventional about it. On the other hand, whenever Churches speak publicly about economic questions they avoid the tendency to make American capitalism absolute, however much this may be done by American public opinion. Here and there is the realization that no economic system that now exists can properly be treated as wholly the expression or wholly the negation of Christian principles. In general, Bennett sees greater openness of mind on Communism and socialism in church than in business circles. He sees also a new theological revival in America, not to be equated with European quietism, nor with Biblical authoritarianism, nor with literal Biblical eschatology, yet appreciative of new European social activism. In his words: "There is renewed emphasis upon the uniquely Christian revelation and a more widespread appropriation of the traditional Christian teaching about sin and redemption. Events have undercut what tendency there was to substitute confidence in human progress for the Christian gospel" ("The American Churches in the Ecumenical Situation," in *The Ecumenical Review*, autumn, 1948, p. 63).

The main issues between Christianity and Communism, in Bennett's view, are three: the Communist atheist absolutism, the Communist method of dealing with opponents, and the Communist estimate of the ultimate status of persons. Communist strength lies in its promise of a new order, in its offer of an interpretation of life, and in its revolutionary method. From Bennett's standpoint, the real power of Communism is based upon the fear and privation following the destruction of so much of Europe, upon the desire of peasants on several continents to be rid of feudal forms of oppression, upon the aspirations and resentments of the colored races, and upon the unsolved problems of capitalism. It is these sources of Communist power to which American Christians should direct major attention. They should begin at home and prove that it is possible to prevent mass unemployment without having recourse to tyranny from right or left, and that the institutions of freedom are not merely " forms," as Communists allege, but that they really are the means by which society can be continuously corrected in the interests of justice. The strength of Communism consists also in the fact that it provides a faith for living for millions of people, especially young people, who have never encountered any faith that put so much meaning into life and which so adequately related their social aspirations and ideals to an interpretation of the world. In Bennett's words:

" There is no other faith that can compare with Communism except Christianity. Christianity, when its full meaning is not hidden by one-sided teaching or distorted by alliances between the Church and privileged groups, is a faith that can meet the need of those who struggle for more equal justice in the social order. It will also prepare them to be radicals in any new order, for it will help them to understand how quickly new institutions and new collocations of power may become the source of new forms of injustice. It will also enable them to relate all that they may do for the transforming of society to the depths of their personal lives and to the ultimate purpose of God. The first responsibility of the Christian community is not to save any institution from Communism, but to present its faith by word and life to the people of all conditions and of all lands that they may find for themselves the essential truth about life " (*Christianity and Communism,* p. 128).

There are, after all, valid elements in the Communist criticism of Churches and of culture that claimed to be Christian. Not, however, the closed society of the Communist, but the open society of the Christian keeps the power of old and new regimes alike under criticism and provides the means by which injustices can be corrected. As Bennett sees it, we must not identify Christianity versus Communism with capitalism versus Communism or with America versus Russia. In his words, " The Christian view of man forms the basis of the Christian support of the two essential elements in Western democracy: government by the people and political freedom for minorities in a context of spiritual and cultural freedom " (*Ibid.,* p. 122).

The relation between Christianity and Communism is not merely a matter of definitions; the conflict and the contest are existential and immediate. In India, for example, Communism is the real and inviting alternative to Western culture. In dealing with Asia, Bennett insists, the military objective, which is prir ary to ۱ʓ, is truly secondary. As he puts it, " As we think of Asia cannot we give less attention to deliverance from Communism and more attention to deliverance from the poverty, landlordism, and corruption, which are the causes of Asia's Communism? " (" Has India an Alternative? " in *The Christian Century,* February 28, 1951, p. 266).

Both in theory and in practice, however, Christianity is forever set against the Communist idolatry which is its essential character — an idolatry that excuses ruthless treatment of opponents. In our own land we must be similarly set against capitalist idolatry, equally ready and eager to offer human victims upon its altar (Cf. " The Christian Answer to Communism," *Theology Today,* October, 1950, pp. 352–357).

In Bennett's view, the Christian Church remains the earnest of the new order that God is now creating out of our half-finished fragments. The power of " Christus Victor " will be increasingly released in the struggles of men for economic justice, for political freedom, and for a world order that can deliver humanity from war. With men of faith everywhere Bennett shares, and invites us to share, " an ultimate confidence that God, known through Christ, is the Lord of the world, that he is the Lord not only of the past but also of the future. . . . The design of God will be fully manifested as God brings to fulfillment what he has begun in Christ. Because Jesus Christ is the center of history, he is also its goal. The Kingdom which has come among us through him is to come fully at the end of history" (*Man's Disorder and God's Design,* Outline of Preparation for the First General Assembly of the World Council of Churches, John C. Bennett, Editor, p. 21. London, The Student Christian Movement Press, Ltd., 1947).

Wilhelm Pauck

A THEOLOGY OF CRISIS AND CONTINUITY

F*ully* as important as other American theologians is Wilhelm
Pauck, professor of Church history at Union Theological Seminary, New York. In particular, he is a profound interpreter of Protestantism as an existential faith, its frequent loss of character in our
time, and the necessity of its renewal. Let us first examine his life,
then three main movements in his mind: The Strength and Weakness of Early Barthianism; The Anguish of Freedom; and The
Protestant Task.

Existential Dilemma

Like Tillich, Wilhelm Pauck was born in Germany. He first saw
the light January 31, 1901, at Laasphe, Westphalia, the son of Wilhelm and Maria (Hofmann) Pauck. He graduated from the Real
Gymnasium at Berlin-Steglitz in 1920, received his licentiate in
theology at the University of Berlin in 1925, and the doctorate in
theology *honoris causa* at the University of Glessen (1933).

He married Olga C. Gümbel-Dietz May 1, 1928. He came to
America in 1925, and was naturalized in 1937. He was appointed
professor of Church history at Chicago Theological Seminary October 1, 1926; professor of historical theology at the University of
Chicago in 1939; and professor of history in 1945. He was exchange
professor at the University of Frankfurt, Germany (1948–1949), and
is now professor of Church history at Union. He is a Congregationalist.

He is a member of the Quadrangle Club, the American Society of

Church History (was president in 1936), and the American Theological Society, Midwestern Branch (was president, 1943). His work is consistently characterized by exact scholarship, broad sympathy, and deep insight.

THE STRENGTH AND WEAKNESS OF EARLY BARTHIANISM

Anglo-Saxon theology, it is true, has often provoked Barth's ridicule. On the other hand, the same theology in recent years has received more sympathetic attention from the European rediscoverer of transcendence. Barth, along with Nels F. S. Ferré, believes in inevitable universal salvation, in a God who includes, and does not exclude, history; for this and other reasons, his interpreter and critic, Emil Brunner, today considers him " new."

In the late twenties and early thirties of this stormy century Barth startled the theological world with an unabashed emphasis upon the primary reality of God, as against the primary reality of man's thought about God. The full strength of Barth's position was not clearly understood in America when Wilhelm Pauck wrote his book *Karl Barth: Prophet of a New Christianity?* (Harper & Brothers, 1931). As far as I know, there has been in America no other equally full and equally fair treatment of this controversial Swiss theologian, though a later study is needed.

For friends and enemies alike, Barth's rediscovery of transcendence in an age of immanence made him inevitably the beginning of a new theological era. With profound penetration Pauck examines why. Pauck himself started as an ardent Barthian. He could almost say of Barth, " There but for the grace of God goes God." Barth and truth were two words for the same thing. From Barth a strong breeze of God-centered religion blew again through Europe and America; the Barthian universe was filled with hope: God is, and God is God; yet the historical process as such seemed to be underestimated. Barth appeared to lose immanence altogether, as the age which preceded him had lost transcendence.

As a disciple, Pauck has understood early Barthianism from the inside; he can still appreciate Barth's contribution. Yet, as one who has moved outside Barthianism, Pauck sees what Barth seemed not to see, his apparent neglect of this world in his preoccupation with God.

Barth's central teaching, as Pauck understood it in 1931, was simple: God is absolutely Other, completely transcendent to human thought and experience, yet God is not, as the deist pictures him, indifferent to the world. Barthianism approaches deism nonetheless. Barth's God may not be totally indifferent to history, but Barth's disciples have often been. Brunner described Barthian transcendence as epistemological, not cosmological. The idea was clear nonetheless; God must not be identified with our ideas about him, and he is not a human experience. Our greatest wrong is to reduce God to the forms and boundaries of our ideas and experiences. This is another way of saying that we must never confuse or identify or equate our thinking with God's. What is this but a recovery of the First Commandment?

True religion is neither easy, comfortable, nor peaceful; it involves the endless torment of baffled love; its object cannot be attained. God forever transcends our thoughts and our emotions. At times Barth's God seems almost the Great Unavailable, and therefore the Wholly Irrelevant. On the other hand, Barth's idea means no more and no less than this: God's knowledge is greater than, and better than, our own; we can never claim absolute identity between our ideas and his. The point is clear enough in our knowledge of earthly things and persons: we experience them, but never fully grasp either their meaning or their mystery. Barth was anxious to destroy the modernist reduction of God to inner experience or intuition, the liberal effort to make God a member of the good will committee of the local Rotary Club. The sentimental reduction of Deity to humanity was, to Barth, sacrilege, idolatry, the sin against the Holy Spirit. As a witness, Barthianism has permanent value; it was, and is, a bulwark against the idolatrous attempt to reduce God to the measure of any human thought about him. God's Work, Jesus Christ, is the only source of the knowledge of God, for it is God's knowledge of himself. Other knowledge may not judge Jesus Christ; all knowledge is judged by him.

Barth's hue and cry for transcendence, for God as objectively existent, was needed then, and is needed now. To talk about God as though he were less than our ultimate concern is not to talk about God at all.

In Barth's view, death reveals God; it is the proof of human futility, the demonstration of human insufficiency. By death we are frustrated, thrown down, hemmed in. To beat our heads against the fact of death makes revelation possible; we must conform to the fact of death, but cannot. We must accept our insufficiency, but will not. We see the glades of Paradise beyond death, the blue sky which stretches farther than our lives, but cannot escape our fate. Man is mortal — that is his limitation; man refuses to accept his mortality — that is his false claim of divinity, his sinful pride. In Barth's view, the Christian doctrine of personal immortality is not a denial of the terminus of death, the fact of human limitation, the divine "No" to man's claim of infinite knowledge and power. To continue as a human person after death would still mean to be less than God — in knowledge as well as in virtue.

As Barth sees it, Jesus, the historical man, was not the Revelation of God. The cross was, and remains, the Revelation. The most sublime figure in history demonstrated that the utmost reach of human life is contrary to the nature and goodness of God and must be destroyed. Barth saw truly with Isaiah that God's ways are not our ways, his thoughts not our thoughts. Our best is but a fragment. God's energy thrusts us forward from behind, while God's truth, greater than our own, draws us onward from ahead. God's truth is precisely ahead of us, not behind us — ahead of the whole process and ahead of each individual person, in science, in dogma, and in life. The break between God and man in Barth's thought is complete and humanly unbridgeable.

However, even in Barth's view, man can love and adore God and live for him, though human activity in God's service is of no value to God; it adds nothing to him; its absence detracts nothing from him. Love, adoration, and good works are offered as recognition of the true situation. Man cannot experience God, but he can experience his lack of God, his finitude, and in anguish cast himself upon the Invisible Mercy. Our human glory is precisely that we are able to adore the Ultimate which we can neither know nor experience. This adoration, which we call faith, lifts us above our humanity; we cannot escape, but we can transcend, our limitations. Thus, from the beginning, if only in what seems to be a one-sided way, Barth recognized human glory, man's ability to adore One who is immeasurably beyond him.

Unfortunately there appeared to be an unacknowledged self-contradiction in Barth's skepticism of man-originated theology. He rightly condemned the human assumption of finality, human arrogance, the belief of human reason at any point or in any person or Church that its truth is infallible. The prophets thus condemned Israel's idolatry. Protestantism was born in a similar condemnation of Roman idolatry. Barth condemned idolatrous human reason, but did undeniably and strenuously use his own reason to discern the meaning of revelation. This is not, I think, as serious a criticism of Barth as it appears; it simply means that to him there was an all-important distinction between human reason humbly *receiving* God's self-revelation, and human reason as the *originator* of truth. Think we must, yet never confuse our thinking with God's. This insight from Nels F. S. Ferré makes the issue clear. Barth insists that human thinking must not confuse its truth with God's truth, but he continues both to think and to affirm that what he thinks is true. Two things are clearly necessary to growth in knowledge, whether of things, of groups, of persons, or of God: criticism and commitment, skepticism and faith. Commitment without criticism is idolatry; criticism without commitment is paralysis. Absolutely necessary for man is constant and ruthless criticism of every idea and experience to the end of correction toward God's truth and commitment to it — the perfect truth we cannot grasp, the perfect truth that grasps us. Only with undiminished criticism and commitment can we hold reality before our minds, yet recognize that it is essentially other than, and better than, anything we think or experience.

Barth accepts *a* system of theology — his own. In his defense it must be said that he accepts his theology not because it is his own, but because it takes fully into account God's primary self-disclosure.

To accept our theology — as the best we can think at the moment — is holiness and hope; the door is open to fuller truth, to divine reconstruction, to the growth of good in process and person. To accept our theology, our grasp of absolute revelation, as final is new idolatry. Pauck ends his book with acceptance of the Barthian witness, but with rejection of any human claim of finality — even in the understanding of the revelation. As Ferré once expressed it in conversation, " Barth is not *exactly* God." Pauck accepts Barth's chasm between man's best and God's truth, but considers revelation a dialogue, not a monologue, made possible by the priority of grace.

THE ANGUISH OF FREEDOM

A mature study of historic Protestantism and an analysis of the contemporary dilemma are provided in Pauck's book *Heritage of the Reformation* (The Beacon Press, 1950). The volume both asks and answers the question: what is the Christian gospel for today? In this writer's view, it answers the question for tomorrow as well. The book contains three sections: The Reformation, Protestantism, and Liberalism. Careful reading discloses that the first section might well be called, " The Anguish of Freedom "; the second section, " Anguish Without Freedom "; and the third section, " Freedom Without Anguish." Precisely through " the Anguish of Freedom " God is now creating process and person as rapidly as the will to do God's will takes possession of human life. " Anguish Without Freedom " is another term for the doctrinal idolatry so often characteristic of Protestant history. " Freedom Without Anguish " is an exact characterization of easygoing liberalism.

Our stormy transitional century calls for serious thinking, and Pauck accepts the call. With care and love he interprets the minds and hearts of the great Reformers — Luther, Calvin, and the neglected Butzer. Pauck steadfastly resists the temptation to confuse subjective with objective history. What actually happened in sixteenth century minds and events can never be fully known. Our knowledge of what happened is inevitably selective, subjective. The idea that there is no connection between the two is a myth. Some connection between fact and interpretation is possible in creative scholarship, which is patience and persistence with imagination. No one but God knows absolutely what happened in Luther's mind, or in the minds of the citizens and first citizen of Geneva. Nonetheless, Pauck seems to know as much as any living man about sixteenth century religion, and to understand as well as any what he knows. Inevitably, Pauck finds his own modified crisis theology present if not dominant in the original motif of the Protestant Reformation.

Luther's determinative religious experience is hardly characteristic of Protestantism as a whole. Few Protestants since Luther have been trained exactly as he was trained; few have faced the alternatives that he faced as he faced them. Nonetheless, the divine-human encounter, however described in form and content, has been central in Christian theology since Paul; indeed, more often than not theology has been a postscript to the encounter. Men never personally confronted with God the Almighty, with the anguish of freedom and decision, have normally espoused extreme liberalism or extreme authoritarianism (whether Roman or Russian). A personal encounter with Almighty Love made Luther Protestant, as it made Paul Christian. Luther came to believe that nothing remains for man but a naked longing for help and a terrible cry of fear and loneliness, and he knew no human infallibility that could help him. The true Protestant, since Luther, never believes that he possesses grace; he rather recognizes that grace possesses him. This is the determinative and distinctive genius of Protestantism; without it, liberalism substitutes freedom without anguish, and authoritarianism (whether ecclesiastical, doctrinal, or political) substitutes anguish without freedom for the Christian anguish *of* freedom.

Pauck may be insufficiently aware that not every man is a Paul or a Luther. The Spirit of God descended upon John, as upon Jesus, like a dove; upon Paul like a desert cyclone. Men grow within and into faith, as well as through radical departure. Yet the soul's despairing discovery of its own inadequacy, and of the inadequacy of any political or ecclesiastical institution or any inspired knowledge or doctrine, as Luther experienced it, can never be absent from genuine personal Christianity. To an extent not fully known, though often experienced, liberalism has frequently lost the spiritual depth of generic Protestantism, and without it has become freedom without anguish, pious tentativeness, feeble and nebulous uncertainty.

Pauck finds that secular subjectivism has interpreted the religious element out of the Reformation, and placed all its eggs in the basket of economics. The religious meaning of the Reformation arose out of Luther's struggle for the assurance of divine mercy, his disappointment in the medieval means of salvation, his rediscovery of Biblical hope speaking to human despair. The real causes of the Reformation were religious. Luther came to the faith that became Protestant Christianity long before the beginning of the Reformation. He was forced to defend his faith against the ecclesiastical claim of infallibility which had kept its authority but lost the Bible. Out of Luther's defense, step by step, the Reformation became a reality. In so far as modern Protestantism is uncertain of its faith, it must, like Luther, plumb the depths of anguish to new spiritual reality.

Pauck is particularly helpful on the development of ecumenical theology. The point is simple: unity seems to be, and is, humanly unattainable; every special theology is determined to be adopted as the definitive ecumenical view, ignoring the transtheological conversation which must reach greater truth through the anguish of freedom; yet with God all things are possible — defeatism is the denial of God. Every segment of the rising ecumenical Church seems to believe that its own doctrinal orthodoxy will be adopted as the creed of Christendom if it argues for it long and stubbornly enough. In Pauck's view, hope for the world and for man lies not in defensive movements toward further fragmentation. As Jesus put it, the things that are impossible with men are possible with God. The Church of the future, which does not now exist, awaits the openness to fuller truth of present isolated and fragmentary orthodoxies — whether of the right or of the left, whether liberal or orthodox.

The Protestant Task

Pauck recognizes the seriousness of the Protestant predicament in our time, perhaps because his own field of concentration is the scholarship of the Church rather than Biblical scholarship. In particular he finds both Protestants and Catholics distorting the Reformation, which must be allowed to speak to our condition in its own idiom. It is popular today, for example, to accuse Luther of being the father of authoritarianism on the one hand, and of individualism on the other. For this reason Pauck is grateful for Barth who, in his view, has attacked both modern Protestantism and modern Catholicism, and brought all theology once more face to face with the main issue of Luther's thought — the priority of God to man's thought and man's work. Otherwise put, the real issue of the Reformation was salvation by divine action (by grace and faith) or by human action (good works) — that is, salvation by divine forgiveness or by human self-sufficiency. It is not Luther but Niebuhr, in Pauck's view, who is the father of the idea that salvation is always in principle, never in fact. Luther took a more serious view of the activity of God as directly engaging man and history. For this and other reasons, Pauck finds American scholarship behind in both Church and Biblical research (Cf. "Luther and the Reformation," in *Theology Today,* October, 1946, pp. 314-327).

If Lutheranism has its troubles in this century, Pauck believes that the old Calvinism, under the modernist impact, has also largely disappeared from the American scene. From his point of view, this is to be hailed as an inevitable and good historical achievement. What is needed now is a prophetic form of Christianity as powerful today as was the theology of the Reformers in the sixteenth century. This is, in his view, a different thing from a return to the Reformers' faith. To achieve the new prophetic Christianity, both liberalism and orthodoxy have necessary roles to play. In Pauck's words:

" I recognize that Protestant theological liberalism is today in a state of crisis. . . . I disagree . . . that this liberalism is about to die, for I am of the conviction that the historical point of view which liberalism has introduced into Christian thought is a permanent achievement and that its present tendency to criticize and to rethink its own theology is a sign of its true vitality " ("The Prospects of Orthodoxy," in *The Journal of Religion*, January, 1947, p. 49).

Three things, as Pauck sees them, characterized Calvinism: a God-centered faith, obedience to law, and churchmanship. Calvinism was never centered in theology as was Lutheranism. We can, and must, learn from Calvinism, without succumbing to the frozen authority of the sixteenth century. To Pauck, it is true that Calvinism had a God-centered faith. It is also true that the religion of modern men has often tended to assume man-centered forms. It is further true that, whenever man tries to deify himself, he is, sooner or later, brought to a fall and is threatened with destruction. Religion should therefore be theocentric and not anthropocentric. But from this it does not follow that the forms of theocentric religion must be of a certain historical kind. If it was good and right and honest to say that papal authority is not of the essence of Christianity, it is also right and honest to admit that Biblical literalism is not of the essence of the Christian gospel. Theological dogmatism finds itself opposed by prophetic religion as well as by enlightened reason. As Pauck puts it: " In due season, all orthodoxies that try to arrest the march of truth will be dissolved. . . . A self-critical orthodoxy is a *rara avis*" (*Ibid.*, pp. 51, 53).

It is the liberals, in Pauck's view, whose careful researches have enabled the Reformers to speak for themselves to our condition, without the static of intervening and distorting tradition. It is the liberals also who have enabled us to see that it is no longer really important to us whether we are Anglicans, Lutherans, or Calvinists, but whether we are Christians. The necessity of liberalism is just the fact that we have the timeless gospel in time-bound forms, and the task is to distinguish the permanent from the passing. Orthodoxy tends to freeze a particular form of the gospel and give it the dignity of the gospel itself. To quote Pauck directly:

"We ask questions . . . to learn the difference . . . of the dynamic from the static, of the living from the dead.

"Being of such a mind, we turn with fresh attention to the creative periods of Christian history, to the age of the New Testament and to the Reformation. We do not turn back to them as if we would escape from present responsibilities, but we hope to obtain guidance from them to the divine sources and the human resources of the Christian faith, aware of the fact that we must bring it to a concrete expression in the life of our times by means which our ancestors, including the apostles and the Reformers, could not possibly know" (*Ibid.,* p. 54).

If the interplay of criticism and commitment is essential in our patient listening to the major voices of the Reformation, it is not less essential in our attempt to deal intelligently with the Protestant-Roman conflict in our generation. To this end, Pauck examines some obvious differences between Protestants and Roman Catholics. Catholics emphasize big churches, while Protestants meet in plain halls. Roman Catholics find their objective authority in a priestly cult; Protestants find their objective divine authority in the gospel. In the Protestant view, when the Word is rightly preached, there is a church, though the inward hearing by the Holy Spirit is not neglected. To Protestants, the Church is a free, dynamic, social movement of believers, centered in the divine reality as pictured in the gospel, in Jesus Christ as the New Testament presents him. Protestantism therefore stresses personal fellowship among individual believers responsive freely to the sovereign Word of God, though the Word of God is never identifiable with its historical witnesses, not even the Bible. Not a religion of, by, and for a priestly class, but personal commitment and mutual service among individual believers characterize all true Protestantism, now as in the past (Cf. "Roman Catholicism and Protestantism," in *Theology Today,* January, 1948, pp. 457–473).

Nonetheless, Protestants must think through the modern criticism of Protestantism by Roman Catholics, to separate the false from the true. Pauck considers four major lines of attack upon Protestantism offered by Karl Adam: (1) Because the Reformers revolted from the Church and broke its unity, modern man, the Protestant man, has lost a sense of the Christian verities; (2) Protestantism is responsible for the crisis of modern civilization, especially in view of (3) its individualistic spirit, and (4) its loss of membership in the community of the Church. To all this, Pauck offers profound and penetrating comment. In his view, Protestants have opened their minds more fully to the cultural achievements of modern man than Catholics have ever been permitted to do. Protestant thought has become "modernized" and, as long as its vitality lasts, it will continue to be "modernized." The belief in any human infallibility is near blasphemy. In Pauck's words, "The 'objectively given tradition' of the Roman Catholic Church is . . . nothing divine; it is the human product of the Roman Catholic community acting through its hierarchical leaders " ("The Roman Catholic Critique of Protestantism," in *Theology Today,* April, 1948, p. 39). Roman Catholicism has thus frozen or sanctified the human achievement of the Middle Ages. Indeed, it was the force of the Reformation that caused the Roman Catholic Church to sanctify Thomism in self-defense. As Pauck puts it:

"We conclude that the Roman Catholic leaders of the sixteenth century are not without responsibility for the breakup of Christian unity and that the Roman Catholic conception of this unity is based on an arbitrary definition of the nature of Christianity. Protestantism therefore cannot be justly accused of having become emancipated from true Christianity. What it has done is that it has set itself against the Roman Catholic delimitation and distortion of Christianity that is embodied in the superpersonal and superhistorical 'tradition' " (*Ibid.,* p. 41).

As Pauck sees it, the Roman Catholic Church certainly would not want to concede that Protestantism was the decisive Christian movement that shaped the cultural motives of modern men or that Protestantism so eliminated Roman Catholicism from the common life as to make it impossible for it to influence modern civilization. As a matter of fact, Roman Catholics have always outnumbered Protestants and the institutions of Roman Catholicism have at all times been more powerful than those of Protestantism. Why, then, should one not ask why Roman Catholicism was not able to prevent modern man from getting into the predicament of humanist isolation? In Pauck's words:

"Roman Catholicism can adopt only with great difficulty the modern scientific and historical world view which no one who has ever come under its sway will voluntarily surrender. By failing to relate the Christian religion openly to the spirit of the modern generations who succeeded in devising a new conception of man's place in nature and the universe, Roman Catholicism has estranged itself from innumerable modern men " (*Ibid.,* p. 42).

Individualism, which Roman Catholics believe originated with the Protestant Reformation, in Pauck's view actually originated with the Renaissance first, the Reformation second. The Renaissance was a cultural revolt from the medieval Church; it blossomed on Roman Catholic soil; and it emancipated reason from ecclesiastical authoritarianism. The Reformation was at one and the same time a movement against Roman Catholic heteronomy and humanistic autonomy and for a new theonomy. Roman Catholics thus fail wholly to understand Protestant practical personalism, the Protestant emphasis upon the right and duty of private judgment in religion, and continue to assert and to practice depersonalism, the right and duty of the priest and the hierarchy to pronounce definitively upon faith and morals. In Pauck's words:

"The lines between Protestantism and Roman Catholicism are thus sharply drawn. What to Roman Catholics appears as a diminution of the fullness of Christianity, namely, the Protestant rejection of priestly authority for the sake of personal encounter between man and God, is for Protestants the guarantee of the freedom of Christian faith. The Roman Catholic suspicion that Protestant religiousness is individualistic is not justified. Upon closer examination, it turns out to be nothing else than an expression of an inability to understand the religious reasons for the Protestant opposition against clericalism and ecclesiastical authoritarianism " (*Ibid.,* pp. 44, 45).

Where the Roman Catholic Church is primarily a regimen and a regimentation of priests, the Protestant Church is a free fellowship of believers. In Pauck's view, it is of the essence of Protestant Christianity that because it is impossible to be a Christian in solitariness, although becoming a Christian is an event taking place in the secrecy of the individual soul, the true mark of the Christian life is the fellowship of service and mutual sharing. In the Roman Catholic community the Church vanishes, and only a priesthood is left. Roman Catholicism is therefore a priesthood of pastors, Protestantism a priesthood of believers. And Pauck hastens to emphasize that it is Protestantism, not Roman Catholicism, that has proved its interest in modern social reform — in Spain, in South America, everywhere.

As Pauck sees it, the religiousness of Protestants is essentially dynamic because it is centralized only in ever new encounters of individual believers with the free, unbound Word of God. The religiousness of Roman Catholics is essentially static, because it lives by the divine substance embodied in the sacred organism of the institutional Church, which is believed to be of divine origin and character. Nonetheless, to Pauck, there remains one basis, and one basis only, of unity — between Catholics and Protestants, between dogmatists and liberals of every shade of theological and political opinion — a basis of unity which is the central issue to all equally: Jesus Christ is Lord, that is, he remains active in and through all our fragments, yet above all our institutional forms and not identical with them.

To conclude: Pauck's important contribution lies in three central insights: (1) man's necessary realization of his own limitation — in knowledge, whether religious or secular, and in virtue; (2) man's anguish of responsibility to participate humbly in God's unfinished work, casting himself and his fragmentary achievements perpetually upon the divine mercy; and (3) the endless necessity of the interplay of criticism and commitment if Protestantism is to remain creative — appreciative of the past but not fettered by it, alert and responsive to the present divine/human demand for freedom and faithfulness in fellowship.

Harris Franklin Rall

A THEOLOGY OF RATIONAL FAITH

We *have it* on the authority of Confucius that the cautious seldom err. Recklessness has rarely been regarded as a Christian virtue, though now and then a saint or a martyr has moved beyond caution to venture. To my mind, an important American voice, uniting caution and commitment, is Harris Franklin Rall. As a mediating theologian, his position has had less glamour than the better publicized extremes. Yet he is no in-betweener. He is a Christian, a liberal Christian. In an age longing for dogmatic virility, a liberal Christian seems timid and uncertain, almost apologetic for his faith, an exponent of the mild God and the sinless man. Yet Rall's liberal Christianity offers needed restraint to the mock-heroics which often accompany oversimplified dogmatics. He looks before he leaps, but leaps, and is therefore a committed member of the fellowship of Christians. The substance of his theology is not thin. This writer finds in his life and his works an indispensable Christian dynamism, the forward look, a complete dedication to the struggle with the present for the sake of the future. Four major movements seem evident in his mind: Christianity Is Judaism Plus Jesus — An Early Liberalism; Salvation Is Historical Creation; Christianity Means No Human Finality; and Robust Theism.

Iowa Discovers the World

One hardly associates Iowa and theology in the same thought, yet one must learn to do so. Harris Franklin Rall was born in Iowa, at

Council Bluffs, February 23, 1870, the son of Otto and Anna (Steiner) Rall. He received his A.B. degree (1891) from the State University of Iowa, where he was elected to Phi Beta Kappa. The same institution gave him the M.A. degree the following year. Yale Divinity School conferred his B.D. (1897), and as a Yale fellow (well met) he studied at the University of Berlin (1897–1898) and the University of Halle-Wittenberg (1898–1899), receiving the A.M. and Ph.D. degrees. In 1899–1900 he was both graduate student and lecturer at Yale.

He has three Doctor of Divinity degrees: from the University of Denver (1914), Ohio Wesleyan (1915), and Garrett Biblical Seminary (1940). Ohio Wesleyan gave him an LL.D. in 1934.

He married Rose St. John, August 14, 1897, and there were two children: Mary Elspeth and Frances St. John. The second child is now deceased. Rose St. John Rall died June 11, 1921. A year and a half later (November 30, 1922) Dr. Rall married Maud St. John.

Ordained to the Methodist Episcopal ministry in 1900, he was pastor of Trinity Church, New Haven, Connecticut (1900–1904), then of the First Methodist Episcopal Church of Baltimore (1904–1910). From 1910–1915 he was president of Iliff School of Theology at Denver, and from 1915 to 1945, professor of Christian doctrine at Garrett Biblical Seminary. He is short in physical stature, like Charles H. Dodd of Cambridge and the ancient Zacchaeus, yet with both he has climbed the sycamore tree and seen the Lord.

JUDAISM PLUS JESUS

Rall received his training well before the First World War, when this century's tragic upheaval had not yet produced theological pessimism on the one hand or hostility to religion on the other. There is a clear continuity with the long past and the longer future in his work — an awareness of history sometimes missing in men preoccupied with tragic depth in human behavior and the extremes of immediacy. His early theology is mild, and, in the light of Barthianism, seems an irreducible mimimum. This writer has gained a new respect for liberal Christians, often discredited today. They are in no haste to accept every weird innovation in religion. They are actually conservative in spirit, anxious to hold fast that which is good, not easily made enthusiasts of any sudden " ism." The virtues of liberalism, lost to view in our decade of extremism, must be regained. I am certain they will be regained, though the depth and height of maximum Christianity we must never again lose.

In 1928, Rall published, with Samuel S. Cohon, of Hebrew Union College, an excellent and meaningful little book: *Christianity and Judaism Compare Notes* (The Macmillan Company). Neither Rall nor Cohon turned propagandist, yet neither sought compromise. There were no polemics and no apologies. Mutual good will prevailed in both historical treatments. Rall's idea of Christianity at this period would not have been accepted by large sections of Protestantism; it would have been totally rejected by larger sections of Roman Catholicism; yet it was marked by an authentic awareness of the Christian tradition. Rall's Christianity seemed more than Judaism-plus-Jesus, but not much more, though certainly no less. The common ground between Christianity and Judaism remains theologically vast, though overshadowed by cultural difference. Rapport between Christianity and Judaism is a perennial necessity; when this rapport ends, Christianity ends with it — else the New and Old Testaments are uncreatively separated, and with them the seminal transcultural conversation of the last two thousand years.

SALVATION IS HISTORICAL CREATION

Three Rall books are a permanent contribution to the union of theology and history: two define salvation in historical terms, and the third accents the necessity of social change.

Faith for Today (Abingdon Press, 1936) sought to explain Christianity, and its conversation with modern complexity, to the confused average man. Not every reader was less confused when he finished reading it, but communication involves powers of reception as well as powers of expression. As the book describes it, salvation is the achievement of the most inclusive integration of values. The idea is applied to the individual, though it is as truly applicable to the total historical process. In the achievement of integration, psychology, sociology, philosophy, and religion work as allies, though religion provides the motive and power. The gospel is thus, as Paul understood it, the power of God unto salvation to everyone who believes. Rall possibly underestimates the motive and power for salvation which issue from nature and mind outside religious awareness; he sees clearly, nonetheless, that true religion offers the direction of purpose for the drive of process. The book, as all theologies turn out to be, is a word study. Faith, religion, Christian religion, science, God, evil, man, sin, salvation, prayer, Bible, church, and immortality receive fresh treatment — always recognizably Christian yet always probing, reaching out, open to the more and the better.

Rall's definition of faith anticipates Tillich's belief-full realism.

"Faith rests upon experience, but transcends it; it sees what this experience means and trusts it. . . .

"If our final business in life were logic, then our first concern would be proof; but our first business is living, and that demands faith. In Bergson's word: 'Speculation is a luxury, while life is a necessity'; so we have the right to that which is necessary to the business of living. . . .

"The root of faith is inner conviction. . . . In the broadest sense faith is trust in a world that is not seen and willingness to act upon it" (Pp. 17–19, 60).

Faith is self-transcending empiricism; it involves and does not escape empirical evidence, yet sees beyond the present God's creative future. Science and religion are not enemies but a division of labor: science deals with the world of sense data; religion, with the world of spirit, of persons, meanings, and values. Science looks toward the past and the present; religion, toward the future. Science examines the process; religion, its meaning, purpose, and goal.

Essentially the same idea, with greater emphasis upon religion as creation, is presented in Rall's latest book, *Religion as Salvation* (Abingdon Press, 1953). Rall the liberal Christian indicates his appreciation for the positive contribution of neo-orthodoxy.

Of special interest in our day, when freedom of speech and freedom of thought seem to exist only in the Declaration of Independence and the Bill of Rights, is the book Rall edited in 1937, celebrating the twenty-fifth anniversary of Francis John McConnell as bishop of the Methodist Episcopal Church and as president of the Methodist Federation for Social Service — lately under attack. Titled *Religion and Public Affairs* (The Macmillan Company), the volume broke completely with every worship of the economic *status quo*. The book would be banned today from the State Department's European libraries, or the attempt to ban it would be made; it describes appreciatively the struggle of labor for civil liberty and social security, the rise of the worker to political power; only thus, in its view, has the public mind come to full consciousness. The book challenges the capitalist system, perceives the growing cleavage between owner and laborer, and calmly asserts that a capitalist economy can be perpetuated only by doping the public mind. The volume worships no God of things as they are, rather the God of things as they must increasingly become; it does not equate the economy of the United States with the Kingdom of Heaven, yet maintains that democratic process toward the achievement of social change, the rise of the proletariat, is to be preferred to violence. Reinhold Niebuhr (today helping to distribute Ford millions) felt then that the power of ownership would not be yielded without coercion. This volume is milder in method, but strictly forward-looking in purpose. Francis John McConnell, then my own bishop, is presented with great fairness as the epitome of progressive Christianity at grips with history; McConnell saw clearly that divine creation is not complete, that at best we are only en route to the fulfillment of God's purpose. Religion must be vitally concerned to further the growth of democracy, in content as well as in method — all present excitement about " pink " churchmen notwithstanding — or cease to be Christian. As Rall describes it, wholeness is not now in our possession, is ahead of us, not behind us; requires growth toward the future, the better, which is God's will. Satisfaction with today's meager achievement, in economics, in science, or in theology, is treason against the permanent Christian revolution. No defense of the *status quo* is Christian. Our American political economy is on trial, is a means, not an end; must prove itself an aggressive instrument of social change toward the City of God. Hope exists in a Christian minority who are militantly prolabor; hope is delayed by a churchly majority of nonworkers, who think of religion only as personal inclination, not as a social revolution toward the will of God in history.

The volume is as opposed to secularism as to the *status quo,* if the two are not the same; it seeks a social leadership of trained souls, a force for unity. The book escapes both the theological right which ignores the world and the merely political left which ignores God. This volume deserves rereading and rethinking today, when Christian criticism of the *status quo* is confused with the Communist attack. The basic issue now before us is this: Can Americans distinguish between social criticism in the name of Christ and social criticism in the name of proletarian dictatorship? between skepticism of present achievement from men who would obey the First Commandment, and skepticism from men who would disobey the Tenth?

No Human Finality

Two additional books emphasize and advance the cause of historical theology. Rall's *Christianity: An Inquiry Into Its Nature and Truth* (Charles Scribner's Sons, 1940) received the Bross fiftieth anniversary prize of $15,000 — the largest cash award ever made in America for a religious book. Naturally, the volume is Rall's magnum opus, his full presentation of evangelical liberalism. It unites wisdom from the past with courage for the future. Rall affirms that the Christian norm (*agape*) is true and final, precisely because it accepts no human finality, rejects all that is less than love, endlessly demands growth toward the stature of Christ in the soul, and the universal fellowship in society.

The finality of Christianity is the conviction that nothing complete, nothing exempt from criticism, now exists on earth. Christian finality may not be identified with Christian communions, creeds, or codes; it can be identified only with God's future for this world, the future that is still unachieved, still unfathomed; the future that was made flesh in Jesus and shed abroad in the Church by the Spirit. Rall does not defend literalism, yet he is certain that essential Christianity is true — at one and the same time our critic and our comfort. He understands that no demonstration can force the knowledge of God upon an unwilling mind. Not that the knowledge of God is wishful thinking; it is rather thinking backed by willing and feeling. Always faith remains faith when the mind has done its best; faith is not acceptance of external authority in default of knowledge. Faith without knowledge is faith without good works and therefore something less than love.

Theology could not be less dogmatic than it is in Rall; this is the quiet strength of Christian liberalism. He persuades and does not bludgeon. He unites the opposite ends of every paradox, but does not join things mutually exclusive. He resolves the tensions between individual and group, activity and rest, religion and ethics, permanence and change, the otherness and the akinness of God with one idea — the relativity of our present apprehension of the absolute. The absolute is real. The absolute moves on ahead of us. The absolute is all-powerful and all-wise Love. The absolute is hope through and beyond our present half-truths.

Rall offers breadth of mind and sincerity of welcome to ideas less liberal, and more liberal, than his own — the charity of the Christian liberal. He seeks for man the highest and fullest life — God's future — and finds no man and no movement in complete possession of the truth that possesses us. He is therefore both rationalist and mystic, both naturalist and supernaturalist, both institutionalist and individualist. In his view, most of the conservative-liberal quarrels of the last century were beside the point and are now of the past. God finds fragments of His truth everywhere, among liberals and conservatives alike. The forward look and the forward movement, which make growth possible, unite argumentative enemies as evangelical friends in a common crusade — to make reason and the will of God prevail. Rall regards naturalism as the attempt of science to serve as a philosophy, yet appreciates the function of science in our half-finished world, that both theology and science are instruments

in God's hands to further his creative enterprise — the one to increase our grasp of purpose and power, the other to increase our
mastery of process.

According to Paul (Charles Scribner's Sons, 1944) applies Rall's
conception of Christianity as beyond all human finality to the life
and thought of Paul. Christianity is a permanent revolution; Paul
was its illustration in Jerusalem and Athens and Rome. What now
exists is grasped, changed, transformed, by the grace of God received in faith and working through love. Almost alone among first
century disciples, Paul understood that Christianity is not a new
religion, but the fulfillment of religion, not a new faith but the
meaning of faith. This world exists to be created, completed, in the
imago Dei. Rall examines Paul fairly and objectively, considers him
a man of his day sharing first century culture, yet transcending his
day and ours in his vision of God's historical enterprise.

One learns from Rall that the meaning of Paul is revolution, the
worship of Paul reaction. Not human infallibility but divine grace
expressed itself in Paul's life and thought. The volume was a Religious Book Club selection, and deserved the honor. Paul's thought
has specific relevance for our time, for it was less a system of doctrine than a creative force, a divine vitality breaking through to
man and history. The book evolved from four Rall lectures on the
Ayer Foundation at Colgate-Rochester Theological Seminary. Not
primarily for New Testament scholars or professional theologians,
the book has value for both. Paul is understood as a theologian who
saw beyond Rome the City of God. Paul was a first century man
who yearned to share with others his unique experience of God; he
is less a finished product of the past, as conservatism has so often
presented him, than a promise of the future, a human soul fully
committed to God and the growing fellowship. Paul therefore remains a permanently valid illustration of transforming grace, the
divine love which possesses us and draws us forward. Paul did not
possess finality; finality possessed him — and drew him irresistibly
onward. One feels the same way about Rall. Salvation is the gift of
God, the gift of life, God's endless help, God's endless deliverance
from personal and world evil. Salvation sends shafts of the future

into the present — through grace, faith, love, the Spirit, and the Church. The present is the predawn; salvation is sunlight from the future — right relation with God whom we know through Jesus Christ. Christianity has two centers of interest: God and salvation — for person and process. The cross was the cost of human delay, man's aggressive movement toward the past. The Church is the fellowship of the future amidst the fragments of the present. At times Rall is redundant, yet each reiteration boldly restates the hope of history. Rall does not seek to save Paul, but to let Paul save us — move us freshly toward the *telos*. He perceives an inconsistency in Paul: he asserted human equality, yet denied equal status to women. As Rall sees it, not every Pauline utterance is relevant to our day. There is peril in modernizing Paul, but greater peril in failing to do so.

Paul's thought is neither an eclectic confusion nor a simple system, but more; it is the breaking forth of creative grace into history.

Rall is always a robust theist — with a liberal vocabulary. A weak and conditioned God, as Tillich has understood, has to look out for himself. Our hope in and for history is that God *is* God. Rall is never interested primarily in the sufficiency or insufficiency of man, but in the sufficiency of God, the pervading grace which widens creatively through the world.

Rall insists that two things, often held apart, must continuously be held together: (1) the primary reality of God; and (2) the endless incompleteness of our knowledge of God. Similarly, two additional factors, often separated, must be continuously united: (1) the primary reality of God; and (2) the permanent claim upon us of God's unfinished work in man and in world-making. To Rall, true religion is therefore not an escape, either from history or psychology, either from society or the soul, but the salvation of both by divine grace.

ROBUST THEISM

Christianity, as Rall understands it, is a faith, a fellowship, a way of life, and a way of social and personal salvation. But it is all this because of its understanding of God. The greatest subjects man can consider are: God, what he is, how he works, how we may know him, what he means to us; man, his sin and need, his nature and destiny; the meaning of history as we see it in Christ; the Church and the Kingdom of God; God's way of life for men and nations; our hope for the life to come. The treatment of all these subjects is inevitably determined by one's view of the first.

God, as pictured in the historic Christian faith found in the evangelical churches, Rall asserts, is the God of all *power*. He is the source of all things. He was before all things. On him all things depend. The order of nature is his will and wisdom; he guides the stars in their courses. He moves in human history, guiding and judging and saving. His purpose and power are in each single life. His highest power, however, is seen not in his work of creation and rule, but in the might of his love and truth and righteousness, over-coming evil and bringing his Kingdom upon earth. Its highest ex-pression is Christ, the power of God unto salvation.

But God is not power divorced from love. To Rall, God is good. This is the heart of our faith — that goodness and power are one. The power that rules this world, and all worlds, is good — that goodness is on the throne of the universe. The goodness of God is holiness, above all sin. It is justice and righteousness, and as such forever set against all evil. It is love seeking to give, to save, to bestow on God's creatures his own life. His love is pure and un-selfish; it does not depend upon our deserving. Christ is the su-preme revelation of God's goodness. We know what the Father is like because we have seen his spirit in the Son. Christ is God's goodness at work in the world.

But God is also personal spirit. In Rall's words:

" Calling God a person does not mean that we are bringing God down to our level, or making God in our own image. Quite the con-trary, it is God who, in his goodness, has created us in *his* image. We are finite persons, persons in the making. He is infinite and perfect. But because he is Person and we are persons, we can share his life and have fellowship with him " (*The Christian Faith and Way*, p. 10. Copyright, 1947, by Stone & Pierce. Quotations by permission of Abingdon Press).

It is obvious that we of the West were brought up to believe in God. Yet calm reflection discloses that something in man calls for God; the world of nature, of order, beauty, evolution, points to God; the world of right and good points to God; further, we can believe without proving God. Whatever we think, we have to act, and we have to act in order to know. In Rall's view, the problem is not how to prove God but how to know him. God made us and speaks to us. Continually God reveals himself through action. Revelation has two sides — God speaking to man, and man hearing God.

Man's view of God, issuing from the highest insight in the Bible, determines his view of the rest of the Bible. The Bible begins with God, a God who not only speaks but acts. The Bible is therefore in a very special sense God's book; it is also man's book; and always it is a progressive book. Rall urges three things as essential to a full Christian understanding of the Bible: one should read it, obey it, and make Christ its center. He suggests further that we should obey the truth as far as we see it, since the same God who spoke to men of old speaks to us now, and his Spirit will guide us into all truth.

On Rall's terms, in his relation to this world God is both far and near; he is present in nature, continuing his creation of our unfinished world; his thoughts are the laws of nature; he is the creator of the heavens and the earth; he uses always the way of growth which includes, and does not exclude, the way of crisis; and finally, God made the world for man. Hence, in Rall's words:

" The Christian faith does not look at the material world as evil. Man may misuse it. He may let the world of things hide from him the world of the spirit. He may give himself to greed and lust and thus become a slave where he should be master. But when man uses the world as God intended, then it will minister to mind and soul as well as to health and comfort. We are not to hate the world nor flee it. We are to take its goods as coming from God's hands and be grateful " (*Ibid.,* pp. 27, 28).

Never does Rall lose sight of the fact that God is the Lord as well as the Life of the world. The order of nature is a help, not a hindrance, to man. How much more to him whose thought and will created the order of nature! The order of nature is God's instrument. A miracle is therefore to be understood as an event, or series of events, in which God's saving purpose and action for man are especially manifest. It does not imply that God is not present in other happenings. It does not mean that God has to violate his own order or break his own laws. The Bible does not speculate or offer us a theory; it simply shows us a God who is master of his world, a living God working mighty deeds in the achievement of his purpose in and for man. And God is totally concerned, with plan and purpose, for individual man and for whole civilizations. He seeks only, and ever, the best for us — in every dimension of life. "God is working in this world not merely to save individuals but to redeem all human life and make it over according to his gracious purpose" (*Ibid.,* p. 31). God offers us commands, directions for the right running of our human machinery, but even more he offers us his help. He speaks through his servants today as he did yesterday; he gives strength and blessing to those who do his will; he rules and overrules for good. He is, and will remain, the God of saving help for nations as well as individuals.

In Rall's view, God is a greater factor than evil. Even in our workaday world, the great problem is not that of evil but of good. For the human race, God's purpose is a family of God, dwelling together in justice and mercy, faith and freedom. But his purpose cannot be achieved ready-made for us; it must grow in us. Freedom is the only way to moral goodness; and moral goodness is the meaning of social solidarity. It is God who has bound us together. Pain and suffering are realities, but they do not stand by themselves; without sensitivity, which makes suffering possible, we should have no feeling-awareness of the world about us, that is, no life. Pain is, in basic intent, a danger signal, and sorrow is a school of the spirit. The greatest leaders of our race have been those who have learned through suffering. Endless slumber, of mind and spirit and body, is the only alternative to toil and struggle; conflict and danger are necessities to the highest life. In any case, Christianity is not primarily an explanation of evil but a way of overcoming it, of using it for the creation of good. Because Christ used the cross for the creation of a new humanity, we have the assurance of a final victory of good over evil.

All men, in Rall's view, are creatures of the earth, but they are also social and spiritual. Men differ through heredity, environment, and their use of freedom. Even more important than their differences, however, are the things men have in common. From the Christian idea of man came the principles which underlie all true democracy: freedom belongs to man; man can be trusted with self-government; the State exists as servant of men; every right brings with it a responsibility; men and nations must work together for the common good or go down in a common destruction.

Sin is wrongdoing — something more than ignorance and weakness. Further, sin is what we are, not merely what we do. Sin is saying no to God and his creative purpose for man; sin is saying I. Destruction and death, social and personal, results from sin, for sin separates us from God, that is, from life, and therefore from ourselves. In the midst of the sin of the world, Rall reminds us that " God is here, and God is greater than evil. Man is not left alone. Man can see and repent and receive the help of God. There is a way that leads through struggle, out of sin, into light and life " (*Ibid.,* p. 47). As responsible individuals, living today and tomorrow and facing real alternatives, we know the full meaning of sin only as we see it in the light of God. It is God who gives our life its real meaning. In him we know what we should be, our real destiny. He shows us the great world purpose which is his will and our good, and how each life has a part to play in his work. To sin is to refuse his righteous will, his purpose for this world, his love for us, his right to our life.

Salvation, as Rall conceives it, is something positive. It is more than escape from suffering or death or damnation; it is gaining life. It is realizing God's purpose for man. God saves us by bringing us into right relations with himself and with men, and thus making us whole within. The life which flows in from God must flow out to our fellow men; we have this life of love only as we live it. If a man does not love his brother, and his enemy, then the love of

God is not in him, and he is something less than a child of the Father. " Grace, faith, love — without these three there is no true religion, no salvation. God reaching down to man, that is grace; man making answer to God, that is faith; man moving out to his brother, that is love " (*Ibid.,* p. 56).

Man, God's half-finished handiwork, needs remaking — both personally and racially. It is through God himself that we are being made over, that we are becoming new men; the new life comes from him. We do not lift ourselves by our bootstraps. We do not make ourselves over. As there is no seeing except as light shines upon us, and no strength of body without food, so there is no life of the spirit except as it comes from God the Spirit. God is saving us both in sudden crises and in slow growth toward his full fellowship. In both the long pull and in the sudden need, we receive God's help through worship, through a growing grasp of his truth, through human fellowship, through work and prayer. Always we must remember that man may perish alone; he can be saved only with all other men.

Christ remains to us the truth, the way, and the life incarnate in Jesus, reconciling the world unto God. In Christ we see, not an angry God being reconciled to man, but man being reconciled to God by God's own deed of love. God was not murdering his Son. The death of Christ was caused by the sin of man; it was suffered to deliver man from sin. In Christ, from first to last, whether we define him as human, as Lord, as Saviour, or all three, " we meet the living God " (*Ibid.,* p. 79).

The Holy Spirit, in Rall's view, is God in us — for all men and for all life. However, the Christ Spirit is not our possession; it is we who are grasped, and may be possessed, by the Spirit. There is one God; Christ is his new revelation; the Holy Spirit his living presence.

The Church, which is the fellowship of Christ's followers, began with the calling of Israel, came to its defining life in Christ, has passed through the fires of history as his fellowship, is both divine and human, and inevitably expresses itself in visible forms, despite the dangers of formalism and idolatry. In Rall's excellent words:

" The Church is here to bring to men God's word as it comes in Christ: the word of mercy in the gospel, the word of truth and love and righteousness as the way of life, the word of help here and of hope for the life to come. It is here to build men up in the Christian life through worship and nurture, through personal guidance and help. It is here to serve, ' not to be ministered unto, but to minister,' and in that ministry to serve all people in all lands and in all ways. It is here to exemplify in its own life as a Christian fellowship what man's life will be when the Kingdom comes and the will of God is done on earth as in heaven " (*Ibid.,* p. 87).

As Rall sees it, there are three main obstacles to the recovery of some sort of visible union in the Church — tradition, wrong ideas of the Church, and pride.

The Kingdom or rule of God is the overcoming of evil, the making of a new humanity after the likeness of God. The Kingdom is therefore both present and to come, both inner and outer, both a gift and a task. In the end truth is stronger than error; love is mightier than selfishness and hate. It is not ours to know the day or the hour of fulfillment. In Rall's words of hope:

" Statesmen and scientists in increasing numbers are saying that the nations must learn trust instead of fear, must work together instead of pursuing individual ends, must show good will and regard instead of suspicion and hatred. . . .

" A Christian social life is no mere fruit of man's effort; it is God's work and God's gift. This is why we are not discouraged. God is seeking to save a world, not a few individuals — not just to take the souls of men out of a wicked world but to save our humanity and all its life in this world. And we must not despair of the power of the gospel, the power of truth and love and God's own Spirit " (*Ibid.,* p. 110).

The alternative to God's direction for us is no direction at all, or a wrong direction. As Rall sees it, the social optimism of yesterday has been ebbing fast. Science is no longer the new messiah; the technology which increased our power and multiplied our comforts now appears as a weapon threatening world destruction. We have seen appalling manifestations of the depths of evil in man. There has been widespread increase of the mood of anxiety, frustration, and fear. Men are turning to psychiatrists and to books that promise peace of mind. Our mental hospitals doubled the number of in-mates within a score of years. In large world areas there is possible or actual revolution caused by want and by a growing desire for free-dom. There is exploitation by selfish and self-appointed saviors. This has brought constant warfare and two or three world wars with the threat of an incomparably more terrible kind. As perhaps never before, mankind is aware of the power of evil and the need of help. The Church is waking up to the challenge, is beginning to see that God offers genuine salvation both individual and social. Body and spirit, heredity and environment, individual decision and achievement, all enter into the making of man. Christianity must be freshly concerned with a sane eugenics, as also with social environ-ment. Individualistic religion of the pietistic or mystical type has often overlooked these, as has that theology which sees in religion only the vertical dimension, that of the soul and God. Biological heredity, cultural heritage, social and physical environment, these all enter into God's work for the making of man; man does not live and grow *in vacuo.* God has created this order in which man's life is set, an order which brings not only problems for human life but needed conditions and means for its achievement.

The hour of breakdown, social and personal, the hour of judg-ment, is always a threat hanging over us, collectively and individu-ally. Nonetheless, for those who believe in the God and Father of our Lord Jesus Christ, the ultimate purpose of breakdown and judg-ment, of punishment, will be seen as disciplinary and redemptive. Through the total experience of growth and breakdown, the goal of God is a new humanity, new in the spirit of true sonship, new in all the relations which make up life. The objective of all-power-ful love is new men in a new world.

On Rall's terms, the Christian view presents a God who is not only power and inclusive order but gracious purpose as well. His goal is not merely ordered being, but beauty and truth and good-ness. The highest embodiment of these is in rational, ethical, per-sonal beings like men, living together in a fellowship of faith and love and righteousness. To these ends God has worked through ages of cosmic development, through millenniums of human history on this earth. It would surely be an irrational world if these divine objectives, now but half-realized, were never to be attained, and the whole enterprise, achieved to this midway point at such cost of time and toil and pain, were in the end to be cast as rubbish in the void.

The basic issue now before the whole life of man, and before each individual man, is to hope or not to hope. In Rall's words:

"The ground of our hope is God. He is the transcendent God, the God of holiness and might, infinitely above the human and finite. He is more than the sum of human goodness and finite forces. It is well to stress this against all naturalism and humanism and mere programs of reform. But it is just as necessary to know that this transcendent God is the living God, the God who works, the God who dwells with men in love and saving help. Our hope is not in man, and it is not measured by signs of progress. Our hope is not in a divine force which shall sometime 'smash' the evil and place the saints in seats of power. It is in the power of redeeming love: in love that is mightier than selfishness, in truth that will win out over error, in righteousness which abides when oppression and injustice destroy themselves. . . .

"Our hope is in God, but our problem, and God's problem, is man with his ignorance and sin. . . .

"The Kingdom is God's gift, but its coming waits for men who will see it, receive it, and embody its rule in their own life and in all the associations of life. We can only say then: God's rule is here where his will is done; God's rule is coming as men receive Christ and live his life. The rest we must leave with God" (From *Religion as Salvation,* Harris Franklin Rall, pp. 227–229. Copyright, 1953, by Pierce & Washabaugh. By permission of Abingdon Press).

ALTERNATIVE TRENDS

W. Norman Pittenger

A CHURCH-CENTERED THEOLOGY

I*n any hour* of social and intellectual confusion Christianity is bound to seek its own clarity, to take stock of itself, to establish or re-establish its center, to find — and, even more, to be — itself. The same thing occurs in biology: when a unicellular organism faces in extreme form the challenge of survival, it enters a spore stage — it develops a hard exterior and retires from the world of conflict; it thus meets the world of conflict by withdrawing from it. Survival is thus actually achieved; hence, the spore stage, in itself negative and world-fleeing, in the long run is affirmative and world-relevant.

It is inevitable in the twentieth century, not least among history's confused eras, that there would, and should, rise a strong Church consciousness. A recovery of a sense of the Church is a perpetual need in Christendom; those who aid that recovery render invaluable service. No one has all the truth; each theologian must be content to contribute the truth that is clear to him.

The strength of Church-centered theology is its consolidation of Christian gains, its accent upon clarity in thought, vitality in faith, and purity in love. Church-centered theology improves the *quality* of the Christian product; it makes stronger churches and stronger Christians in an hour of challenge.

The weakness of Church-centered theology is its inevitable pessimism about the world it is committed to redeem; too quickly it casts the world out of the Church. It builds a high wall between sacred and secular spheres, and considers God at work only in the sacred, and the secular beyond his interest. Church-centered theology accents charity toward the world, even identity with it in its hours of tragedy, but does not regard the salvation of the world as the primary objective; rather, the salvation and extension of the Church seems the central concern.

Nonetheless, the Christian world is perpetually indebted to Church-centered theologians. Unless the Church *is* the Church, hope must turn to hopelessness.

The Church is the fellowship in Christ and the Holy Spirit, but our churches are also societies of self-righteousness and *status quo* worship; both Church and churches must increase their participation in the present-tense activity of God. To Church-centered theology God's present activity is the redemption of the few, the restoration of part of what has been lost; Church-centered theology thus underestimates God's present activity as the creation of universal brotherhood, the achievement *through* and *for* freedom of what history has not yet known.

A splendid representative of Church-centered theology is W. Norman Pittenger. The definably Christian structure in faith and sacrament is always his first love; in this necessary mission to America, he renders conspicuous service. Let me tell you a little about his life, to locate him in time and space, then present his ideas in four dimensions: The Gospel of, by, and for the Church; Beyond Liberalism and Neo-Orthodoxy; Salvation *from* the World; and Classical Christianity.

ONE FOOT IN HEAVEN

William Norman Pittenger was born in Bogota, New Jersey, July 23, 1905. He is one of the younger American theologians, though three years older than Nels F. S. Ferré. He is the son of Charles Henry and Clara Louise (Van Norman) Pittenger. He received the S.T.B. and the S.T.M. at General Theological Seminary in New York City (1937 and 1940).

He spent four years (1928–1932) as a newspaperman — hence his lucid style. He was ordained a deacon in the Protestant Episcopal

Church (1936) and priest (1937). He has been fellow and tutor at General Theological Seminary since 1936; lecturer in religion at Columbia University (1941–1948); instructor in New Testament at St. Faith's School (1937–1942); lecturer on theology at Windham House, New York (1938–1942); and chaplain of the Episcopal Guild of Scholars since 1939. Since 1941 he has been vice-chairman of the Episcopal Church Congress, examining chaplain of the Diocese of New Jersey (1939–1944), a member of the study commission of the World Council of Churches (since 1940), and instructor in apologetics at General Theological Seminary (since 1945). He is a member of the American Theological Society, the Society of Biblical Literature, and (of special interest) the Church League for Industrial Democracy. He is primarily devoted to the salvation of the Church, but at times also to the salvation of the world. He represents a strong American Anglo-Catholicism, regards nonapostolic-succession clergymen as innovators belonging to a ministry "changeable at will, without regard to historical developments . . . an instance of expedient human planning . . . sheer novelty, innovation without identity . . . likely to lead to conclusions that bear little resemblance to the original reality" (*The Christian Sacrifice,* pp. 18, 19. Oxford University Press, 1951). Roman Catholics, of course, look upon the Anglican ministry exactly in this light.

Every Christian ought to take the Church straight — at least occasionally. Though definitions differ, Pittenger is one man who likes the Church undiluted.

The Gospel of, by, and for the Church

In Pittenger's emphasis, the Christian gospel is the creation of the Christian Church. The Bible is the Church's book; it cannot be understood except within the experience of the Church. Indeed, the Christian view of Christ is the creation of the apostolic witness. The gospel was created by the Church, is maintained by the Church, and exists for the Church. The world is beyond the pale, has status only as a mission field for prospective church members. The Church itself is not a universal fellowship in Christ; in Pittenger's view the nonapostolic-succession churches appear to be illegitimate children of the Holy Spirit.

Pittenger's first book, *Approach to Christianity* (Morehouse-Gorham Company, Inc., 1939 — published in England by Geoffrey Bles at 3s 6d), is incorrectly titled (most books are). It is a splendid summary of classical Christian ideas, not an introduction; from beginning to end it attempts to build a bridge from Catholicism to modernism. One end of the bridge is planted on the terra firma of Anglo-Catholic theology, but the other does not quite touch the modern bank. In all honesty, it has no need to do so. A clear summary of Christian ideas is valuable in its own right. Pittenger attempts too much in too few pages, and says too little on each subject. Nonetheless, as a quick outline of Anglican Christianity, the book is excellent. Free Church folk of all shades should read it, if only to acquaint them with the thinking of a Church which existed before their fragment.

In the first book the gospel approaches but does not reach the modern mind. In the second book, *Christ and Christian Faith* (Round Table, 1941), Jesus is the Lord of the Church, not the Lord of the world. However, no better treatment of Christ's true humanity and true deity has appeared. Chalcedon lives again. The years 451 and 1941 are not in conflict. The Christian appeal is not philosophy, not theology, not even an ethical code, but the great person in whom men have found, and now find, life and strength. That Christ came to give life to the total historical process is not emphasized in Pittenger. It seems to be exclusively for the Church that God acted in Jesus. Beyond the Church, any blessing that Jesus imparts is incidental or accidental. God acted in Jesus, we agree; but was not this action for the sake of the world? As Pittenger sees it, faith in Christ rests, not upon the historical Jesus but upon the apostolic witness, the total impact of his personality upon the early Christians. Our knowledge of Jesus is mediated to us by what he meant to his followers, by what he still does in and for the Church. The New Testament reports the flaming conviction of the Christian community that, in Jesus, God had indeed visited and redeemed his people. With this Pittenger view all Christians will agree. Each man, through his own experience of Jesus against the background of his own time, will decide the meaning of Christ for himself and the world. Pittenger is rightly opposed to any reductionist effort to denature the incarnation. Partial divinity does not represent the fullness of God's decisive act in Christ. Jesus is not " the man who dared to become God," but the " God who dared to become man and to choose Jesus for his supreme revelation." Other men — Gandhi, for example — may receive and impart God's message; Jesus was one with God.

The idea is not emphasized in Pittenger that the incarnation is not alone the revelation of deity, but the revelation, as well, of the future of humanity.

Pittenger asserts that our knowledge of God in Jesus is congruent with our knowledge of God's cosmic purpose; hence, we accept the apostolic witness to Christ. The reader may ask: Is it not the other way around? Is it not through our experience of God in Jesus that God's cosmic purpose becomes clear to us?

Pittenger is particularly helpful in his view that the incarnation illustrates and focuses, yet also quickens and intensifies, the activity of God for his Church. God's reason in slow motion is our revelation, our impulse to victory. The incarnation, neither the redemption nor the creation, is the center of Pittenger's interest. There is little of tragic depth in Pittenger's view of man. Tragic sinfulness is the painful cost of creation through freedom. The incarnation and the atonement together mean a new step in God's creative enterprise — to make of the world itself one Church. Pittenger sees this through a glass darkly; his real interest is not the world to be created, but Jesus as the Church's private possession.

A specially valuable book is *The Christian Way in a Modern World* (Cloister Press, 1944). Pittenger's sympathies are wider than his theology. His sympathies embrace the world the Church is committed to create; his theology embraces only the Church. The book is an outline of Christian theology for laymen. To Pittenger, Christianity is three things: a way of believing (we are what we think), a way of adoring (we are what we love), and a way of living (we are what we do). The book devotes its entire attention to plain central Christianity as "a way of believing" — the incarnation, the atonement, the Trinity, the Catholic Church, and the Bible. The volume speaks to, but not with, the modern mind. It is a monologue, not a dialogue. It is interested in the Christian mind, which is well and good; but may not the modern mind add its penny's worth to the conversation? The book presents splendid capsules of orthodoxy with Christian charm. As I finished it, I asked myself a question: Is the modern mind the deadly enemy of the Christian mind — or its protégé, critic, and ally?

Beyond Liberalism and Neo-Orthodoxy

This movement in Pittenger's thought seems a genuine breakthrough to a creative future — yet its basic appeal is to the unity of the early Middle Ages. However, no finer treatment could be written of the necessity of moving beyond the half-truths of liberalism and neo-orthodoxy to new dynamism. The book should be required reading in liberal and neo-orthodox seminaries. The Pittenger pessimism about the possibility of a Christian world is still with us, but it is not accented. His dynamic orthodoxy itself offers genuine hope. In the long run, William Temple may shine more brightly in the firmament of theology than Barth, Brunner, and Niebuhr. Pittenger has listened to Temple. But Temple, more fully than Pittenger, preached the creation of the world as God's enterprise. To Temple, the Church included the world; to Pittenger, the Church excludes the world. Nonetheless, Pittenger renews his wholesome effort to meet the historical situation. Indeed, he has learned much from the liberalism he rejects — its breadth of sympathy, its openness to the more and the better. To him, neo-orthodoxy is a needed corrective which needs correction. Anglo-Catholic theology, as he sees it, corrects and supplements the liberal and neo-orthodox fragments, and adds its own important insight to the ecumenical movement.

One wonders whether Anglo-Catholicism, with its insistence on the apostolic succession as the "one thing needful," desires to contribute to ecumenicity — or to determine it?

Neo-orthodoxy, as Pittenger views it, is so persuaded that man is a sinner and will stay that way that it cuts the nerve of action. Salvation never quite saves. As Newton Flew expressed it to the writer at Cambridge's Wesley House, " With Niebuhr you feel that the skirts of salvation are always just disappearing around the next corner." To Pittenger, the ancient faith, which he presents as dynamic orthodoxy, is the modern need; it insisted upon divine transcendence as much as Barth and company, but also upon divine immanence along with the best of the liberals. As this writer sees it, Pittenger considerably overestimates the classical emphasis upon immanence. In his view, the ancient faith taught original sin, but not total depravity. Man was capable of responding to the salvation offered him in Jesus Christ; man could even become a candidate for sainthood. Pittenger admirably describes the balance, comprehensiveness, and sanity of classical orthodoxy — its ability to weave many strands of truth into one tapestry. The historic faith proved historically valid, is today as contemporary as the morning newspaper, and will be fully adequate a thousand years from now; it is the hope of the future.

Pittenger believes the current revival of orthodoxy the most significant trend in American religious thinking; as he sees it, few reputable theologians are willing to be called liberals. The outstanding theologians are either confessional, neo-orthodox, or orthodox. Liberalism is on the way out because it presented an impersonal God and a sinless man.

Pittenger approves the neo-orthodox view that man is not only depraved, he is perverted. He needs a redemption which must come to him from beyond. But the neo-orthodox God is so transcendent that He seems out of touch. The reader may well inquire: Was it not human history itself that was united with the Word in the incarnation?

Pittenger shares fully the neo-orthodox rediscovery of the importance of the Church, the necessity of its independence from sociology. He sees orthodoxy in our time as both a blessing and a curse: if it could develop a more hospitable attitude toward natural truth and goodness, correct the errors of secular humanism, and supplement the inadequacies of liberalism, it would be entirely a blessing.

There is real breadth in this Pittenger book — a healthy desire to move beyond exclusive immanence and exclusive transcendence, to unite liberal breadth with neo-orthodox depth. The Amsterdam spirit is here, and the Evanston spirit as well.

Not everyone will agree with Pittenger that parochial schools offer the best solution to the problem of Christian education, but this writer does so heartily — for the sake of the world, not alone for the sake of the Church. Our task is not to neglect the world for the sake of the course, but to keep to the course for the sake of the world.

SALVATION FROM THE WORLD

From my point of view, Pittenger should have stopped writing with *The Historic Faith and a Changing World* (Oxford University Press, 1950). His latest book, *The Christian Sacrifice* (*op. cit.*), returns to the Church-centered theme of earlier volumes.

His Body the Church (Morehouse-Gorham Inc., 1945) presents the Roman Catholic doctrine of the Church, in itself consistent, but hard for Protestants and most Anglicans to swallow. The Church is divine only; Jesus is human only; Christ is the creation of the Church. Is Christ not rather the perception of the Church? The humanity of the Church is not a Pittenger theme. His ecclesiology seems docetic only. To him, the Church is the New Israel guided by the Holy Spirit. The result of the fact of Christ was the fact of the Church. These Bohlen lectures at Philadelphia Divinity School stress the corporate interrelatedness of Christians in the mystical body of Christ — the social humanity of the incarnate God. Pittenger considers the Church's sad division natural and superficial; beyond it he sees the reality of supernatural unity. The Church, as the fellowship in love, continues the work of God in Christ, enacts in liturgy the meaning of the Christian event, safeguards with dogmas the truth of the original drama, extends in daily conduct the supernatural life. One may inquire: Does truth need to be safeguarded by authority? In Pittenger's view, the Church, to be Christian, must possess unity, holiness, catholicity, and apostolicity. Clearly the Church is not the Church without integrity of .being, continuity between dogma, worship, and ethics, and an ordered ministry. The distinction between mechanical and spiritual apostolicity is not emphasized.

Pittenger asserts that the Church must be universal in three senses: comprehensive in content of faith; world-wide in mission; and adaptable to every time and clime without loss of identity. The central Christian core can sustain wide peripheral difference, and must do so; in different ages different doctrines are useful. The Church ecumenical, in Pittenger's view, includes the faithful departed as well as Christians-still-in-the-making.

The nature of Pittenger's theology becomes strikingly apparent when he asserts that the Church ecumenical must acknowledge the pope as the first Christian bishop. The reader may feel that reunion will indeed include Roman orthodoxy, with or without the pope, but also Russian orthodoxy. The reader may ask: Is not the total world God's growing Church? This idea eludes Pittenger. The Church to him is Monophysitic — always and only divine. He plays down the Church's humanity, its involvement for purposes of redemption with the total historical process. Humanity seems a mere instrument of divinity, not a serious divine enterprise — a means, not an end.

Similarly, Pittenger's idea of the Kingdom of Heaven is entirely otherworldly; it never can, and never will, come upon earth. The Lord's Prayer petition, "Thy will be done on earth as in heaven," seems meaningless to him. Man's true society is God alone. This society is exclusively beyond history. To Pittenger, Christus Victor is the Lord of the Church, not the Lord of the world.

Nonetheless, Pittenger's view of partiality and persistent sinfulness among the members of the Church is genuinely realistic. True also is his view that the Church as the society of charity is always in, yet never of, any human society.

Pittenger sees the possibility of a world of peace and justice produced by a relatively more satisfactory ordering of human affairs; this, he declares, has nothing to do with the Kingdom of God. He similarly ignores the perpetual Christian theme that without the penetrating and healing grace of God no relatively better ordering of human society is achievable. In his view, the unfolding of a finished creation in and through and by means of the historical process is impossible, even to divine grace, which seems a denial of omnipotence.

There is liberalism in Pittenger's snow blindness to all apocalypse and crisis. His idea of final triumph is clearly docetic, does not embrace this world; it is attained without grappling with the tragedy of man's demonic deification of his nation, his century, his culture, his church.

In *Living Faith for Living Men* (Cloister Press, 1947) Pittenger attempted again to plant one end of his Anglo-Catholic bridge solidly on modern soil. Of the ten chapters, eight rehearse basic Christian ideas; the first and last assess with insight the contemporary historical dilemma. The crux of the modern problem, in Pittenger's view, is the mechanization of life — man's estrangement from God and the moral law. The reader will inquire: "Is not this estrangement inevitable in a split sacred/secular world? Pittenger sees three urgent needs in our time: for cosmic security, for salvation from loneliness, and for power to live with dignity. True faith, Pittenger feels, meets these needs by offering a trustworthy reality, fellowship instead of loneliness (the meaning of the Church), and creative energy.

Salvation, as he defines it, is the integration of personality — spiritual health and spiritual growth — through total contact with God. To achieve this integration in us, Jesus Christ brings God near and makes him real, demonstrates God as Almighty Love and shows us what human nature can become, gives us the Holy Spirit, the power to achieve our destiny as sons of God. Salvation also as integration of the corporate life of man through total contact with God, achieved and empowered by Christ and his Spirit, is not mentioned. Personal salvation is obviously basic, but the transformation of history is hardly of second importance.

As Pittenger rightly understands, we cannot be full Christians without the Church. The reader may wish to add: Nor without the world. Is not the Church both end and instrument in the creation of one *agape* community beyond all our subagapaic fragments?

Pittenger defines heaven as man's fellowship with God through love; he defines hell as the absence of this fellowship. These terms, focussed by Pittenger exclusively upon the individual, seem equally applicable to the total movement of human life.

Salvation *from* history characterizes Pittenger's latest book, *The Christian Sacrifice,* a study of the Eucharist in the life of the Church. Eucharistic theology offers a steadying changelessness in our restless century. Continuity with all Christians is demonstrated in Holy Communion, the central act of the Church. However, as Pittenger sees it, the Holy Communion embraces only the Church; it is not a demonstration of man's unity with nature and history; it is something less than the promise of final fulfillment, the foretaste of the future in the present. Paul and John, in Pittenger's eyes, were better teachers about the Eucharist than was Jesus; the effect was, and remains, more definitive for Christians than the cause. " The full intention of God in the actions that the historic Jesus performed in the Last Supper included more than the human mind of Jesus himself may have foreseen. . . . The task of Paul and John was to bring into clearer light the divine intention " (Pp. 39, 40). When the Church is gathered for the Lord's Supper, Christ is as truly present as in the days of his flesh. One must ask, " Only there? " Is Christ not our Lord at every moment, whether we are together or apart? Is he not the Lord of all history, of the total human pilgrimage toward freedom in fellowship?

In Pittenger's view, every form of ministry not directly and visibly within the apostolic succession is departure from the Holy Spirit; it is therefore either deadening and enervating originality or shattering heresy. Further, the Eucharist imparts its value automatically; in the *action* of the Eucharist, not in the thoughts or feelings of communicants, the memorial is found. The reader may inquire: Not even in repentance and faith, in new commitment to love and hope? A family at dinner is physically and spatially gathered; further, its unity is demonstrated regardless of its members' private feelings. To be sure. On the other hand, there is no communion if each member withdraws into his private world and ex-

cludes, or hates, the rest of the family. The family itself is, or ought
to be, a miniature Holy Communion, a foretaste of the final whole-
family reunion at one altar. To Pittenger, the sacrament is not a
memorial but a sacrifice. Once again, however, he asserts that the
Church alone is divine, that there is no divinity in the world beyond
the Church. The apostolic succession, which provides the one duly
authenticated ministry in Christendom, excludes Coptic Christians,
Armenian Christians, and all of us hillbilly Protestants.

In conclusion: Pittenger seems to exclude the world that God is
now creating through and beyond the Church. Yet Pittenger's love
of the Church as the community of charity in and of the Holy
Spirit is, and will remain, the Christian norm. God's purpose is our
hope; his will is our peace; his patience is our salvation.

CLASSICAL CHRISTIANITY

At best, terms are slippery, and categories inevitably elastic. The
term "classical Christianity" undoubtedly means many things to
many people. The term as classifying the theology of W. Norman
Pittenger suggests three particuar things. First, a clear tendency to
select as the starting point or final reference of thought, not the
events recorded in the Gospels, but the great creedal formulations
of the fourth and fifth centuries; in other words, the events of the
Gospels are interpreted in the light of the creeds of Nicaea and
Chalcedon, rather than the reverse. Secondly, a conception of the
purpose of God which may seek fully to embrace this world with
charity, yet has its eyes not primarily upon the world as God's central enterprise but upon the achievement of salvation for the elect in
the world to come. And thirdly, a healthy openness, in principle
and often in practice, to the actual problems and interests of the
world outside the Church. To summarize these three characteristics
of Pittenger's thought most simply: his point of beginning and
ending is not the gospel but the great interpretative creeds of the
Church, which ought to be regarded as testimonies, not as tests,
of faith; the central interest of Christianity is vertical and otherworldly, however much it may look upon the struggles of humanity

with charity; and finally a genuine interest in, and regard for, the world which may be improved by the light of faith, but cannot be redeemed. Where some classical Christians assume an increasing asceticism toward the world, Pittenger seeks genuinely to draw near the world with the challenge, and invitation, of the Church.

His point of view, therefore, may indeed be roughly described as, at one and the same time, Roman Catholic and modernist. Its Roman Catholicism is the content of the creeds; its modernism, a sincere attempt to relate creedal Christianity to modern knowledge, and to present the creedal faith in modern language. The word "reality," in the Pittenger vocabulary, is very similar to its use in the realism of the Middle Ages; the word refers to God who is absolute perfection. To Pittenger, therefore, "Christianity is a life lived in a special relationship with the great Reality which is man's most intimate yet most ultimate environment, a relationship which is realized through that Reality's active self-disclosure in Jesus Christ" (*Approach to Christianity*, p. 1).

Pittenger acknowledges willingly that we cannot give neat, ir-resistible proofs for the Christian faith. It is not possible to offer absolutely convincing arguments for the affirmation that the great Reality is the Christian God of love, that he has supremely revealed himself in the divine/human life of Jesus Christ, that we may know him intimately in prayer and sacrament. But this we can do. We can speak of the unanimous witness of the saints, the testimony of nature and history, the purpose which seems to flow through the world, the moral goodness and sublime holiness of noble souls, the appearance of Christ himself. We can ask men and women to rec-ognize that these point toward, even if they do not quite con-clusively prove, the Christian view. When we have done that, we can legitimately ask for the act of faith, the living trust, that will turn converging probabilities and reasonable theories into a reality which endures and deepens as life is enriched and dignified.

About religion, thus defined, science, in Pittenger's view, has nothing to say. Indeed, science is of great assistance to religion. Not merely does it show us how, as a matter of fact, God works on several important levels of his creation, and so enlarges our knowl-

edge and aids us in comprehending the divine plan. More important than that, it makes impossible any religion but the highest and
purest. It rules out superstitious and magical ideas of the way in
which the great Reality works in the world, and replaces them by or-
derly and consistent ideas. This is a very great service, for the result
is a deeper and truer vision of the nature of God himself. And to
know God, in the most intimate sense, is the whole meaning of
religion.

If the meaning of religion is to know God, the method of the
Christian religion, in Pittenger's accent, is to know the creeds —
inwardly as well as historically. To Pittenger, the creeds, taken as
great historical statements of the faith (with all their imperfections
and infelicities), unite us with the Christian past and emphasize
our continuity in the Christian life. Anyone who accepts the fundamental beliefs may join in that life of the Church. The conviction
that Reality is love, that he reveals himself through many channels
and supremely in Christ, that Christ is still active in the world in
the " fellowship of the Holy Spirit," that sins may be forgiven, that
personality persists through death, that all life is to be redeemed by
Christ's spirit — this is what matters. When we repeat the creeds,
we unite ourselves with a great company of witnesses in confessing
our allegiance to the faith that overcomes the world.

To Pittenger, God is prior to our knowledge of him, and his
knowledge of himself is therefore prior to our knowledge. Hence
the human drawing aside of the veil, the life of human reason, while
legitimate, is at best a secondary way of knowing God. The action
from our side is not the main thing, however necessary; rather, God
takes the initiative; it is he who moves to reveal himself to us in
nature, in history, and in persons. With this Pittenger view, all believers in God as the Lord of history will inevitably agree. As Pittenger has understood, we may reasonably assert that there is really
only one religion — the growing apprehension of God, following
upon his self-disclosure to men. It starts very humbly, and rises
gradually to grander and grander conceptions of the great Reality.
Finally, it reaches a climax and a fullness in Christ.

There is no theistic finitism in Pittenger's theology, but divine omnipotence does not mean that God is the author of nonsense. In Pittenger's excellent word:

" What the omnipotence of God really asserts is that the divine Reality possesses all the power there is; it belongs to him and to no one else. Yet that power is delegated by him to men, as well as to lesser orders of being, and it may very well be used against him if their wills are not aligned with his will. And God's own employment of his power is in accord with his nature, which is positive goodness. He never uses it arbitrarily, selfishly, harmfully. He is the union of power and love, and his most mighty power is his boundless love " (*Ibid.*, p. 31).

Pittenger finds no final conflict between divine omniscience and human freedom. To him, God is like a professional chess player who knows all the moves that an opponent *may* make; he knows also that he will win the game. Yet his opponent is perfectly free to play as he will, but the possibilities are limited and the end of the game is obvious.

The problem of evil is a problem indeed, to Pittenger as to anyone, but he recognizes that there is a purpose of righteous love at work in the world, that somehow good is " the final goal of ill." He is fully aware that belief in the loving Reality immensely increases the problem of evil, yet also holds out a hope which makes the struggle against evil worth the trouble.

In the *consensus fidelium,* authority and freedom go hand in hand in the recognition that " it is God who is beforehand in all our seeking " (*Ibid.*, p. 134). If freedom has its dangers, so also has authority. " Christianity has no more dangerous enemy than anything that would narrow or restrict it " (*Ibid.*, p. 136). From Huxley, Pittenger quotes a useful line to picture the whole response which Christianity demands in individual men: " It does not take much of a man to be a Christian, but it takes all there is of him " (*Ibid.*, p. 143).

The Christian faith, as Pittenger understands it, focuses finally in a Kingdom which is outside this world, yet its charity necessitates its realistic movement toward the more and the better within history. In his challenging words:

"The professing Christian will . . . co-operate, so far as he is able, with all movements which make for the improvement of social, industrial, economic, and political conditions. He will realize that the Christian religion has profound social implications, and he will seek to do his reasonable share in bringing it about that the spirit of Christ prevail in the entire fabric of social life. Although the end of man is eternity, and God's Kingdom is finally to be sought outside this world of time and space, the Christian Church rightfully seeks to establish among men a social order that will reflect, so far as this earth can reflect, the mind of Christ" (*Ibid.*, pp. 141, 142).

Pittenger quotes Samuel Butler to the effect that "there are some people who would be equally horrified at hearing the Christian religion doubted and at seeing it practiced" (*Ibid.*, p. 147). He refers to a London priest, who was asked why he worked to improve the plumbing in the slum hovels within his parish, and replied, "Because I believe in the incarnation" (*Ibid.*, p. 149).

The Christian must move out into the world, not alone in action, but also in imagination — in art. Christian art, as Pittenger rightly understands it, is not primarily the presentation of the Holy Family, or of moral themes; it is not primarily designed even to edify; it is rather a depth criticism of life. Art as the criticism of life is an inevitable activity of man, simply because to make no judgments is to be inhuman. With Christianity as the ultimate standard, art can help Christians to come to grips with the world, both in appreciation and in discrimination. (Cf. "Art and the Christian," in *The Christian Century*, Dec. 31, 1947, pp. 1612–1615.)

The immediate problem of the Christian in the world, to Pittenger as to Kierkegaard, is to live in absolute relation to the absolute and in relative relation to the relative. The religious category is therefore primary; the ethical category, secondary. Greater guidance in specific ethical conduct, Pittenger believes, is to be found in the voice of the Church than in the voice of Jesus. The problem, differently stated, is to keep in living union a total commitment to God and Christ together with the necessity of accommodation and compromise in the application of broad principles to narrow situations. From Pittenger's standpoint, we are pilgrims in this world, yet we must use our minds; we are not, and must not allow our-selves to become, moral robots. For example, neither literalism nor rigorism nor libertinism provides the answer to the Christian's understanding of modern marriage and divorce; rather, a living tension between absolute commitment and actual human situations. (Cf. *Compromise and Morality,* in *The Christian Century,* Nov. 30, 1949, pp. 1422–1424.)

In Pittenger's view the flow of history, as such, is never God's central enterprise. Rather, the Church must recognize that it is fully in, but never of, the world. In his words:

" There is no reason under the sun why the Christian faith should be *adjusted* to the new pattern of things. . . . One of the worst evils of the now much-decried 'liberal era' in religious thought was found pre-cisely at this point. If Christianity were not being adapted to the think-ing of the *laissez-faire* capitalistic world, it was being adapted to the newer optimistically conceived liberalistic world. If it did not serve as a means for condoning the evils of an 'acquisitive society,' it served as a dynamic for producing a 'socialized society.' In either case, the whole-ness, independence, and self-identity of Christianity were minimized or lost " (*The Historic Faith and a Changing World,* p. 5).

Against the expediency, which Pittenger considers the assumption behind the assumptions of modern thought, we may, in his view, be happy that Christianity is no longer taken for granted. If the Christian position is believed today, it is believed — rather more often than yesterday — because it is felt to be *true,* not because it is the " atmosphere " that one naturally accepts in a given cultural situation.

The American scene is neurotic, as Pittenger sees it, yet he finds hope in the fact that liberalism is dead, at least in the seminaries, among the leaders of thought, and among the younger ministers. Orthodoxy is on the way in. Yet orthodoxy has its own dangers, even to Pittenger. One of these dangers is the " extricationist " view, the desire to withdraw from the world in which the Church is com-manded to bear its witness. The Church must reckon realistically with the five convictions that define the uniformity of our culture: the belief in expediency, the belief that truths are unknowable, the belief that all men are equal, the belief that things are the essential realities, the belief in self-expression and self-fulfillment. The liberal faith, not identical with the convictions of modern culture, believed in the Fatherhood of God, the brotherhood of man, and, as one man put it, "the neighborhood of Boston" (*Ibid.,* p. 57). The liberal creed, to be precise, was this: "I believe in the Fatherhood of God, the brotherhood of man, the leadership of Jesus, salvation by character, and the progress of the human race" (*Ibid.,* p. 56).

In 1920, Karl Barth and neo-orthodoxy began to appear, emphasizing both individually and socially the depraved, self-centered, proud, lustful, egocentric quality of man the sinner, man's need for redemption which at best could be accomplished only in principle, the extreme or radical transcendence of God, that finite and sinful man cannot reach God, that God must come down to man, and has done so in Jesus Christ. To Pittenger, orthodoxy of the newer variety has minimized Jesus as a human model, has asserted also the limited power of human reason, that revelation is not human inspiration but God's act and speech, and has emphasized a strong eschatological element. However, one of the virtues of neo-orthodoxy is that it has rediscovered the Church. As Pittenger views the neo-orthodox message, we stand under the mercy of God, but above all we stand under the judgment of God. Human life reaches its finality in death, a fact that signifies both the limitation of man as a mortal and the utter necessity for his finding his meaning, if his life is to have significance, in something other than self. The resurrection, to neo-orthodoxy, is therefore not a fact but a symbol. Pittenger therefore believes that neo-orthodoxy is not quite orthodox, in the light of Christianity's formative and normative creeds. To Pittenger, man is not totally depraved; the image of God in man is damaged, but still real. And, against the neo-orthodox emphasis, Pittenger asserts both the immanence and the transcendence of God. The neo-orthodox pessimism receives straightforward criticism in Pittenger's words:

"The newer 'orthodoxy' has approached the whole question of religious faith from the side of man's dilemma rather than from an attempt to make place for religion in a total world view in which science is dominant. The obstacle to faith is no longer the supposed contradiction between evolution and creation, between a scientific world and the religious sentiment, et cetera, such as agitated the minds of many of us when we were young. The real obstacle now is what might roughly be called a cultural one — that is, it is the problem of relating a vigorous religious faith to a cultural situation in which man's problems seem not only to be insoluble by concerted human effort, but to be insoluble altogether.

"The cynicism of the 'intellectuals' of our day seems to be close to the position of the 'new orthodoxy'; for both begin with a thorough pessimism about man" (*Ibid.*, p. 78, 79).

Liberalism, however, has been unable to criticize modern American thought, since it has been primarily a reflection of modern thought currents. Neo-orthodoxy has been able to criticize the modern cultural stream, but must not overwork the ability. There is grave danger for democracy itself in neo-orthodox pessimism.

Pittenger speaks a wholesome word on behalf of human reason, human will, and human desire:

"Even if it be true, and unquestionably it is true, that human reason is profoundly limited and that man's conclusions must always be watched lest they be spoiled by 'special pleading' and 'wishful thinking,' it is also true that the human reason is the only instrument that may be sufficiently checked so that the margin of error can be restricted. Even when we have admitted the imperfection and perversion of the human will, it is still true that the will accomplishes all that is done by men in this world; even if our desires are all too frequently directed toward that which is bad for us and for our human brethren, we do desire and can desire only that which *seems* good to us, however limited and fallible our judgment may be. In fact, human nature with its worst tendencies and most reprehensible drives is still not without *some* good — it can discover truth, if only occasionally; it can will the right, if only now and again; it can love the good, if only infrequently" (*Ibid.*, pp. 93, 94).

Pittenger feels that both liberalism and neo-orthodoxy have missed a golden opportunity. In his view, what might roughly be called post-Reformation theology has been given a remarkable opportunity to work through, experimentally, a variety of possible points of view; it has emerged from this movement with the possibility of approximating the balance and proportion of the pre-Reformation theology — not the Roman Catholic position (Pittenger insists), but the traditional Catholic position classically expressed in the age of the Fathers and not too unworthily stated in what Von Hügel called "the golden Middle Ages," the time of Thomas Aquinas, Bonaventure, and Duns Scotus. Anglicanism, in Pittenger's view, offers the middle way between liberalism and neo-orthodoxy, providing a healthy continuity with the best of the past.

We are challenged by a new society in which individualism is ended, and State control of the whole of life, including education, is increased and will increase. As Pittenger puts it, " We have become a unity with an overwhelming weight of mass authority and a strong tendency to smother the individual in that mass " (*Ibid.*, p. 110). The future may have a concern for social justice, but it will be in every sense collectivist, with a this-worldly perspective. Religion, in such a society, is regarded as useful to the new leviathan and to mental health; its own characteristic influence is diminishing. In this new society, with its good side in making a place for the common man, the Church is freshly challenged to be itself, to be the Body of Christ.

In Pittenger's view, the liberalism of yesterday tended to merge Christianity with national life and interests; the newer orthodoxy tends to make a complete divorce between them. Historic Christianity has seen the need for balance, and has insisted that while the Church is not part of secular culture or identified with the society surrounding it, it has its message and mission to that society. Its work is to bring the supernatural charity of God in Christ straight into the midst of the relative justice, if there be such, of the world, so that light and life may be generated for the sons of men. This does not mean that history, as such, can be saved. In Pittenger's words:

" After all, we have no guarantee anywhere in the Gospels that the Christian faith will soon win the entire world. It is a relatively modern idea that things are getting better all the time, so that in the end the whole world will become perfect . . . and then, presumably, become a freezing uninhabitable planet! No; our task is to do our work as we see it, when we see it; to leave the future to God and not to ask that what *we* think to be right shall necessarily come to pass " (*Ibid.*, p. 151).

The Church's business, as Pittenger sees it, is therefore vertical, not horizontal. "We have said little about the Church's concern for the social pattern. We do not believe that the Church's principal task is in this direction " (*Ibid.*, pp. 152, 153).

The need of our time, to Pittenger, is therefore dynamic orthodoxy, which recognizes the fact and priority of God, that man is a finite creature who pretends more and is thus a sinner in rebellion against God. Man's body unites him with the world; his soul unites him with God. Yet man remains precisely a body-soul unity, in spiritual/temporal tension. Dynamic orthodoxy insists upon God's action in history, and upon the hope of glory (of personal immortality), and the fear of everlasting damnation. Nonetheless, dynamic orthodoxy, as Pittenger conceives it, is entirely hospitable to whatever new truth may come from any direction; it is not " the kind of orthodoxy Erasmus once described, that took ' the new learning to be synonymous with heresy,' and so made ' orthodoxy synonymous with ignorance ' " (*Ibid.*, p. 168).

Finally, the Christian society is the community of the elect, en route through this world to a better one, yet commanded to leaven this world with divine life. " The Christian Church is called to be both the ark of salvation, in that it gives to men the certainty of life in God, and the continuing agent of redemption, in that from it and through it health-giving influences stream out into the whole world " (*Ibid.*, p. 181).

Louis Berkhof

A THEOLOGY OF BIBLICAL LITERALISM

T*he* meaning of Christianity is revolution — forward to the un-achieved will of God. The worship of Christianity is reaction. Nothing human is complete, final, or infallible; nothing human is above criticism. The failure to recognize our human fallibility uniformly results in *rigor mortis*. Ecclesiolatry is familiar enough in our day — the denominational claim of infallibility — and the Roman sect is not the only example. The attempt to save the Church and neglect the world seems also ecclesiolatrous.

Another form of distortion, less familiar today but still with us, is bibliolatry — the claim of absolute Biblical infallibility. Louis Berkhof specifically states that he believes in God only because an infallible Bible tells him that God exists. To believe in the Bible first and God second — is not this idolatry? From this beginning, Berkhof moves toward personal immortality, a " saved " Church, and a millennial after-history; this world, which God " so loved," means little or nothing to him. He mentions divine immanence, but immanence, as he treats it, is verbal only — empty of content; a word, not a fact. Once or twice he declares that God's Kingdom is present as well as future, that the millennium is not a canceled present but the present transformed; nonetheless the context and tenor give this world only the status of an illusion. He seems more preoccupied with the Bible as the Word of God than with either God or the world. To him, the Bible is a lawyer's library, a set of infallible proof texts — unambiguous utterances of Omniscience.

Nonetheless, Berkhof, a careful scholar, draws attention to the actual words of the Bible, often enough neglected; few men will prove more stimulating and informative. His surveys of theological and doctrinal history are painstakingly exact and immensely useful. Knowing his exact point of departure and arrival, you can estimate for yourself the trend of the argument if God's world and God's work as well as God's Word were taken seriously.

Berkhof's argument for Biblical infallibility and the Roman argument for papal infallibility are identical: " God would not allow man to proceed without an exact blueprint; hence, the Holy Spirit guarantees infallibility."

First a quick look at his life, then a patient analysis of three aspects of his one-dimensional thought: Systematic Infallibility, Christ Died for the Elect Only, and A Plea for Authoritarianism.

A Theological Career

Louis Berkhof was born October 13, 1873. His parents were Jan and Geesje ter Poorten Berkhof. In 1900 he married Reka Dijkhuis, and there were four children: Grace, William, Jeanette, and John. Mrs. Berkhof died in 1928. In 1933 he married Dena Joldersma, and there have been two children: Joanna and Wilma.

He graduated from the theological school of the Christian Reformed Church, Grand Rapids, Michigan (1900), and received the B.D. degree at Princeton (1904). From 1904 to 1906 he studied (by correspondence) at the Divinity School of the University of Chicago.

He was pastor at Pearline, Michigan (1900–1902) and at Oakdale Park Church, Grand Rapids (1904–1906). He became professor of exegetical theology (1906), and professor of New Testament studies (1914), in the theological school of the Christian Reformed Church. He was president of Calvin Seminary from 1921 until his retirement (1944), and from 1926 professor of systematic theology. He delivered the L. P. Stone Lectures at Princeton Theological Seminary (1920–1921).

There are many doctrinal differences among theologians of the infallible Bible — heated controversies between premillennialists and postmillennialists, dispensationalists and nondispensationalists, infralapsarians, and supralapsarians, predestinarians and nonpredesti-

narians. Berkhof is postmillennial, nondispensationalist, infralap-
sarian, and steadfastly predestinarian. These are matters of life and
death to friends of the infallible Bible. Premillenarians, extreme dispensationalists, supralapsarians, and nonpredestinarians will not be
satisfied with Louis Berkhof as our only representative of proof-
text theology. I myself would be happy to include additional Biblicists in this family album. The "predestined" length of this
volume necessitates many sacrifices. In any case, there is no funda-
mentalist scholar more thoroughgoing than Berkhof. In the main,
infallibility means the same thing to all representatives of the school,
though interpretations are many-colored — and each is regarded as
final. Indeed, I find Louis Berkhof more helpful than the stout defenders of the faith once for all delivered to Scofield.

Systematic Infallibility

Some Biblicists maintain with gestures that theology is an evil
science, that one should take the Bible straight — undiluted with
interpretation. The view that the Bible must not be interpreted is
itself an interpretation. In actual practice no one has excluded all
interpretation; rather, the inevitable interpretations are sometimes as
confused and contradictory as they are varied. Louis Berkhof has no
sympathy with the lethargy of mind that leaves an interpretation at
war with itself. The attempt to systematize Biblical interpretation,
in his view, is an unavoidable necessity for thinking men. Berkhof
recognizes, with genuine humility, that his truth and God's truth
may not be identical. To quote him directly:

"There seems to be a lurking fear that the more we systematize the
truth, the farther we wander from the presentation of it that is found in
the Word of God. But there is no danger of this if the system is not
based on the fundamental principles of some erring philosophy but on
the abiding principles of Scripture itself. God certainly sees the truth
as a whole, and it is the duty of the theologian to think the truths of
God after him. There should be a constant endeavor to see the truth as
God sees it, even though it is perfectly evident that the ideal is beyond
the grasp of man in his present condition" (*Introductory Volume to*

Systematic Theology, p. 15. Wm. B. Eerdmans Publishing Company, 1932).

Berkhof may be naïve in his effort to exclude all "erring philosophy" from his own, or any other, analysis of Biblical meaning; he is certainly right in his understanding of the theologian's task — the attempt to think God's thoughts after him.

Six Berkhof books endlessly repeat the story of Western theology — and invariably he casts his vote with Calvin. Four constitute a ponderous but rewarding reading course in systematic infallibility: *Introductory Volume to Systematic Theology* (1932), *Textual Aids to Systematic Theology* (1942), *History of Christian Doctrines* (1937), and *Systematic Theology* (1938) — all published by Wm. B. Eerdmans. To read these books exercises the eye as well as the mind; it is also to penetrate every minute distinction in theological history, to listen with fear and trembling to long anathemas against liberal departure from Biblical infallibility, to hear the all pro, and no con, of Reformed "dialectics." Berkhof's understanding of Schleiermacher and Ritschl is one-sided but helpful. He has read many contemporary American theologians — some with tolerance, none with approval.

Berkhof surveys in every volume the theological ground from Origen, Lactantius, and Augustine, through John of Damascus, Peter the Lombard, Anselm, Abélard, and Aquinas, to Melanchthon, Zwingli, Calvin, Watson, and Gerhardt. He explains technical terms and insists that Church dogmas, like the dogmas of science, possess a certain authority, though they possess also the added authority of real or supposed revelation. A dogma, in his definition, is any teaching regarded as true by an official group and formulated by some competent body. Unfortunately this definition makes a dogma of every weird teaching in the history of thought. Some group has approved and formulated every contradictory possibility. Berkhof has little sympathy with Schleiermacher's theology of experience or with Ritschl's theology of faith; his own appeal is always to the objective and infallible Bible. He stresses the necessity of dogma against religious relativism; he finds modern Christianity without

Scriptural subject matter, without dogmatic reflection, and without official definitions by competent ecclesiastical bodies. In his view, a Church without dogmas would be a silent Church, a contradiction in terms. A silent witness is no witness at all — though deeds sometimes speak more loudly than words. Dogmas, however, are never made to order; they grow out of the experience of the believing community. Berkhof rejects Kant's idea that God is the object, not of science, but of faith. To him, the Bible makes God an object of science. Berkhof is all faith and no skepticism. He agrees with Barth that the task of dogmatics is to test the language of the Church about God, to examine the agreement between divine revelation and Church proclamation.

Berkhof always organizes the theological subject matter as follows:

I. God (Theology)
II. Man (Anthropology)
III. Christ (Christology)
IV. Applied Salvation (Soteriology)
V. Church (Ecclesiology)
VI. Last Things (Eschatology)

Religion, as Berkhof understands it, is the impact upon life of God's relation to the world, theology the impact upon thought of the same relation. Special and general revelation form the basis of our knowledge of God. The seat of religion is neither the intellect, as Hegel believed, nor the will, on Kant's terms, nor the emotions, as Schleiermacher thought, but the heart. Since man was created in the divine image, an image not wholly lost in the Fall, he can respond to God's objective self-revelation. The Bible is the Holy Spirit's chief instrument. Through the inward testimony of the Holy Spirit the Christian is convinced that God is faithful in his revelation; therefore, as a matter of course, the Christian accepts the testimony of the Scripture concerning itself. Special Providence, watching over Scripture, has preserved its divinity and infallibility.

Unlike Berkhof, the reader may see in the Bible both infallibility and fallibility, and therefore the necessity of skepticism and faith — to separate light from darkness. Light shines through, but darkness and distortion weaken our apprehension. "The light shineth in darkness; and the darkness comprehended it not" (John 1:5, K.J.V.).

Berkhof's proof-text method is clear in the book *Textual Aids to Systematic Theology* (1942). Our knowledge of God and salvation, he insists, depends absolutely upon the inspired Word of God. No reliable system of truth is available apart from the authoritative Word. The Bible is the source of theology. Man cannot discover God. There is no way from man to God — only a way from God to man. Man can obtain knowledge of God only in so far as God reveals himself. If man would know God, he must study God's revelation with a believing heart. Berkhof acknowledges that even in the Bible man cannot know God perfectly; nonetheless man can obtain in the Bible a knowledge that is perfectly adequate.

In assembling Biblical proof texts, the Old and the New Testaments are to be used as allies, not as enemies (the error of Marcion and the Gnostics); the two Testaments are two activities of one God who emphasizes different aspects of his truth in law and grace, in the prophets and the apostles. Four principles are important in the use of proof texts; the Bible is to be used as a whole; one must always consult the context; one must always be exact in quotation; and one should avoid doubtful passages. Berkhof approaches the Bible as a Supreme Court judge approaches the United States Constitution; the effort to distinguish greater from lesser value seems forbidden. In his view, the theologian's task is simply to mobilize the proof texts like soldiers, organize them in military divisions called theology, anthropology, Christology, soteriology, ecclesiology, and eschatology, and march forth in strength to meet the foe, with singing and the sound of trumpets.

In the *History of Christian Doctrines* (1937), a companion volume to *Systematic Theology,* Berkhof re-examines the Apostolic Fathers, the Gnostic and Ebionite perversions, the reforms of Marcion and the Montanists, the apologists (Justin, Tatian, Athenagoras and Theophilus), and anti-Gnostics (Irenaeus, Hippolytus, and Tertullian), the Alexandrians (Clement and Origen), dynamic and modalistic monarchianism, and the diverse interpreters of the atonement (Anselm and Abélard, Duns Scotus and Socinus, Grotius and Armenius). The volume illustrates Berkhof's contention: the Bible is infallible and unalterable, but the dogma of the Church is changeable; as a matter of fact, it has undergone many changes in history. That which is unchangeable is not subject to development and has no history. With this principle Berkhof defends the Bible and attacks the Roman Church; papal theology cannot change and is therefore nonhistorical; Reformed thought, able to distinguish between the divine and the human, has undergone change. Berkhof never perceives the nonhistorical character of Biblical infallibility. True, we have this wine in earthen vessels; but to Berkhof the Bible is all wine and no vessel.

His most thorough work is the one-volume *Systematic Theology* (1938). It is more ponderous than profound, yet in every sense scholarly; it raises most of the questions and examines a wide variety of answers, yet proceeds from the view that Creation took place in six twenty-four-hour days. He mentions that God is immanent as well as transcendent, but never refers to immanence again. The world, the historical process, does not appear in the book from first page to last. Berkhof's Bible, like his universe, is static. The treatment follows his usual distribution of the great themes — God, Man, Christ, Salvation, Church, and Last Things. You do not begin, as Tillich does, with man the question, nor with God the answer; Berkhof begins, continues, and ends with the Bible. It is his only epistemology; it is not a dialogue with man, but a divine monologue.

Divine light breaks through Berkhof's pages; you feel that the man is a saint in a strait jacket. He stresses the divine decrees — predestination, creation, preservation, and the original covenant of works. Man's happiness rests upon obedience, simply. Berkhof's conception of the atonement is therefore penal and substitutionary, a matter of legal disobedience and legal substitution. The reader may not share Berkhof's view that man has no claim whatever upon God. Surely man has one claim upon God — God's own love for what He is creating. Berkhof is totally opposed to any form of Pelagianism, ancient or modern. But surely Pelagius understood one thing better than Augustine — divine immanence; and Augustine understood one thing better than Pelagius — divine transcendence.

Berkhof insists that Christ is King of the total universe, but only "in the interests of the Church" (*Systematic Theology*, p. 410). The government of the world is of no importance for its own sake. It is the Church, the elect only, that God is saving; the world is neither more nor less than raw material. As Berkhof sees it, Christ has completed the redemption of the few; he has not opened the door and extended the invitation to all men.

With Ferré, Berkhof considers both creation and redemption the work of the Holy Spirit, though he does not make Ferré's distinction between the preparation of the Spirit of God and the fulfillment of the Holy Spirit. To Berkhof, not to Ferré, God instills saving faith into the few who are foreordained to life, and foreordains to damnation those to whom he does not impart faith; Berkhof then refuses to consider the charge of divine injustice. Similarly, God grants the grace of final perseverance to those whom he effectually calls. Man has nothing to do with it one way or another. The work of God in the soul, however, is never complete in this life; perfect sainthood is therefore impossible.

Berkhof places the Word (the Bible) above the sacraments as a means of grace. Salvation *begins* with the hearing of the Word; it is merely *continued* by the use of the sacraments. Berkhof, like Calvin, rejects Roman transubstantiation, Lutheran consubstantiation, and Zwinglian memorial; the sacrament is present-tense fellowship with God and the Church. Christ is present in body and blood but not physically; the man of faith experiences a real communion with the whole Christ in glory.

Berkhof has little patience with the premillenarians who insist upon two or three Second Comings of Christ, three or four Last Judgments, and two or three resurrections. As he sees it, the Second Coming of Christ is a single event, preceded by the calling of the Gentiles, the conversion of a remnant of Israel, the great apostasy and tribulation, the revelation of Antichrist, and signs and wonders. The Second Coming is personal, visible, physical, sudden, glorious, and triumphant — but no man knows the hour. The Second Coming brings quickly to pass the resurrection of the dead, the Final

Judgment, and the regeneration of the heavens and the earth. Berkhof is not a gradualist with the liberal postmillenarians. His view is simple: Christ will return at the end of the world to introduce the future age, the eternal state of things; he will inaugurate and complete two mighty acts — the resurrection of the dead and the Final Judgment. The final forensic judgment will render to every man his due. The Jews will be judged by Jewish Law, Christians by the law of Christ, the Gentiles by the law written in their hearts. Heaven and hell are places; both are permanent.

Berkhof rejects the Lutheran idea that the present world must be destroyed to make possible an entirely new creation. With Reformed theologians, he believes the new creation will be the present process renewed, transformed. The joys of eternity are not spiritual only; in some manner the body will remain; hence there will be recognition of loved ones, social intercourse "on an elevated plane," and a hierarchy determined by deeds. Nonetheless, each man will participate in perfect happiness forever. Berkhof's final society seems static, a stately minuet at a young ladies' finishing school — something less than a wild dance of Chestertonian joy.

Two useful little books reduce the heavy Berkhof systematics to beginners' English: *Manual of Christian Doctrine* (1933) and *Summary of Christian Doctrine* (1938). Classes of younger or older probationers might well be exposed to these volumes — they raise most of the questions inevitable in Christian theology; unfortunately, the historical process goes into complete eclipse, but the teacher can add something for himself. Berkhof is stimulating and helpful whether or not you agree with him — indeed, more so if you do not. Persons raised in the more liberal Churches, where human sinfulness and the call to repentance have not been whispered, *ought* to read Berkhof. The cure might be worse than the disease, but the dimension of transcendence added to the liberal awareness of time and history should prove creative. Precisely this has often happened: James Luther Adams passed from childhood fundamentalism first to atheism then to creative faith.

CHRIST DIED FOR THE ELECT ONLY

To say the least, there is nothing in Berkhof about inevitable universal salvation. As he sees the Scriptures, they offer no bright hope for all men. Only the few will be saved. The greater part of mankind, in his view, was foreordained to damnation from the beginning. Humanity, as such, is not God's serious enterprise; rather God is interested only in the salvation of a handful, a holy remnant. All Berkhof's books accent this theme, but four in particular seem filled with it. *The Assurance of Faith* (1939) presents personal immortality, not for the many, but for the few. Berkhof stresses the good point that saving faith contains an element of trust. However, trust, as he conceives it, rests not upon the character of God but upon the written promises of the Bible — divine I.O.U.'s Many liberal Christians today find security, safety, and joy in God's Agape; Berkhof finds serenity in proof texts. He urges men to make their calling and election sure, but explains that man cannot save himself; however, he can make his calling sure *to his own consciousness.* Personal salvation, having nothing to do with subjectivity, is an objective reality whether consciousness perceives it or not. Nonetheless, we may increase our faith by studying the Bible, praying for the guidance of the Holy Spirit, attending the sacraments, hearing sermons, and cultivating good works.

The surrounding gloom of the world is Berkhof's theme in *Riches of Divine Grace* (1948). These ten expository sermons are dedicated "to Dena, my devoted wife." The world is without hope, a meaningless nether region; out of it a small group will be redeemed by divine decree. The small circle of the saints will enter the city that has foundations, whose builder and maker is God. There is no awareness that the total world is, and must increasingly become, the City of God. The elect share Abraham's covenant: "I will be thy God and the God of thy seed." Only men in Christ are heirs of the promise. Berkhof stresses, in pietist form, a wholesome morality: we are called to be righteous seven days a week, to eliminate the blasphemous white line between sacred and secular. However, we merit nothing by our ethical purity; by faith alone we appropriate

Christ, his righteousness, and his sanctifying grace. Our hope lies
in hearing, and heeding, the Bible.

Vicarious Atonement Through Christ (1936) restates the penal
substitutionary theory of the atonement, and analyses the historical
alternatives. To Berkhof, only the penal substitutionary theory is
scriptural. Anselm's satisfaction theory was better than the earlier
ransom and capitulation theories, but in Anselm's view God's honor,
not God's justice, was to be satisfied. Abélard's moral influence
theory was superficial; it did not deal realistically with the fact of
objective disobedience. Duns Scotus' acceptation theory denied the
necessity of an atonement. Socinus' example theory left sin unpun-
ished. Grotius' government theory, halfway from Socinus to Calvin, satisfied neither God's justice nor man's desire for deliverance.
In Berkhof's view, modern rationalism has done away with the
atonement altogether. The moral influence theory, dominant in our
day, makes the whole matter subjective. Repentance alone is necessary for forgiveness; no objective justice exists to be satisfied. Nowhere does Berkhof recognize that the wrath of man crucified
Christ; that human inertia rejected God's incarnate call to growth
in love; that the past nailed the future to the cross; that in all things
God works for good with those who love him; that the future
shattered the present in the resurrection, endlessly breaks and shakes
all present achievement, and is shed abroad in the shattered present
by the Holy Spirit. Berkhof rejects Schleiermacher's mystical theory
(atonement by incarnation), is sympathetic to John McLeod Camp-
bell's theory (vicarious repentance), but insists that law as well as
love must be satisfied.

One's conception of sin determines his theory of atonement; to
Berkhof, sin is voluntary, man's willful departure from God's
known will; sin is positive transgression; it is therefore guilt, liable
to punishment. Punishment is not merely a natural result of sin;
it is legal, and therefore demands a legal atonement. The reader
may feel that, in Berkhof's view, God seems more of a tyrant than
a father. To Berkhof, God is angry with the sinner. Christ is the
sin offering for believers only. Christ atoned for the elect both by
active and passive obedience; he therefore extends to the blessed

both negative forgiveness and positive acceptance. Sovereign election means that the elect can never be lost. And to those foreordained to be damned God shows some kindness. The atonement was sufficient for all, but God never purposed to save all.

Berkhof's posthistorical focus is clear in the book *The Second Coming of Christ* (1953); fulfillment follows, it does not involve, history. There is no recognition of what might be called Christ's five "second comings": at Pentecost, the gift of the Holy Spirit; at conversion, personal participation in Pentecost; at the death of the saint, to be absent from the body is to be present with the Lord; at the decline and fall of an idolatrous nation (Rome, for example) or an idolatrous Church (the judgment of the Reformation against the Roman claim of infallibility); and finally at the establishment of universal freedom in fellowship through and beyond tragedy. The fifth of these is Berkhof's only interest. Since he does not understand that crisis is a stage in process, he is convinced that only cataclysm can usher in the Kingdom. One sudden event will complete the work of redemption. Berkhof would have us bear in mind that God's ways are higher than our ways, that His thoughts are not our thoughts.

A Plea for Authoritarianism

Berkhof seems a voice out of the past — the short past; he does not go as far back as the historical realism of the Reformers. His is an imitative voice, less vital in historical terms than either Luther or Calvin. There is greatness of soul in him, but it labors within a Nessus shirt of inviolable infallibility. You feel that Biblicism was a by-product of the early Reformers as they hurled themselves against Rome's frozen finality; in Berkhof the creative venture is long past, and Biblicism is frozen.

Three of his books deal heroically with the modern stress on immanence, but never comprehend it. Transcendence without immanence and transcendence distorted into Biblicism, form his cry in the wilderness. In 1946 appeared his address *Recent Trends in Theology*, delivered in 1943 at Moody Bible Institute and later at Calvin

Seminary. Apart from the Bible, he asserts, man has neither genuine religion nor worthy theology. He is right, I think, that there is no theology without religion nor religion without theology. To him, theology is the reflection of the Church on the Word of God. Those who bow before the authority of the Bible must join battle with those who place human reason on the throne. Enthroned human reason to Berkhof is blasphemy; to many Christians, resistance to reason is resistance to Logos. Berkhof approves Walter Marshall Horton's condemnation of liberalism, but deplores Horton's modernist method, his appeal to reason. Berkhof parts company with Barth and Brunner because they consider the Bible a mere witness to the revelation, not the revelation itself. Berkhof reports fairly the theocentric theology of Erich Schaeder, and the homocentric religion of Lippmann, Barnes, and Dietrich, but rejects all equally for their rejection of the Bible as final authority. There is some truth in Berkhof's contention that modernism lacks a central principle of its own, that it proceeds by negation, that it is a vacuum clothed with piety. The modernist's Christ is merely an exceptional man. Man is not fallen but evolving. There is no special revelation. Berkhof makes short shrift with the social meliorists Gerald Birney Smith and Shailer Mathews. He finds that Schleiermacher, though dead, yet speaks in the voices of William James, Wobberminn, Hocking, and Fosdick; in all alike moralism replaces dogma. In short, the modernist methodology, necessitating the subjective, the experimental, the historical, and the scientific, has everything Berkhof lacks.

Two books in 1951 continue Berkhof's attack on self-sufficient human reason; both plead for a return to Biblical authority. *Aspects of Liberalism* champions Calvinism against modernism. Berkhof is aghast that the social gospel gives no attention to immortality or the millennium, but concerns itself with the salvation of history. More to the point, in his view, the social gospel " imposes on man a task to which he is not equal, when it summons him to change the world into a Kingdom of God " (P. 33). Berkhof thus grasps the weakness of man-centered optimism. Calvinism's principle of authority is the infallible Bible, God speaking, while rationalism's authority is human reason, man thinking. The source of theology to Calvinism is God's special revelation — to modernism, man's feeling of absolute dependence; modernism thus provides knowledge not of God but of religion. Calvinism versus modernism simply means sovereignty versus rational integrity, transcendence versus immanence, supernatural versus natural, redemption versus evolution, legal satisfaction for sin versus moral education, bliss in heaven versus God's will on earth.

Berkhof insists, with Karl Marx, that religion is the most stabilizing influence in the world. Without religion, declares Berkhof, the world would lie in chaos. The reader may reply: With religion, the world sometimes lies in *rigor mortis*. Modern religious confusion, says Berkhof, seeks ecumenical union at the expense of truth; it is both the effect and the cause of departure from the infallible Bible. Calvinist education, in Berkhof's view, is the best now available; it offers confidence in God with subjective calm, rather than confidence in man with confusion and fear, disappointment and disillusionment. Men are by nature Pelagian, by grace Augustinian; modernism deals only superficially with sin and guilt. Neo-orthodoxy has rediscovered sin, but is adrift from the Word of authority.

From several points of view the book *The Kingdom of God* is the most valuable of Berkhof's works, though it is neither long nor heavy. It analyzes the development of the idea of the Kingdom, especially since the eighteenth century. The Kingdom idea has moved from premature identification with the visible Church (the Roman distortion of an Augustinian insight) through many sea changes to future hope. The Reformation, as Berkhof sees it, taught the spiritual nature of the Kingdom. Kant stressed its ethical nature; Ritschlean classic liberalism developed the Kingdom's this-worldly character. Schweitzer and others rediscovered the eschatology of Jesus; subsequent reaction to Ritschl reintroduced the Kingdom as religious hope. Berkhof's L. P. Stone Lectures at Princeton Theological Seminary (1920–1921), plus a lifetime interest in the subject, form the basis of this book.

In the New Testament as Berkhof understands it, the Kingdom meant the " reign of God," an operation of sovereign grace, not a product of human activity — the divine creation of new men, new conduct, and new secular life. There is a long step toward historical seriousness in Berkhof's view, repeated again and again in this volume, that the Kingdom is both a present and a growing reality, both a possession and a hope. Transcending all national boundaries, it is world-wide in scope. The end, as Berkhof conceives it, is the transformation of the whole life of man and society in harmony with the will of God. Surely nothing less is acceptable as the future of process, since God is God. This harmonious future, as Berkhof understands it, can only be introduced by cataclysm and catastrophe — not by educational gradualism.

In Berkhof's interpretation, Augustine did not actually identify the Kingdom with the visible Church. The City of God, in Augustine's view, was larger than its historical and ecclesiastical embodiment. Common ground existed between the Church in heaven and the Church on earth, but the two were not coterminous. Later Roman centuries, misreading Augustine, considered the medieval Church the millennium. The papal and hierarchical Church became the Kingdom — an idolatrous usurpation. The Reformation, in reaction against an omnipotent Church, asserted the Church invisible — the community of the elect. The visible Kingdom was rescheduled toward the Second Coming of Christ.

Albert Ritschl and the Enlightenment accented human reason with its questioning of the Bible; it substituted ethics for dogmatics. Kant's ethical community became the foundation of modernism. In Schleiermacher the Kingdom became the goal of ethical activity; God was somehow divorced from the world, though the Kingdom, not innate in man, was implanted by Christ. Ritschl confused and finally identified divine grace with ethical activity. To Ritschl, the moral union of mankind was at once the purpose of God and the goal of history. The Christian community, producing ethical humanity, is the Kingdom. The same community, organized for public worship, is the Church. The organized Church is a means, the Kingdom the end. In Ritschl's thought, Berkhof believes, the Kingdom replaces God. The reader may reply: In Berkhof's thought, the Bible replaces God.

The Kingdom in this world was the next development; is not this the meaning of the gospel according to Karl Marx — the social organization of humanity as the final goal of history? The eighteenth century accent on the worth of man, and the nineteenth century emphasis upon evolutionary process, together considered the Bible a book of social reform, and led directly to Fremantle and Rauschenbusch.

Berkhof speaks an appreciative word on behalf of the social gospelers. He considers their work an inevitable reaction to a one-sided neglect of ethics and an exclusive individualism. " Jesus and the apostles teach us to look upon the Kingdom as a future hope indeed, but also as a present possession and as a new order introduced into the world " (*The Kingdom of God,* p. 75). Berkhof insists, however, that no one for whom the Word of God is the final court of appeal can accept the modern view. The distinction between man and God is blurred with Washington Gladden's idea that divinity is finite in man, and humanity is infinite in God.

In short, if proof-text theology could see that cataclysm is a stage in creation, the following paragraph would present, with some accuracy, a new confidence in history under God:

" That Kingdom will undoubtedly be identical with the Kingdom that is now in process of development. Yet its appearance will not be merely the final stage of the process now in operation. No more than the sanctification of the individual Christian is completed in this life by a gradual process, will the Kingdom of God grow imperceptibly into its final form. Sin will still abound when the end of the present dispensation comes, and will even be alarmingly prevalent. We are taught to look for a great cataclysmic change at the coming of the Son of Man, a change so great that it can be called ' the regeneration.' . . . The Kingdom that is now invisible will then appear in royal majesty. The present spiritual Kingdom will pass into a higher external form, including all that is true and good and beautiful in the present creation and resplendent with heavenly glory " (P. 85).

Henry N. Wieman

A THEOLOGY OF EXCLUSIVE IMMANENCE

Henry Nelson Wieman "saves" the goodness of God by denying His existence (as transcending the process). The motive is pious, but the achievement seems self-defeating.

Nonetheless, many Christian thinkers will feel that Karl Barth and Henry Nelson Wieman make a necessary team of opposites. The reader may believe that omnipotent love transcends and directs, but also sustains and drives the creative process; that the process is of primary importance to God; that he is at work *within* it and *upon* it. In Wieman's thought you have all process and no transcendent Purpose; he believes that the creative process *is* God, which has hitherto been called idolatry. The reader may respond to Wieman: The creative process is God's, a wholly different concept, though it includes, and underscores, the value of the process. The opposite of Wieman is any theology that exalts Purpose and belittles process. Put together the immanence of Wieman with the transcendence of traditional theology, and you have a full view of the transcendent *and* immanent God.

First a look at his life, then an examination of four elements in his thought: The Revolt Against Unreason; Religion Is Creative Evolution; The Creative Process Is God; and The Creative Versus the Created. He is important and valuable — in epistemology as a champion of rationalism, in metaphysics as an alternative to exclusive transcendence. Religion which involves neither divine nor human reason (neither Logos nor logos) is blasphemy. He is equally valuable in his total commitment to history, his complete break with all theologies of escape. He sees that the sacred/secular distinction is schizophrenic; there is one world, and all of it divine. Wieman shatters the barricade between Church and world. Finally he defines and advances historical movement, the creation of the possible out of the actual, the divine enterprise. Wieman's idea of salvation by history, despite Reinhold Niebuhr's disapproval, seems half of Christian truth: God is at work from below; God is the energy of the process, it is He who drives history irreversibly forward toward the Agape community. Salvation is of Jehovah, who is immanent as well as transcendent, historical as well as spiritual. Add Barth to Wieman, and you have a thing called Christianity — you may have heard of it. It takes two men to make a church; even more, it takes two men to make a Christian. At best we are half men, and often half-baked to boot.

BREAK WITH TRANSCENDENCE

Henry Nelson Wieman, like the two Niebuhrs, was born in Missouri, and like Reinhold, he can never quite be shown. He was born at Rich Hill, August 19, 1884, son of William Henry and Alma (Morgan) Wieman. In 1907 he received the B.A. at Park College, Parkville, Missouri. In 1910, the year Leo Tolstoy and Mary Baker Eddy died, Wieman was a student at San Francisco Theological Seminary, and in 1910–1911 a student at the Universities of Jena and Heidelberg. Harvard gave him the Ph.D. in 1917. He has a D.D. from Park College (1929), and a Litt.D. from Occidental College (1930).

He married Anna M. Orr, January 15, 1912, and there are five children: Florence Margaret, Nelson Orr, Marion Isabelle, Robert Morgan, and Eleanor Brunhilda. Mrs. Weiman died in 1931. In 1932, Weiman married Regina H. Westcott, a Ph.D. in psychology, author of many books on religion and the family, and coauthor with her husband of *Normative Psychology of Religion* (1935). One of her books was titled *Does Your Child Obey?* (1943). Every husband is a child to be raised, a problem to be solved, and success is not inevitable; after fifteen years, Weiman's second marriage ended in divorce. His third wife is the former Laura Matlack.

Wieman was professor of philosophy at Occidental College, Los Angeles (1917–1927). Then for twenty years he was professor of philosophy of religion at the Divinity School of the University of Chicago and is now professor emeritus. He was professor of philosophy at the University of Oregon (1949–1951), and at the University of Houston (1951–1953).

He was visiting lecturer at McCormick Theological Seminary (1926–1927), the Taylor lecturer at Yale (1930), the Mendenhall lecturer at DePauw (1930), the Swander lecturer at the Theological Seminary of the Reformed Church (1930), the Carew lecturer at Hartford (1938), the Earl lecturer at Pacific School of Religion (1932), and the Ayer lecturer at Colgate-Rochester (1947).

He is a member of the American Philosophical Association, the American Theological Society, the American Association of University Professors, and the Quadrangle Club. He is a Unitarian. No one has all the truth; Wieman has spent a lifetime developing his fragment, and an important fragment it is.

THE REVOLT AGAINST UNREASON

Method is not identical with content, but often determines it. Method produces metaphysics, and it is often produced by it. Thinking is always circular, though it may acquire treasure en route. You end where you begin, and you begin with your conclusion. " Home is the sailor, home from the sea, and the hunter home from the hill." American theology has often involved empiricism in method, and naturalism in metaphysics. God has had some difficulty securing a visa to enter the empirical-naturalist world. To enter at all, he has usually had to assume a disguise and appear incognito. Measurement is fine, but so is meaning. In the long run it may be wiser to start with measurement, but meaning ought not to disappear into measurement, lest measurement have no meaning. If meaning is excluded, why start at all?

Wieman's method predetermined his metaphysics, or vice versa, yet both forbid the assumption of finality; both guarantee openness to further light. He simply discovered and used the two necessities — skepticism and faith — with neither watered down. Either alone leads nowhere. Neither can maintain itself without the other. Unfortunately, like Brightman, Wieman's area of investigation is too small; he applies skepticism and faith only to immediate experience, and bypasses altogether the historic experience of the Christian community.

Wieman's first book, *Religious Experience and Scientific Method* (The Macmillan Company, 1926), established his philosophy; the volume stressed the reciprocal role of science and religion, the inadequacy of either without the other, cleared away theological debris, and made religion functional. The book, not always convincing, has two values: it recognizes the necessity of thought (another word for "faith"), and the equal necessity of doubt (another word for "skepticism"). Reason and faith are two words for one serious attempt to understand, to see — an effort which requires courage to achieve, and humility to doubt one's achievement. To look with courage and humility at natural process is to be a scientist. To look with courage and humility at the meaning of process is to be a philosopher. To look with courage and humility at the Purpose and Power that sustain and direct process is to be a theologian. To look with courage and humility at the blueprint of the future made flesh in Jesus Christ and the initial Agape community is to be a Christian theologian. Wieman looks with courage and humility — but neither at Purpose nor Power nor blueprint. A small beginning makes a small ending. He begins with the process; with the process he ends. Precisely this is his value — he sees what he is looking at. Further, he will accept no religion that seeks escape from its historical function.

Wieman's 1927 book, *The Wrestle of Religion with Truth* (The Macmillan Company), carries the argument a step farther. Divine reason and human reason are basically alike; divine reason is neither unreason, nor antireason, nor suprareason. There is genuine kinship between the mind of God and the mind of man, though one is the ocean and the other a drop of water. Part truth has thus a real, not an illusory, relation to whole truth; whole truth is available only to God. Wieman's revolt against unreason and antireason and simple nonsense is heroic; he is limited by the fact that his admirable method is never applied *with* or *within* the Christian community.

He never asks or answers the question: What does Logos mean to Christians? He begins, and ends, with generalized immediate experience. He does not see that the total experience of the Christian community is a case history to be investigated with courage and humility. Theology is precisely the study of the case history of the total Christian community — a vast but intelligible unit of scientific anaylsis. Wieman has every right to generalize from immediate experience — not only a right, but a duty. However, his asceticism against the Church's understanding of itself, his allergy to theology, excludes the Christian case history from his view — and Christianity from his conclusion. His courage and humility focus exclusively upon process; not skeptical of his own conclusion, he dogmatizes against the existence of Purpose. Dogmatic and exclusive immanentism is Wieman's premature finality. In this, Wieman's second book, God had not disappeared completely into process; Wieman tests and validates the worship experience. Worship, as he sees it, is rationally justified, though not recognizably Christian. He attempted piously to give back what science had taken away. The book is general rather than particular; it lacks the precision of measurement necessary to scientific introspection. Wieman's outburst against mathematics betrays his own dynamism. He worships science in general, but evidences little familiarity with any science in particular. "Religion," as he describes it, has no connection with any existing religion. God never seeks to make himself known; man is the only seeker. God is not a conscious Personality, but an emotional term for the evolutionary process. The book's positive value lies in Wieman's continued revolt against unreason — his insistence upon logos. For some reason, he perceives no connection between logos in general and Logos in particular — the Christian conviction that Agape, the Logic of the world, was made flesh in Christ and the Church.

Religion Is Creative Evolution

Religion is creativity in person and process. Wieman sees clearly the divine thrust from below. The divine thrust from beyond, Agape, the pull of Purpose, is invisible to him. Half the truth is thus clear in Wieman. He presents his practical process-theism in the book *Methods of Private Religious Living* (The Macmillan Company, 1929). Ten chapters present ten methods of increasing personal creativity; they offer soul-searching by common sense. Wieman's religion is wholehearted response to the evolutionary process; the process does not belong to God; it is not God's activity; it is simply God. Private worship dedicates person to process; religion releases energy in and for society; evolving social brotherhood is the divine enterprise; common things have uncommon dignity; every crisis is a stage in process; fellowship is the goal of process; joy is the zest of creative living; prayer is communion of the part with the whole; religion is process touched with emotion.

Wieman's 1931 book, *The Issues of Life* (Abingdon Press) contained his Mendenhall Lectures at DePauw. True religion is a passionate quest of the utmost value in and for existence. His healthy rationalism is sensitive to the compulsive lure of God — but neither Wieman foot is in heaven. The reader may feel that rationalism is more mature than irrationalism, to be sure; but the assertion of reason in a universe regarded as without reason is itself irrational, however heroic. Rationalism in a world believed nonrational is premature maturity. In a nonrational universe, irrationalism may be closer than rationalism to reality. God is rational, but every present conclusion of rational man is part thinking, short of the glory of maturity. Not to see that all present maturity is premature is to lose altitude, to abandon skepticism, and to commit idolatry.

Wieman at this point preferred John Dewey to Sigmund Freud. Later, in his development of "creative" theology, he robbed John to pay Sigmund. In Wieman's view (1931), Freud considered religion a rationalization of man's anxiety. Dewey considered religion a sense of the possible and a commitment to achieve it. Wieman defends no escape from reality; he believes rather in religion as adjustment to reality. The reader may respond: Reality includes not only what is *existentially,* but also what is *ultimately.* It is clear that Dewey provided the substance and Wieman the voice in the view that true religion is not the remaking of reality to fit the human heart, but the remaking of the heart to fit reality — with reality regarded as process without Purpose. To Wieman, religion must know the actual, perceive the possible, and labor to change what is into what can become.

Wieman begins, not with the solution, but with the problem — our current confusion and complexity, our recurrent cynicism and ennui, our disillusionment and despair. Wieman believes himself emancipated, but seems only unbuttoned. To him, there are no eternal verities, only proximate and relative goods. In this world of directionless change, only one thing can command supreme and undivided devotion — the quest for value. To Wieman, the quest is its own reward, its own goal; there is no other. Religion, God, and worship increase the joy of the quest in a universe of absolute relativism. Religion is wholehearted dedication to the highest achievable values in a world alien to value. Religion offers no unique experience, no privileged truth. The truth of religion is the truth of science; poetic imagery, on Santayana's terms, has no truth of its own. Religion knows no avenue to truth save scientific observation, hypothesis, and experiment. God is not a Person, but the matrix of persons. God is the actual and the possible; hence, the greatest possible good is truly achievable by human effort. God is not a Person; he is the structure of the physical, biological, and social world. Evolution is God. He is not an ideal, but the growing actual. Ideals are human guesses; they may or may not aid the evolutionary process. Wieman is against humanism; in his view, man is exclusively a child of nature; his task is not to shape the process, but to be shaped by it.

Wieman seems a simon-pure optimist. His universe is going to turn out well, but it has no conception of its goal. Wieman knows more than the process about its Purpose. His universe is all motor and no mind, a diesel locomotive hurtling through space with neither engineer, nor brakeman, nor destination. In this view, is not wreckage more logical than arrival? Is not this the essence of faith completely blind? Nonetheless, with blithe optimism, Wieman believes the culmination of the process will be fulfillment above the fog of our dreams. Toynbee also believes that God's will is always other than, and better than, our own — but Toynbee's universe is mind as well as motor.

Prayer, to Wieman, is the outreach of human personality toward greater value; it is neither the vain repetition of the Gentile nor the romantic reverie of the pantheist; it is worshipful problem-solving, the application of the scientific method to the good life.

Wieman has confused the activity of God with God; nonetheless, he has seen, more clearly than other American theologians, that religion and evolution are, and ought to be, two words for the same thing. We are half-finished souls in a half-finished universe. The will of God is ahead of us, not behind us, nor presently achieved among us. To be religious is to grow, and to do so wholeheartedly.

Wieman's optimism is not Rotarian complacence. With Dostoevsky he recognizes tragic realism, the painful cost of creation, the crisis of decision in every man and every generation for or against forward movement. Religion is neither comforting nor comfortable; it demands the ruthless sacrifice of the good for the sake of the better. A hand or an eye may be the cost of entrance into the Kingdom of the future; the part must surrender to the whole.

To Weiman, God is the fire that burns and the torrent that destroys; wreckage, sorrow, and great suffering pave the road that leads farthest and highest. Wieman's trouble is simple: In his world of absolute relativism, how does one distinguish between what is high and what is low? There is no point from which to measure high or low, far or near. One man's high is another man's low — in an insane asylum of assorted solipsisms. Wieman's universe is traveling with the speed of lightning — nowhere. Nonetheless, he has seen one truth often neglected: religion is evolution toward universal freedom in fellowship, the *imago Dei*.

THE CREATIVE PROCESS IS GOD

In contrast to Wieman, the reader may believe that the creative process is creative as well as process; that it has not only drive, but also a demanded direction; that the drive of process is divine immanence, its demanded direction divine transcendence.

Eight books present Wieman's exclusive immanentism, his insistence that the long night of exclusive transcendence come to an end. The process is real; our experience in nature and history is desperately serious. There is no suprahistorical hope in Wieman, no search for escape from the process through personal immortality. His expectation of the Kingdom of God is not posthistorical. The Second Coming is now. Through the agony of freedom the Kingdom is created, and God is not Creator, but the process of creation. The Kingdom is actuality, for it embraces the present; it is also possibility, for it drives toward the future. Wieman's God is not more than the process; he is not the Purpose of the process; he is the process. The reader may reply: God is the strength of the process, but also the Power and Purpose that direct it. The universe is humanity's schoolroom — in the hands of omnipotent Love. When God is considered coterminous with the universe, as John Dewey understood, the God of saints and heroes is dead. To say that the universe is God is to recognize divine immanence — to believe in half of God. Wieman is not an atheist, but a demitheist. Like Moses, he has caught a rear view of the Almighty; unlike Moses, he has failed to see God face to face. The Agape made flesh in Jesus and the Church has somehow escaped Wieman's attention.

Is There a God? (Willett, Clark & Company, 1933), a symposium, appeared at the bottom of the depression, and remained there. Henry Nelson Wieman, of Chicago; Douglas Clyde Macintosh, of Yale; and Max Carl Otto, of Wisconsin, conducted a triangular debate. It was never clear whether the subject under discussion was "the God of Abraham, Isaac, and Jacob," or one of many dwellers on Olympus, or the pantheist's fathomless universe. The central theme was subject to change without notice. No contestant discussed omnipotent Love, God transcendent *and* immanent. Macintosh seemed to be saying: We need God; therefore he exists. Does not his existence precede, and explain, our need? Macintosh did not say so; his argument was more apathetic than apologetic. Max Otto, with greater consistency, denied the existence of the supernatural. Otto rightly rejected the merely otherworldly God; God immanent as well as transcendent is the strength of Otto's rejection;

God is the life in all that lives, the existence in all that exists — as well as the Love that directs all existence. In the name of sense Otto rejected nonsense. Wieman attempted to be positive where Otto was negative, but held a similar view. Both Otto and Wieman believed in the complex of forces working for enlightenment; Wieman, unlike Otto, simply called this complex God. The volume destroys heteronomy (a split universe), but does not achieve theonomy (a sacred universe); it stops with autonomy (a secular universe). No contestant raised the question: Is the universe meaningful or meaningless? The evasion of this question places secularism itself in peril. To think is both a duty and a right, but to think a senseless universe makes nonsense of your thought. To Wieman, the question of God's existence is a dead issue; that is, existence itself is God, therefore God's existence is undebatable. Wieman defined God as the energy of process; he failed wholly to realize that God is not only the push of process but also the pull of Purpose.

Whitehead's "process *and* reality" loses altitude in Wieman's "process only." Is not God more than the shadow of our own infirmities? Is he not the strength and the Lord of history — our Saviour and our Song?

In 1935, Henry Nelson Wieman and his second wife, Regina Westcott Wieman, published *A Normative Psychology of Religion* (The Thomas Y. Crowell Co.). The book ably describes the historical function of religion. Its good theme is character education in a secular world; it thus presents to theology an important and necessary new dimension — educational psychology. Christian fire and faith are not in these pages, but neither is Christian fanaticism; another fanaticism, dogmatic immanentism, is given its day in court. To the Wiemans, Christianity as Christians have conceived it is neither more nor less than quaint and archaic mythology. One feels that the attack on nonhistorical religion is necessary and constructive. Neither conservatives nor liberals were happy with this book, yet both needed it. Too often, Christian education has placed all its eggs in the basket of right doctrine, has ignored the mechanism of human personality, the microcosmic process which God takes seriously. The Wiemans insist that religion was made for man — man actual, not man theoretical; that persons are not means but ends.

The book is filled with social passion. Religion that does not mean the creation of one world is irrelevant. We applaud! However, to the Wiemans, as to Jean Jacques Rousseau, the social war between good and evil is entirely external; it is not inside men. In any view, this is nonsense. For good or ill, individual man is more than an innocent bystander; he is a participant as well as a product — and often enough a problem. If the individual has no part in the play, why write this book to instruct him?

The volume substitutes the psychology of religion for religion. Religion, the Wiemans rightly see, is total devotion through search, service, and adoration, to the highest one perceives. There is little critical awareness that the highest one perceives may mean, in actual individuals, sexual indulgence, private profit, political power, the cause of the proletariat, or prohibition. Is not God the transcendent direction of growth as well as growth itself?

Supreme value is the greatest *actual* and *possible* connection between activities; interrelatedness makes all activities mutually sustaining, mutually enhancing, and mutually meaningful. God and supreme value are one. God is superhuman; the conditions of value are cosmic as well as personal. This is not a recovery of transcendence. God transcends individual experience, but not the historical process. God is a unity because the structure of value is mutuality. God is actual; there is realization of value now; the conditions are actual for the realization of untold further value. God represents possibilities beyond all imagination; he is the future of process, but not more than process. The God of personal, conscious purpose has become a cold abstraction. The book suffers from exclusive contemporaneity; the experience of the Christian community through two millenniums does not exist for the Wiemans. The door is closed to fuller theism; the plea for growth is sound, but the reality of direction and demand is dogmatically denied; this is closed seeing, a premature finalism. Robert L. Calhoun's personalistic theism includes the emphasis upon process within the meaningful action of the Lord of history.

In 1936, Wieman and Bernard Eugene Meland pigeonholed

members of the contemporary philosophical community in their book *American Philosophies of Religion* (Willett, Clark & Company). The chief value of the work was not its studies of men (no full-length portraits are given), but its system of classification. The authors found four main trends in modern thought. The Wieman-Meland first category was *supernaturalism* — what Tillich calls heteronomy: God transcends, but is not immanent within, process. The supernaturalists, in the Wieman-Meland view, were opposed to science; they maintained a severe cleavage between divine and natural orders. This pigeonhole included the traditionalists, Machen, Mullins, and Patton, but also, and in many cases incorrectly, the neosupernaturalists, Barth, Tillich, the two Niebuhrs, Pauck, Edwin Lewis, and George Cell. Since this classification, by definition, included God but excluded science, few of these alleged neosupernaturalists belonged in the category. The second category was *idealism*. Values are objectively real — with or without a personal Deity; Royce and Hocking represented the absolutists, Brightman the personalists. The third category, *romanticism,* included ethical intuitionists and aesthetic naturalists. The Santayana illusionism is lumped indiscriminately with the theism of William Adams Brown. Douglas Macintosh and Walter M. Horton, with their empirical and realistic theology, are listed among the romanticists. The category should have included the Saint Paul of theological romanticism — Henry Nelson Wieman. The fourth category was *naturalism*. Neither James Ward, nor Rudolf Otto, nor Robert L. Calhoun belongs in this pigeonhole; they are birds of a different feather — personal theists, though nature is not excluded from their thought. Their naturalism is method, not metaphysic. All reject revelation as a monologue. Philosophy of religion was clearly a confusion of tongues, not less so after these ambiguous classifications. Men are more than pigeons; they are also more than foxes; they are never comfortable in either pigeonholes or foxholes.

The Growth of Religion (Willett, Clark & Company, 1938) presents two views of growth. To Henry Nelson Wieman, " growth " is God; to coauthor Walter M. Horton, " growth " is God's creative enterprise. Christian dynamism is precisely the American contribution to theology. We inherited transcendence from Europe; we discovered immanence on our own. Horton surveys the growth of religion from primitive to modern society; he concludes that the religious purpose is the reorganization of the world into a system of mutually sustained activities promoting the growth of meaning. To Wieman, growth is the meaning of the world; to Horton, God is the meaning of growth. A common concern with immanence linked the two treatments.

The choice confronting democracy in 1941, and now, was and is the growth of freedom and equality or their retreat before hysterical fascism. This profound choice was clearly presented in Wieman's admirable volume *Now We Must Choose* (The Macmillan Company). In the midst of World War II, the book shouted to democracy, "Advance or perish!" Wieman was convinced that the potential strength of the free world — democracy itself — had not been mobilized. Class war had dissipated democratic strength. Rich and poor were fighting for the rich. To preach democracy was good; to practice it would better resist the rebirth of tyranny. Men were defending democracy who had forgotten its purpose. Kierkegaard sought to reintroduce Christianity into Christendom; Wieman sought to reintroduce democracy into the democracies.

The final denouement of Wieman's process-worship is his self-revealing book *The Source of Human Good* (University of Chicago Press, 1946). The source of all value is not a conscious, personal Spirit, but the creative event, the creative process. The idea of a personal God, in Wieman's view, is purely mythological. Spirit is simply matter in motion. Wieman assumes that his theology is Christianity in modern dress; it rather resembles Christianity as Sanka resembles coffee. In the Wieman caricature, Christianity, the body of Christ, has lost weight and is hardly recognizable: " Christ " is gone, " inanity " is left. Nonetheless, Wieman offers in this book a valuable because almost wholly neglected emphasis in Christian thought — a serious view of the obstacles in the path of creative good.

Looking forward from process — Wieman's method — you conclude that neutral energy is God. The reader, in contrast, may believe that neutral energy is indeed God's impersonal presence, his preparatory activity to bring forth selves who may become sons and saints. Raw energy regarded as the whole of God leaves deity without responsibility. In Wieman's theology, "Whirl is king, having driven out Zeus." Man depends exclusively upon the creative event as the source of all good. Nothing more exists. To look beyond the process is to look beyond God. To co-operate with the process is our good; to obstruct it, our evil.

Wieman goes farther: we are to worship the creative process, not the goods it has created. To write off the creative good as outside value is to write off God's work in and upon the process for the creation of the world. To put it bluntly, to worship the creative process is not more idolatrous, and certainly more reasonable, than to worship the bread and wine in Holy Communion. To Christians, Holy Communion unites the future with the present, Purpose with process, spirit with flesh. "Thou shalt have no other gods before me." Neither bread nor wine nor natural process. Created things say to us as to Augustine, "The hand that made us is divine."

As Wieman sees it, the process is to be distinguished from the goods it has created: family, friendship, school, and ordered society, the nation, the United Nations, peace, art, and knowledge itself. The reader may inquire, Are not these goods the creations of transcendent Purpose as well as immanent process? To Wieman, the goods which process has created are subject to change without notice. Man himself creates nothing. His function is to remove obstacles in the path of progress. New values endlessly emerge. The reader may reply: The discontinuity of grace, God's unachieved Purpose, endlessly embraces the continuity of nature and history, and the new is born. Man may also obstruct the process; human life may be debased in interaction with the environment. To Calhoun, God is the biggest term in man's environment. As Toynbee put it, at our first London interview, the society of which man is a part includes God. To Calhoun and Toynbee alike, God transcends the environment, yet is also the life and strength within it. To Wieman, the creative environment *is* God.

Wieman destroys a sacred/secular split universe, and thus renders invaluable service; further, he sees rightly that devotion to the part rather than the whole is demonic. However, as the reader will recognize, Wieman himself gives to process alone the devotion that belongs to Purpose and process together. In this sense, Wieman's one world is not half-scale theonomy but full-scale idolatry, the demonic claim of infinite dignity for finite reality. Wieman rejects the idea of Dewey (and Sartre) that man is more than nature, that man receives and remakes nature to meet his needs. To Wieman, man is one fragment within nature — and neither more nor less.

As Wieman sees it, Christian ideology is mythology, not truth; Christian mythology simply covers naked reality with poetic warmth. The only relevant truth is the creative process; it is not God's theater of operations, but itself God. Wieman believes in God as myth, but rejects God as truth; the source of human good is neither transcendent nor a person.

Have we not been through all this before? Fifty years ago evolution was called God, and was later recognized as an ignored but important dimension of his work. More recently behavior, human interaction with environment, was called man, but has since been recognized as man's public relations department. Wieman makes a metaphysic of the behavior of nature. His God does not know what He is doing. Wieman mistakes the behavior of God for God, as sociology and psychology at times mistake the behavior of man for man.

In Wieman's view traditional morality, when in conflict with the creative process, must undergo revision. The function of morality is to advance, not to hinder, the enterprise. A moral code can become an idol, a substitute for the moral law. A moral code is often the strength of resistance to the achievement of one world — for example, parochial patriotism versus world brotherhood, racism versus humanity, class loyalty versus whole-family fellowship, or private property versus public need. Again the reader may reply: Morality considered as total responsibility in and for God's creative enterprise is one thing; morality considered as co-operation with process is another. The Wieman morality requires the worship of the creative process; thus Jehovah is sacrificed to Baal, direction to drive. The Judaeo-Christian idea of responsibility in marriage, of faithfulness as against faithlessness, the law of love against adultery, on Wieman's terms, seems a present wholesome expediency, but open to slow revision. The creative process is sovereign; moral codes are secondary. In his view, social revolution is *always* divine creation; we must surrender with rapturous abandon, with religious ecstasy. We must never attempt to distinguish between change and progress, between meaning and madness.

Two late books soften the Wieman rigorism. *Religious Liberals Reply* (The Beacon Press, 1947) attacks neo-orthodoxy — its alleged revolt against reason, its retreat from history. These seven essays by seven liberals insist that history is God's serious enterprise. To seek escape from the historical task is simple disobedience. Religion, like God, must be humble enough to grapple at close quarters with the world — to transform process with Purpose. Max Otto's chapter on "The Aggressive Growth of a Religionless Church" urges the wholly necessary surrender of otherworldliness to the conversion of this world. If one must choose between militant immanentism on the one hand, and quietism, pietism, and escape on the other, Otto's secularism has much to commend it. R. G. Sellers would have us "Accept the Universe as a Going Concern." Not in the rejection of His enterprise is God discovered. The book's orthodox rationalism seems halfway toward self-transcending rationalism, or faith. These self-conscious liberals clearly think of themselves as ahead of the sheep, and they are — but not far enough. Is not God's *telos* ahead of us all — whether we are liberals or orthodox? *All* human maturity is alarmingly premature.

There is hope in Wieman's recognition that this is an age of transition. *Directive in History* (The Beacon Press, 1948) deals with the problems of racial and cultural survival in an atomic age. Our situation in the twentieth century is not so desperate as Jewish minorities have often faced, not so hopeless as the world must have seemed to early Christian martyrs. Wieman sees no transcendent Purpose for the process, no goal to correspond with the goad and the road. The present thrusts itself forward into the unknown, the unknowable. We have no idea where we're going, but we're on our way. Nonetheless, Wieman perceives and asserts the reality of hope. Animal hope, moving in a void, may be optimistic, irrational, but hope it is, and God sustains it. One asks only, Which way is forward — in a total relativism?

Wieman is filled with confidence. As he sees it, almighty process can be trusted. Is it not both sublimely and ludicrously optimistic to travel at top speed with no steering wheel? The adventure may not be sane, but it is at least gay. His universe is ultimately purposeless, but hope is in him, and he seeks the better future through history, not in escape from it. And he understands the nature of the better — he calls it creative communication. It is what Christians call the fellowship of love.

THE CREATIVE VERSUS THE CREATED

Few writers have so fully demonstrated the inadequacy of all religion that accents transcendence without immanence as Henry Nelson Wieman. The debt of American theology to him is greater than many have assumed. In a precise sense his theology is concerned, not with God, but with the will of God; to put it differently, his theology accents, not God, as traditional religion has pictured him, but the work of God in and upon the world. Jesus understood that the adoration of God was no substitute for the struggle to accomplish his will. Wieman's theology grasps fully the meaning of Jesus' words.

To Wieman religion is not an end but a means — a method of attaining goods of supreme value which cannot be found in any other way. All that man may ever hope to attain depends upon intelligent adaptation to his environment. Human nature rightly adjusted to its total environment has tremendous possibilities. The problem is to make the right adjustment. Religion is therefore man's way of seeking adjustment to God. But what is God? In Wieman's view, God is the subtle and intimate complexity of environmental nature which yields the greatest good when right adjustment is made. God may be much more than this, even to Wieman, but at least he is this.

Religion as adjustment to the total environment must be distinguished, Wieman insists, from an opposite kind. "According to this opposite kind God will take care of me if I put my faith in him no matter how I may ignore the processes of nature. Consequently I can be stupid without danger, if I am religious; and the more religious I am the more stupid I can be without loss of complacency" (*The Wrestle of Religion with Truth,* p. vii. The Macmillan Company, 1929). Wieman opposes this cleavage between religion and intelligence with all his strength. In his view, to make religion a dear illusion and intelligence a rigorous adaptation to natural processes is disastrous; it works like a deadly poison both upon intelligence and upon religion.

Because religion is self-giving it contains within it the possibility of great tragedy and great triumph; hence, critical intelligence must examine the object of the gift. In Wieman's excellent words:

"Religion is man's endeavor to explore the possibilities of immeasurable degradation and anguish, and glory and blessedness, in order that he may apprehend the best which the universe has to offer and live by it; and to apprehend the worst in order that he may flee it or destroy it or war against it, or otherwise protect himself from it. It is his endeavor to find that adjustment and the most protecting and uplifting Behavior of the universe in order that he may be saved from the worst possibilities and may actualize the best. Religion of this original sort is man's groping into the unexplored possibilities of all being in order to win ultimate salvation and escape ultimate destruction" (*Ibid.,* p. 147).

Mysticism in religion, as Wieman sees it, is an excellent servant but a poor master. The supreme good is attainable, and it can never be attained without the use of religious experience. The mystical experience provides the conditions needed for that radical kind of personal experimentation through which the supreme good must be sought. The immediate good of the mystical experience itself is not the supreme good. On this point many mystics have erred. But when the mystical experience is used to practice religious experimentation, it is an indispensable means to the attainment of the best possible world.

In Wieman's view the good, in any intelligible human sense, is that which provides satisfaction of human need. The ultimate cause, however defined, is good if it is that condition which determines whatever measure of maximum satisfaction humans may ever attain.

In the pursuit of the good, in Wieman's view, it is religion that cherishes and craves truth far more than science. If science should attain the final truth about God and how best to adjust to him, religion would take over these findings and use them continuously and gloriously. But science would drop the matter entirely once the truth had been found.

Similarly, philosophy is a necessity, but not a substitute for religion. The enterprise of religion, as Wieman understands it, will be frustrated and its power shorn if men fall into confusion of thinking concerning the methods and ends of religious living. To lose the power of religion from human life, or have it perverted to destructive ends, because of the inadequacy or confusion of its concepts, is one of the most pitiful and tragic evils that can befall human life. It is the part of philosophy to guard against such disasters. But philosophy can never take the place of religion.

The real battle of the world, and therefore of religion, is the rebellion of created good against the creative good — what Tillich has termed the demonic. To Wieman history is the field in which creative power wins a tragic victory over time and matter and the evil ways of men. However, this creative power must not be understood as in any sense outside history. In his words:

" No transcendental reality could ever *do* anything. . . . Nothing can happen if it does not happen. . . . When the transcendental becomes an event, it is no longer transcendental. We cannot know anything, and nothing can make the slightest difference in our lives, unless it be an event or some possibility carried by an event. . . . The transcendental must be ignored, except as an imaginative construction of the human mind. Since we never shall know everything, the transcendental might be retained as a mystical way of representing what is yet to be discovered. . . . It is better dropped " (*The Source of Human Good*, p. 8. The University of Chicago Press, 1946).

To Wieman therefore, the higher levels of existence sprang from, rest upon, and are undergirded by the lower. Nothing has value except material events. He prefers the Jewish-Christian emphasis upon the sovereign good operating in history to the Greek preoccupation with supreme form, but rejects altogether the Jewish-Christian emphasis upon transcendence. The hope of man, as he sees it, lies in cumulative development through history; and human good can be increased only by progressive accumulation of good through a sequence of generations.

In Wieman's view, there is a creative process working in our midst which transforms the human mind and the world. Transformation by this process is always in the direction of greater good. The human good thus created includes goods, satisfaction of human wants, richness of quality, and the power of mind to control the course of events. But the created good cannot be attained by seeking directly to increase goods or satisfaction or quality or power. These can be increased only by promoting that kind of transformation creative of the greater content of good when created good is interpreted as qualitative meaning.

The creative event, or the creative good, weaves a web of meaning between individuals and groups and between the organism and its environment. Out of disruptions and conflicts which would otherwise be destructive, it creates vivifying contrasts of quality if it is able to operate at all. Thus it can utilize frustration and disaster to create and weave into the web of life's meaning vivid and diversified qualities, thus adding immensely to the richness of its variety and the depth of its significant connections. This happy outcome ensues if the participant individuals provide the conditions under which the creative event can occur. One of the most important of these conditions is the self-giving of the individual to such transformation. In weaving the web of richer meaning, the creative event transforms the individual person so that he is more of a person. In the beginning it creates the human person out of the living organism of the infant. Likewise, it creates and progressively transforms human community and the course of history.

Man can do much to provide the conditions releasing the full creative power of this event, including the self-giving of his own person to be transformed by it and to serve it above all. Also he can remove many obstructive conditions hindering its efficacy. But he cannot himself do the work of the creative event.

Thus, to Wieman, the good that is created, when valued for its own sake, prevents the greater good, and obstructs the continuing creative process. Even qualitative meaning becomes unreliable the moment it usurps the greater good of which it is merely the product and for which it must function as a servant. The good of nationality thus becomes the evil of nationalism; the good of sexuality becomes the evil of irresponsibility; the good of community becomes the evil of collective coercion.

Wieman shouts through his pages with the thunder of the prophet. The service of created good is destruction; the service of creative good is salvation. And the problem is not academic, but immediate, for the total of modern life. When men allow the calm of high happiness to " dome their lives entire," the good of life sinks slowly and imperceptibly but surely into atrophy. The peril, particularly the peril of modern technology, can be escaped by redirecting human endeavor from service of good already created to service of the generating source of all good. The tender growth of emergent good is often undetected and killed because men place their present understanding of value against the source of new and greater value. Present understanding of value is unreliable because of the limited range of human appreciation, because good and evil are distorted by self-concern, and because resistance to change dominates men.

Man in weakness was served by redemptive religion, but modern man is man in power. Power itself, a created good, now threatens to destroy man. It can serve man only if it is subordinated to the service of the creative good. The religious problem is therefore no longer merely individual and solipsistic; it is now social and communal. In Wieman's view, doubtless a few saints and sages and fellowships of faith have lived under dominant devotion to creative good rather than allow created good to direct their lives. No longer is it sufficient for individuals in personal commitment to do this.

To Wieman the bomb that fell on Hiroshima cut history in two like a knife. Before and after are two different worlds. That cut is more abrupt, decisive, and revolutionary than the cut made by the star over Bethlehem. It may not be more creative of human good than the star, but it is more swiftly transformative of human existence than anything else that has ever happened. The economic and political order fitted to the age before that parachute fell becomes suicidal in the age coming after. The same breach extends into education and religion. As Nels F. S. Ferré has understood, the gears of history have been shifted from low to high.

On every page Wieman reiterates the demand that the creative source of value must come first in man's devotion, while the specific values apprehended through the narrow slit of human awareness must come second, if we are to find the way of our deliverance and the way of human fulfillment. This reversal in the direction of human devotion, from created to creative good, is, in his view, not new. It is, he believes, the very substance of the original Christian faith. What is new is the need to reinterpret the creative source of human good in such wise as to render it accessible to the service of the mighty tools of science and technology.

In Wieman's anaylsis of the originating events of our faith, he perceives that Jesus split the atom of human egoism, but insists that the creative good was not something handed down to the disciples from Jesus but something rising up out of their midst in creative power. In the fellowship about Jesus occurred a complex, creative event, transforming the disciples as individuals, their relations with one another and with all men, and transforming also the appreciable world in which they lived. The creative transformative power was not in the man Jesus, although it could not have occurred apart from him. Rather he was in it. The creative power lay in the interaction taking place between these individuals. So long as Jesus lived, the creative event was bound to limits and confined by obstructions which would have prevented it from bringing salvation to man if Jesus had not been crucified. What rose from the dead was not the man Jesus; it was creative power. It was the living God that works in time. It was Christ the God, not Jesus the man. Religious faith is basically an act — the act of giving one's self into the keeping of what commands faith, to be transformed by it, and to serve it above all. Beliefs are incidental. Therefore, Wieman insists, we shall dispense with authority, whether in Jesus or in any other, and continue our inquiry. If we strive in despair of attaining the truth with our minds as now constructed, they may be reconstructed by a creativity not our own. Indeed, man himself must be transcended or destroyed.

Evil, in Wieman's view, is a definite and specifiable character of events; it is what obstructs or destroys the good. He therefore decries any belief in an overruling Providence as undercutting the seriousness of man's struggle with evil. Nonetheless, in the Wieman perspective, we have no knowledge of any evil that can destroy creativity; however, if creative good is absolute good, the evil that opposes it is absolute evil. Final outcomes, as well as all original beginnings, are entirely beyond the scope of our knowing. Clearly, the evil called suffering has a creative part to play. Human living without suffering always congeals into complacent contentment at the lower levels of the social order and complacent arrogance at the higher. Maturity in suffering, particularly in the suffering involved in the experience of criticism, accepts the criticism of others and submits itself to the transformation demanded when the criticism is based on evidence. Otherwise expressed, maturity is the art of putting one's self and all that one can command under the supreme control of creative good — always other than, and better than, any good that has, to date, been created in existence or envisioned in the mind.

In the face of real evils, whether the sin, immorality, and demonry originating in human life, or the inertia and protective hierarchies not caused by men, liberal tolerance and solipsism, in Wieman's view, constitute a miscarriage. In his words: " In our society it is not primarily injustice and hardship that drive men to madness. It is rather hunger for a towering majesty that will deliver them from the inane; men seek it in illusion if they cannot find it in reality — for instance, that of racial destiny. Men must find greatness somewhere, else the humanity dies out of them " (*Ibid.,* pp. 111, 112).

Sin, in Wieman's terms, is any resistance to creativity for which man is responsible. And because we are sinners, we must be broken because there is a good so great that it breaks the bounds of our littleness. Tragedy is the contrast between what might have been and what actually occurs.

Truth, as Wieman understands it, is ancillary to, and derivative from, value. It is discovered by the inquiring mind; it is never created by the inquiry or by any performance of the mind. Truth is created by the creative event, but truth is antecedent, coercive, and determinative for all inquiry. Myth is the forerunner of truth. We know God by intuition — by creativity and the integration of meanings — but we cannot get firsthand knowledge of God until God does something to attract our attention.

Wieman's naturalism is, in reality, energism. That is, minds and organisms come finally from energy, not vice versa. He thus acknowledges as great an indebtedness to Bergson as to Whitehead. In his view, science and philosophy are both rooted in common sense, and both must come back to it to find their solid base. In any case, we cannot step beyond experience to the Great Ultimate. The tests of truth are three — observation, agreement between ourselves, and coherence. All three apply to every proposition alleged to be true, whether in common sense, science, philosophy, or faith. Revelation is not knowledge but the release of creative power to transform the world. The Bible is not a peculiar source of knowledge about God apart from observation. It does provide peculiar, direct, and saving access to the saving power perpetuated in Christian fellowship by symbol, ceremony, and ritual; hence, the Bible is an indispensable agent and condition for this fellowship and this commitment of faith.

Morality, understood as a social standard, not as a personal invention, is a necessity, though ambiguous. It is ambiguous because it may require subservience to created rather than creative good. It is nonetheless a necessity. Man sinks to the subhuman when he fails to maintain the required moral standards. However, when moral practice takes on religious character, the moral law is changed from being sovereign to being a servant. That is, morality has a role to play in creation; it is therefore not static, not an end in itself. Genuine morality, in Wieman's terms, is the struggle to reshape the actual physical, biological, and social conditions of this world so that individuals will be impelled to live sensitively and responsively to each other, undergoing creative transformation of individual personality and social structure. Morality is therefore not to be confused with moralism. The moral struggle itself does not end; when some problems are solved, new ones appear.

In Wieman's view a major tragic blunder of Western society is its belief that the individual is the basic unit of life. Rather the home, a communal structure, is basic. Even the potency of human sexuality plays primarily a socializing role. At this point especially created good often resists creative good — moral standards often cripple abundant love. In Wieman's words: "The real purpose of morals in sex is constructive. It is, or it should be, to guide the sexual impulse into a love so powerful that it shatters and transforms a man's life and brings him into social relations which enrich not only himself and those in his intimate group but also society in its wider ranges" (*Ibid.,* p. 239). Moral standards and love strive together for the mastery, and a problem is created. The solution of the problem, however, is found, not by repudiating the established order or by transgressing its demands, but by changing it slowly so that it will permit the creation of contexts of value more widely and freely. To quote again: "When the nature of value and its source is understood, it should be possible in time to develop standards and a religion and social practices more hospitable to love's fulfillment. Perhaps the world of sexual love is in the making. Sometime a social order and a personal discipline may be reached that will be fitted to bring forth the unexplored possibilities of value resident in love but now hidden" (*Ibid.,* p. 241).

Wieman suggests that the magic of sexual union transfigures two people — why not the whole of society? In sexual joy heaven touches earth. In any case, love going beyond mutuality and community is the gift of grace. Only when the demands of creativity are sovereign over all other demands in one's life can one be sufficiently open, receptive, and responsive to permit abundant love.

An increase of justice and love in our modern economic society, in Wieman's view, will increase rather than decrease social instability. That is, the creative good is dynamic, the created good is static. Wieman sees two necessities in our industrial era: full employment and full production. Similarly, he sees an evil and a good way to achieve these necessities: dictatorship leading to tyranny, and an increase of direction by organized labor, leading to freedom and peace.

Religion as self-giving, as devoted living, must always play its part. To Wieman prayer is answered when, in response to prayer, the creative event transforms the individual, his appreciable world, and his community in such a way as to bring forth what is sought in the prayer. The answer to prayer is the re-creation of the one who prays, of his appreciable world, and of his association with others, so that the prayerful request is fulfilled in the new creation. True prayer is therefore indispensable; it transforms one's neighborhood, one's institutions, and one's faith.

In Wieman's view, the source of human good is not metaphysically transcendental, but it is functionally transcendental. Creative good is, in fact, the actual reality that has done the work and played the part fictitiously attributed in the Christian tradition to something eternal, nontemporal, immaterial, and superhistorical. The creative good is the actual reality mythically represented by the transcendental metaphysics of traditional Christianity.

God, to Wieman, is heteropersonal. He cannot be a person, but is much more than a person. A person is always a creature. God, the creative good, always operates between persons. Nonetheless, Wieman acknowledges that the idea of God as personal may be necessary for devotion. In any case, as Wieman suggests, the creative good is greater than any definition of it, including his own.

To end with Wieman's realistic words:

"Perhaps human nature as it now exists is incapable of moving with creative advance up the heights to be ascended. If so, another creative crisis awaits us in the future, foretold in Christian myth and symbolism as 'the end of history,' 'the Judgment Day,' 'the Second Coming of Christ.' . . .

"Without difficulty, danger, and loss a man will scarcely seek his security in the true source of human good. Always he will seek it in some created good, if not the Hebrew law, then American democracy or scientific method or his health and popularity or his past record or whatever else it may be. These other grounds of security must be seriously threatened or taken away before any man will seek and find his strength, his hope, and his courage in the creative power which generates all value. In this sense, perhaps, despair and recurrent despair alone can open the passage into the ways of forgiveness and salvation" (*Ibid.*, pp. 274, 279).

Edgar S. Brightman

A THEOLOGY OF THEISTIC FINITISM

Brightman insisted that he was not a theologian but a philosopher of religion. I believe he was right; he did not look back upon the process from the all-powerful Purpose pictured in Christ and the Church; rather, he looked forward from the nature of present personality. Not that there is a difference of method between philosophy and theology; I think there is none; the difference lies rather in what is examined. Both are efforts to see; both therefore require the perpetual exercise of skepticism and faith. Whether in philosophy or in theology, skepticism must attempt to separate the false from the true in order that faith may labor to make truth prevail. Think we must — whether we are thinking about religion from nature and personality forward, or from God in Christ and the Church backward. We must think what we think, whether in philosophy or theology, yet at the same time, and all the time, hold our thinking under perpetual critical surveillance. To my mind, therefore, the methods of philosophy and theology are identical; the difference is their subject matter. One sees Purpose and thinks toward process; the other sees process, and thinks toward Purpose.

Brightman, from first to last, did not think back from Purpose and Power, but forward from process and person. Yet so great has been his influence among theologians that he must be examined in this volume with care and love.

"The right to think" describes Brightman's method, and "the right to think forward from human personality" determines his content — a well-meaning deity having trouble, as any person does, with his own unconscious. The real clue to Brightman's immature God, working out his own salvation with fear and trembling, is depth psychology, man's war with his own Given, his own karma, his own unconscious or subconscious. Brightman has created his "God" in man's own image, and is insufficiently skeptical of his creation. His contribution to theology was greater than he knew; he explored a dead-end street and marked it clearly on the map.

Let us look at his life, then at four aspects of his thought: The Liberal Approach; God's Search for His Own Salvation; Rational Ethics and Religion; and Reason Versus Revelation.

Productive Living

Edgar Sheffield Brightman was born at Holbrook, Massachusetts, September 20, 1884, the son of George Edgar and Mary Charlotte (Sheffield) Brightman. From Brown University he received the A.B. (1906), the A.M. (1908) and the Litt.D. (1936). From Boston University he received the S.T.B. (1910) and the Ph.D. (1912). He was given an LL.D. at Nebraska Wesleyan University (1929) and another at Ohio Wesleyan University (1942). In 1910–1911 he studied abroad at the Universities of Berlin and Marburg.

Brightman married Charlotte Hulsen July 1, 1912; May 24, 1915, she died. Three years later, June 8, 1918, Brightman married Irma Baker Fall. He had one son, Howard Hulsen, from the first marriage, and two children, Miriam Fall and Robert Sheffield, from the second.

Brightman was assistant in philosophy and Greek at Brown University (1906–1908), then professor of philosophy and psychology at Nebraska Wesleyan University (1912–1915). At Wesleyan University, Middletown, Connecticut, he was associate professor of ethics and religion (1915–1917), and full professor (1917–1919). From 1919 until his death, February 25, 1953, he was professor of philosophy at Boston University's Graduate School.

He gave foundation lectures at Harvard (1925), Lowell Institute, Boston (1925 and 1934), Duke University (1927), the University of Michigan (1942), Vanderbilt (1942), Ohio Wesleyan (1943), Southern Methodist (1945), and Boston (1950–1951).

He was not a lonely individualist, but an active participant in the

social life of thought. He was a member of the New England Conference of the Methodist Church, of the American Philosophical
Association (eastern division president, 1936), the American As-
sociation of University Professors, the American Theological So-
ciety (president, 1933–1934), the National Association of Biblical
Instructors (president, 1941–1943), Phi Beta Kappa, and Kappa
Sigma. He was a Fellow of the American Academy of Arts and
Sciences, and an honorary member of Kant-Gesellschaft. He was a
member of the University Club of Boston and of Philosophics
Anonymous (no relation to AA).

His thought, not uniformly accepted, has been uniformly stimulating, and therefore of permanent value.

THE LIBERAL APPROACH

Openness of mind, which makes hope possible, is evident in
Brightman from the beginning. His first published book, *Sources
of the Hexateuch* (Abingdon Press, 1918) introduced, explained,
and presented in textual sequence the three main strands of early
Old Testament literature: our old friends J, E, and P. The J (Jah-
vistic or Judean) document, the oldest (circa 850 B.C.), the E
(Elohistic or Ephraimitic — circa 750 B.C.), and P (Priestly Code —
circa 500 B.C.) are printed in full from the American revised text.
Brightman supplies the reader with the necessary accompanying
data. Integrity of mind means honest scholarship. Brightman was
never a liberal turned conservative, but a liberal always. This book
is still useful as a text; it demonstrates the critical method and result in tangible form.

Brightman's lifetime method is evident in his *Introduction to
Philosophy* (Henry Holt & Co., Inc., 1925; revised edition, 1951).
The later edition develops, but does not change, his basic epistemology. The volume raises the central philosophical questions and
presents the diverse historical answers, but emphasizes the Bowne-
Brightman personalistic idealism (the view that ultimate reality is
personal and therefore spiritual). Brightman is always a defender
of his faith, a colorful contestant; he is honest and therefore never

neutral, never a mere mirror of other men's opinions. To him, philosophy requires the synoptic method — the attempt to see life steadily and see it whole. One remembers that Brightman's treatment of the Hexateuch was not synoptic but analytic; that the Law and the Gospels were not analytic but synoptic. The philosophical method is simply the attempt to see: philosophy attempting to see the process in the light of the Purpose is theology; theology attempting to see the Purpose in the light of the process is Brightman's philosophy of religion.

The Brightman standard of measurement is comprehensive coherence. To assume that man can see either comprehensively or coherently is to recognize the kinship between human and divine reason; only God, of course, can see with perfect comprehension and perfect coherence. Nonetheless, man can, and must, see as comprehensively and coherently as possible; we are called inescapably to see *more* comprehensively and *more* coherently, and herein is the grace of growth. Wholeness is an excellent standard, though in itself as static as the Thomist synthesis. Mere wholeness is not enough, unless it contains forward-moving dynamism, aware that present knowledge and ethics are a good deal less than whole. Brightman's standard seems Romanesque rather than Gothic, architectural rather than dynamic. Nonetheless he believed that the synoptic method and the criterion of coherence lead inevitably to personalism (the belief that God is a personal spirit, struggling against resistance) as the most inclusive and satisfactory world view. As this writer sees it, the Brightman method is sound: the issue is the subject to be investigated: to seek comprehensive coherence in the world may lead to personalism; to seek comprehensive coherence in the relation between God and the world may lead to confidence in omnipotent goodness.

Brightman's book *Philosophy of Ideals* (Henry Holt, 1928) established, in Bowne fashion, the objective reality of values. Ideals are not convenient human inventions; they exist independently of man's thought about them. Brightman's personalistic idealism is clearly on the way. Theistic finitism has not yet made its bow, but a personal God, laboring to realize the ideal, is already present.

God's Search for His Own Salvation

Three books present, describe, and defend Brightman's immature God, the God who struggles against the down-drag of his own unconscious: *The Problem of God* (Abingdon Press, 1930), *The Finding of God* (Abingdon Press, 1931), and *Is God a Person?* (Association Press, 1932). Since the dawn of human thought, the divine goodness coupled with the divine omnipotence has run head on into the problem of evil. Brightman does not solve the problem; he merely changes its location. The conflict now shifts to the psychic life of the Deity, and the question is restated: How assimilate within the Supreme Personality the antithetical, the irrational, the material, the gross, the impersonal, the subconscious or unconscious, the Given — what Edwin Lewis calls the uncreative and discreative. To Brightman, God is not the solution of the problem: he is Himself the problem. That is, the resistance to God is *within* God.

Brightman examined with some sympathy the serious doubters of our era of prosperity, the twenties: Lippmann, Freud, Watson, Vaihinger and Sellars, Julian Huxley, Krutch, and O'Neill. Lippmann's sad stoicism in a meaningless world left Brightman cold, though if Brightman's position were true, that is, if God were not omnipotent, Lippmann's "high religion" would have much to commend it. Brightman considered Dewey's humanism insufficient to supplant theism: it had ignored the question of meaning or non-meaning in the world; its chief capital was the blindness of traditional religion to social need.

In Brightman's view modernism had expanded God toward vague pantheism and fundamentalism had contracted God toward finitude. Against both distortions Brightman urged his own conception. To maintain divine goodness, divine omnipotence must go. God is limited by resistance within his own nature — a pervading inertia. This is God's problem — and Brightman's: How control the stubborn resistance to good will within the divine nature? How integrate the divine personality? In a word — how save God? Brightman, a true fideist, believed God will eventually get himself together; nonetheless, at present the deity faces an unresolved and unresolvable inner conflict. God, an adolescent, struggles for self-mastery. Divine and human personality are identical. We struggle. God struggles. God is an enormously large man. However, on Brightman's terms, God is unlike man in one particular: Normal human personality is not completely split, whereas the divine personality is definitely schizophrenic. Brightman thus perceives the actual struggle of immanence, the dualism real in existence. Edwin Lewis perceives the same thing in *The Creator and the Adversary*. To underestimate the existential struggle is utopian; to project it into divinity is final frustration. Brightman pushed the dualism inside God; Edwin Lewis insisted it remain outside; in both, the result is logical hopelessness. Two equal powers struggle for an impossible mastery — whether in God or between God and the world. To both writers, the goodness of omnipotence and the pedagogy of process are not perceived. In all fairness to Brightman, he insisted that evil could never conquer good; rather, that good was always conquering evil.

In Manichaean fashion, Brightman wished to protect God from the contamination of matter. Matter is merely a form of God's conscious experience. But if to personality everything is a form of consciousness, the Given which resists God is also a form of consciousness, and the devil thus exists within the Deity.

The problem involves two questions: Whence the Given? but also, Whence the divine good will? Both are finite. Still further, since fear is inescapable in finitude, a finite God, who must defend himself, must be as often a God of wrath as a God of love; hence, God's " good will " is only the better side of his dual nature, not his single character from all eternity. Are wrath and love two deities in the universe, as Hinduism and Edwin Lewis believe? Are they two equal powers within one deity, as Brightman believes? Or is wrath one form of God's creative pedagogy as Ferré and this writer assert?

Brightman deals with the two-way movement at the heart of religious experience: man's search for God, and God's search for man. And God, like man, must find Himself. God and man exist to find each other. This is similar to Berdyaev's view that man awaits the birth of God in him, and God awaits the birth of man in Him; it is also different, for Berdyaev's God is *unconditioned* freedom. Brightman invites both dogmatic atheists and self-satisfied theists to ignore his work. Atheism is meaninglessness regarded as a meaningful creed, which is contradiction and nonsense. Brightman believes that meaning is structural to the universe, but considers traditional theism inadequate: it ignores world wars and world depressions. Brightman's finite deity is clearly a depression product. To Brightman, meaning is struggling to master nonmeaning, and both exist in God. The book is for honest skeptics. Brightman considered Barthianism a self-destructive denial of human knowledge and a menace to religion itself: man could listen but not commune. God's reason in slow motion is our revelation; reason is common to God and man. On Brightman's terms, unreason is also both human and divine. Two-way fellowship is possible. God is to be found through the realization that we are sought, through the realization also that God is reasonable, through moral commitment, and personal worship. Man fully conscious, fully critical, still finds in the world an Other in whom is his delight. God is vaguely detected at the beginning of the search but more clearly perceived through reason and moral seriousness. Brightman finds divine finitude not inconsistent with divine eternity. God is not abstract timelessness unrelated to history, but endless duration through temporal change. Time is real to him, as to us. No artificial foreknowledge drives men to religious fatalism. Calhoun also stresses duration through real change as basic to God, but, unlike Brightman, finds God all-powerful as well as at work.

Brightman insists that divine finitude is consistent with divine mystery. God's finitude does not breed in man contempt of the familiar. Divine power and love and beauty are not fully known by man. The goodness of God, in the face of human failure, forces Brightman to think of God as finite. In his view, Omnipotent Goodness would have created men who would always choose the good. Is not this an elderly maiden lady's world view? Could Brightman seriously imagine a noneducational process? A good God doing the best possible is the logic of Brightman's experience. He seems to underestimate the divine gift of freedom. Only omnipotence can give freedom, sustain it, correct its misuse, and move through it to fulfillment.

Brightman's thought meant to him a greater appreciation of divine energy and divine availability, an increase rather than a loss of worship. With his heart, Brightman clearly believed in omnipotent love; with his head, in love less than all-powerful. Since he started with man-the-measure-of-God, his conclusion that God is manlike was inevitable.

Rational Ethics and Religion

Without special revelation, the break-through of divine self-disclosure, men can, and do, think about the moral basis of life. Brightman carries into ethics and religion his synoptic method, his criterion of coherence, and his content of personalistic idealism. *Moral Laws* (Abingdon Press, 1933) considers ethics a normative science of the best of human conduct. The purpose of ethics, in his view, is not to describe values, but to evaluate facts — to show where true value lies. His approach is positive: the opposite of each moral law is unthinkable or in conflict with laws already established. Not from above, but from below, a man may build a vigorous ethical life.

Autonomy, the break-through to personal integrity, is a permanent necessity. To think for oneself is both a right and a duty; to find the compelling good for oneself may mean the casting off of external dogmatic authority — whether in science, religion, or ethics. Man must assert himself to find himself — even at the risk of conflict with Church and State, family and God. If independent thought is both comprehensive and coherent, the truth will out.

The good is life in accordance with a mutually self-supporting system of rational principles — generalizations embedded in moral consciousness and brought to light by the science of ethics. Brightman's eleven laws seem reducable to three: the logical law (the will to be free from self-contradiction), the axiological law (the will to an integrated system of values), and the law of personality (the will to wholeness). Indeed, the three are reducible to one: consistency, or comprehensive coherence. Moral law may not always have an unambiguous relation to logical law. Paradoxes invade healthy personalities. The law of altruism requires respect for each self as a potential saint. Consistency, an undeniable virtue, is never fully possessed by anyone; and consistency sometimes makes little minds littler, requires first-class allegiance to second-class values. Responsible love, the Christian moral law, appears more severe than consistent when it defends the weak against the strong.

In *Personality and Religion* (Abingdon Press, 1934) we turn from morals to meaning, but not to the God of Jesus Christ; we turn only to the God man has made in his own image. These Lowell Institute Lectures (1933–1934) present the essentials of personalistic religion. God, as Brightman understood him, is not the deist's dear departed deity. God is very much in the world, and the world very much in God; indeed, the world is almost too much for God. Brightman's value was not his conclusion, but his introduction — his progressive spirit, his willingness to probe, to prove once for all that a blind alley is really blind.

The essential structure of Brightman's thought, for those who will read but one book, is to be found in *A Philosophy of Religion* (Prentice-Hall, Inc., 1940). Consideration is given to four problem areas: religion, God, personality, and immortality. His treatment of diverse interpretations is fair; it is not that he loves other views less, but that he loves his own more. Who doesn't? There are many advantages in Brightman's effort to be fair to himself; he avoids the futilitarian relativism to which "objective" treatments lead, and he stimulates independent thinking. Always he seeks piously to save the divine character by surrendering the divine control. In his words:

"The two forms of theism (absolutistic and finite) agree in the proposition that God is an eternal, conscious spirit, whose will is unfailingly good. The difference between the two may best be brought out by saying that theistic absolutism is the view that God faces no conditions within the divine experience which that will did not create (or at least approve), whereas theistic finitism is the opposing view, namely, that the will of God does face conditions within divine experience which that will neither created nor approves. . . . The first-mentioned view,

then, overemphasizes the perfection of God and declares his whole creation to share in that perfection. The second view expresses so strongly
the imperfections of the creation as to raise questions about the perfection of the creator. . . . Both are rooted in the realities of religious
experience " (pp. 281–283).

The reader may insist that theistic absolutism also means that
omnipotent love is now creating *through freedom* perfect man and
perfect world. Ready-made perfection, which bypasses pedagogy, is
Mrs. Eddy's view.

Epistemology is often the philosopher's stumbling block, and
Brightman is no exception to the rule. Since he begins with human
personality, with human personality he ends. He ignores the content of historic revelation; in addition he dismisses Kierkegaardian
existentialism (personal faith through and beyond reason) with a
shrug. In S.K.'s view, only those who yield their wills may know;
to start with knowing rather than obeying is to fail. Brightman ends
as he began — with a manlike God, struggling to control himself —
a human personality written large. Possibly Brightman presents as
big a God as you can get without historic or personal revelation.
Tribal gods of polytheistic primitivism are similarly available — and
similarly finite — projections of human limitation.

Brightman's 1942 volume, *The Spiritual Life* (Abingdon Press)
is timely, but without war hysteria. Personalism, with its accent on
the mind, and its devaluation of the body, is closer to capitalism
than to Communism, for " rugged individualism " is its essence;
nonetheless, Brightman is opposed to the depersonalization of
mechanized capitalism. Spirit is power from on high; to maintain a
union between the power and its source is the modern task. Brightman's " spirit " is identical with Tillich's " courage to be." Spirit is
an inseparable union between process and Purpose. Spirit is conscious, powerful, noble, rich, courageous, free, rational, social, divine and developing. Whatever is weak or evil or irrational or mechanical is unspiritual. Nothing external can break a man's spirit
until he breaks it himself by surrendering. The last word of spirit
is victory — to human and divine person alike, struggling against

resistance. However, the spirit Brightman describes seems never quite incarnate. The body, and the material world, mean nothing to him until they are mastered by mind. Personality learns nothing from nature. Is not God the life of nature as well as spirit? Brightman's God is spirit only; nature seems alien to God until absorbed and conquered by him. The same ascetic attitude toward nature is found in Edwin Lewis' three eternals: " the creative," " the uncreative," and " the discreative." " The creative " is God; " the uncreative " is nature; and " the discreative " is the demonic — the resistance to be overcome, whether inside or outside God. This Brightman volume remains (in 1955 as in 1942) a word of courage to the free world in its struggle against the powers of darkness.

In 1944, Brightman edited a symposium, eulogizing Albert Cornelius Knudson on his fifty-first year as teacher: *Personalism in Theology* (Boston University Student Supply Shop). Thirteen associates and former students review the philosophy of Borden Parker Bowne, the personalist view of metaphysics, ethics, and education. The volume stresses divine immanence (that God is in the world), and neither affirms nor denies transcendence (that God is also above the world). One thinks of the pantheism of Xenophanes, Zeno, and Spinoza. Reality, which is near, not far away, is vital, accessible, and universal. Personality is the nature of reality. To this writer objection to personalism is justifiable only when human personality becomes the confining measure of divinity — when God is no more, though certainly not less, than man. The Brightman personalism departs from Bowne and Knudson, and he is on his own. The reader may feel that personality in man is a witness to a reality greater than itself and different in kind; a man is not the measure of God, as a dog is not the measure of man.

Brightman's critics commented that he had not treated the world of nature. *Nature and Values* (Abingdon Press, 1945) was his attempt to do so. He stoutly defends personalistic idealism against all forms of naturalism. These Fondren Lectures at Southern Methodist University argue that personalism unites nature and spirit, and makes possible one world. Brightman stresses respect for personality, nature as a revelation of divine personality, and spiritual liberty —

against naturalists on the one hand, and religious irrationalists on the other. To him, the universe is reasonable only as the struggle of God and man against the dark resistance.

Brightman applauds the attempt to supersede the mind-matter dualism of Descartes — the effort of the new naturalists to make the human spirit more at home in the real world. However, he opposes every attempt to supersede traditional metaphysics or his own personalism. The materialists must make a full surrender to the disciples of Bishop Berkeley. Brightman has little use for Dewey's neutral position — equally accommodating to spiritualism and naturalism. As Brightman sees it, naturalism means materialism, and personalism means idealism.

Despite his effort to perceive its independent reality, nature, on Brightman's terms, disappears into mind. As he sees it, nature is implied in the world of sense experience; it gives life to finite persons and takes it away; mind is not a part of nature; nature is divine experience; every energy of nature is a deed of God; nature is in mind; the evidence for nature is in personal consciousness. Brain is the divine personality in action at the level of human personality. Everything is known through personal experience, or not at all. The reader may feel that Brightman's view means this: nature disappears into mind, the impersonal into the personal, the stage into the actors, the world into God. The ultimate problem, to Brightman, is the salvation, not of men, but of God.

Brightman was a devout and practicing Christian, a faithful churchman. Every man believes more than he can define. By passion a saint, by profession a philosopher, Brightman, like Buddha, recoiled from personal sorrow and suffering in the world; he could accept no sentimental view that ignored either suffering or God. He absolved the Deity from responsibility for pain by demoting him from omnipotence. Dichotomy invaded divinity. God, as Brightman conceived him, is under tremendous tension; he attempts to grow in his own grace, but is conditioned by his own immaturities, confronted and partially frustrated by the Given. An exhausting schizophrenia neutralizes the divine good will. God will solve his problem ultimately, but how far off is " ultimately "? Since God is one finite spirit alongside others, how shall the Given be forgiven or mastered? A house divided against itself has no future — not even the house of God. Influenced by Whitehead, Brightman enclosed reality within process, while attempting to enclose process within reality. He did not see that the world is an educational institution God maintains for His children. Reading Brightman you conclude that God has associated too long with man, has become infected with man's double-mindedness. There are sins, and surds, and absurds, but if the divine reason itself is afflicted with irrationality, optimism must yield to despair, and hope is dead. There is no antichrist in Christ. Christ, as Richard Niebuhr understands, is a stronger surd than evil. God the solution is greater than man the problem.

God was a problem to Brightman. Possibly Brightman was a problem to God. In personal trust and love, Brightman's God was an adored presence, the final Disposer of human events, the Judge of all things.

Reason Versus Revelation

Human thought about the world and its meaning always faces a predicament, and the predicament is not always seen. Human reason, attempting to understand the totality of human experience, may and often does, as in Brightman, arrive at the practical certainty that God, the great Person, exists. The predicament then begins to emerge. For if God exists, by whatever process of careful reasoning man has discovered him, he exists prior to the discovery, and prior to the human reasoning that has arrived at its conclusion about him. All theologies of revelation, unless they be the vain repetitions of the Gentiles, the mere explication of dogma, uncritically examined, have perceived that God, though reached at the end of a reasoning process, is prior to the process, the source of its vitality, and the active and interested Lord of the world. If God exists prior to the discovery of his existence by human reason, revelation, God's active self-disclosure, is both possible and probable, and reason must learn to take it into account. Further, if God exists prior to man's thought about him, his revelation of himself is also prior to man's reason about him, though not intrinsically in conflict with ⌐   ⌐ reason.

In Brightman's treatment of religion, this predicament is present but not fully perceived. Brightman thinks coherently and comprehensively and finds that God is real, that God is the great Person, at the end of his process of reasoning. At no time, however, does he recognize that the God whom his reason has discovered existed prior to the discovery. Nowhere does he perceive the priority of God, and of God's thought about himself and the world, and of God's work in and upon the world — to man, to man's thought about God and the world, and to man's work in and upon the process. At the end of Brightman's thought, you have indeed the great Person, but he is permitted to do or say or think nothing for which Brightman has not made room in his thought. The priority and independence of God to Brightman's or to any man's thought about God has been better grasped by Barth than by Brightman, though where Barth discounts the reasoning process that leads to the discovery of God, Brightman rightly insists upon both its privilege and its necessity. Put differently, where Barth begins with the priority of God, and therefore the priority of God's self-disclosure, Brightman begins with human experience, with the attempt to see it steadily, coherently, and whole. To put it still differently, Brightman begins with what might be called the chronological or psychological priority of man's reason, the necessity of man's immediate grappling with the facts of experience, and is thus Cartesian in his starting point; Barth begins with the metaphysical priority of God's existence and God's speech to man. In other words, Barth begins where Brightman ends, with the great Person who is prior to man, and whose Word is prior to man's thought. This in no way discounts the practical necessity of modern man to think, and to think hard, beginning where he can and must, and ending where he will. Brightman's important contribution lies at this point: he insists that human thought, if coherent and comprehensive, will lead inevitably to God as the most satisfactory explanation of the whole of reality. Let us therefore examine, more deeply than we have thus far done, the content and structure of his characteristic ideas.

For all personalists and near-personalists, activity (usually identified with will) is the core of all being. The word "process" seems to personalists barren and abstract as it stands. The only process there is, empirically, is the process of conscious experience, possessing the creativity, the manyness, and the oneness of the ultimate. The personalist therefore confines all his statements to propositions about someone's experience at some time. " Matter " (as something else than active experience), " unconscious process," substance, and the like, being unverifiable in principle, in any actual or possible experience, are excluded from a personalistic universe. Experience always occurs (a personalist holds) in " first person " form and as private. Hence, all knowable being is personal. Since only persons act and only persons are verifiable as defined, only persons exist.

Modern atheist existentialism, it is true, also begins and ends with a world of persons, but Brightman is quick to point out that " Sartre's theory of freedom is personalism gone slightly daffy " (" A Meeting of Extremes," in *The Journal of Religion,* October, 1951, p. 236).

The personalistic conception of religion, on Brightman's terms, is simply co-operation with God, or creative communication, and indeed co-operation with man, though one must remember that there is a distinction between self-experience (" the situation experienced ") and communication with others (who are " situations-believed-in "). Faith need not involve acceptance of propositions believed to be false, or even believed to be beyond knowledge. Rather, to Brightman, faith is simply commitment to the best that is known.

In Brightman's view, God is another Person occupying a vastly different level of experience. " God's unity is not the same as man's unity. He has experienced beyond all that ' has entered into the heart of man to conceive.' He is in a sense *totaliter aliter,* since he cannot be identified with any human persons, nor can human experience exhaust him. But the divine and the human are in creative communication " (*Ibid.,* p. 238). Nonetheless, not only does God transcend man, but man also transcends God. " God and man, for a personalist, are mutually transcendent but interacting and communicating persons. The universe is not one person, but a society of persons " (*Ibid.,* p. 239). First-person experience is, to Brightman, as to Descartes, the type of all process and the key to reality. One can only move from the untested experience to the tested ex-

perience. Even prayer, on Brightman's terms, is a sort of experiment
with the whole of reality. In any case, nowhere does any experience
arise that is not personal experience. "For a personalist, all process
is personal process, all activity will, all nature the personal process
of God's experience, where values also have both their norm and
their creator" (*Ibid.,* p. 241).

Brightman humbly acknowledges that "no writer can express all
of God in one sentence" (*Ibid.,* p. 238). Rather, truth must always
be a co-operative enterprise. "The search for truth must be also a
search for agreement, not for pride of opinion" (*Ibid.,* p. 241).

From a slightly different standpoint, Brightman insists that personalism is the theory that to be is to be a self or a member of a
self. However, personalism may be singularistic or pluralistic, theistic or nontheistic. Following in the footsteps of Borden Parker
Bowne, Brightman describes his own personalism as theistic and
pluralistic. Both to Bowne and to Brightman, personalism means by
the word "self" a unitary, self-identifying, conscious agent. A self
capable of the realization of values may be called a person. The personalist method is always organic, or synoptic, considering synopsis
or comprehensive coherence the ultimate form of intelligibility. This
does not deny the validity of analysis, but rather includes it. A person is incomprehensible as a synthesis of parts revealed by analysis;
parts are understandable only when interpreted through their membership in the whole person to which they belong. Reality is rational,
and hence an organic whole. To Brightman, the clue to ultimate
reality is always the individual person; he finds "the nature of the
whole mirrored in the internal structure of the individuals within
it" ("Personalism and the Influence of Bowne," in *Proceedings of
the Sixth International Congress of Philosophy,* E. S. Brightman,
editor, p. 161. Longmans, Green & Co., Inc., 1927). Brightman thus
discloses his own characteristic procedure, to think from man to
God, from the part to the whole, and to make God conform to what
is found in man, the whole to conform to what is found in the part.
Herein is both the strength and weakness of reason versus revelation,
of personal anthropomorphism in one's thought of God.

The simplicity of the Brightman personalism partly explains its attractiveness to modern thought. You begin with persons; with persons you end. "All reality must be viewed as conscious experience. Personalists think of concrete reality always as self or person. Impersonal idealists explain personality in terms of categories; personalists explain categories in terms of personality. Personalism emphasizes particular, concrete experiences" (*Ibid.,* p. 162).

Personalism is realistic in its epistemology in so far as it holds that idea and object are forever two, thus preventing the merging of self into the world. To Brightman, the sources of personalism are Plato, Aristotle, Augustine, Berkeley, Leibnitz, Kant, Lotze, and Renouvier, though he finds the word first used by Schleiermacher. Borden Parker Bowne was, in Brightman's view, a typical personalist, holding that "all experience is not self-conscious, but all experience is self-experience" (*Ibid.,* p. 163). To Bowne and Brightman alike, the real is rational; a Supreme Person is the ground both of the system of nature and of the society of persons. The universe is therefore perpetually purposive. To be is to act and to act is to will. Both Bowne and Brightman rejected both fundamentalism and positivistic humanism, insisted upon a theistic interpretation of evolution in the light of the immanence of God, upon social ethics, and upon intellectual freedom in religion. Both found "the antinomies of thought on every level solved by personality" (*Ibid.,* p. 167).

Brightman's break with analytic on behalf of synoptic logic was presented with charm and force in his study of *Immortality in Post-Kantian Idealism* (Harvard University Press, 1925). By immortality he meant the survival of individual personal consciousness, and he explained the necessity of a world view before the question concerning immortality could be answered. Both to analytic and synoptic interpreters, in Brightman's view, "the starting point and goal of thought is the interpretation of experience" (*Ibid.,* p. 7). But the two methods of interpretation go their different ways. The present, thinks Brightman, is inclined toward positivism. Men who believe in rational unity strive for and have faith in a vision of the meaning of reality as a whole; that is, they are metaphysical. Men whose minds are meticulous rather than comprehensive are inclined to positivism. Thus, in his words:

"The analytic method reaches its goal when it finds atoms. The synoptic method reaches its goal only when it finds an organism of some sort, a genuine whole to which the atoms belong and from which they derive their meaning. The understanding explains the whole in terms of the parts; the reason explains the parts in terms of the whole.

"Idealism . . . does not reject the atomistic in favor of the organic view; but it regards the organic as the truer, because it can include the truth of atomism, while atomism cannot do justice by uniquely organic properties and laws" (*Ibid.*, pp. 19, 20).

Historically, idealism's apparent indifference to empirical facts laid it open to naturalist attack. But what of the future?

"If merely analytic atomistic logic be the mind's best instrument for attaining truth, the belief in immortality will probably be analyzed away. The conscious person will be dissipated into associated sensations or chain reflexes; the universe will be an aggregate of atoms; there will be no unified meaning of the whole of life and no plan or goal for immortality. Thus the immortal person will evaporate into his constituent atoms, and any question about his destiny becomes an impertinence. If, on the other hand, synoptic or organic logic be the instrument of true thought, then the complex personal life of man may be a true unity; and the cosmos may be an organism with infinite functions which set a career for an immortal soul and provide for it a home. For organic logic, immortality is at least possible, even probable; for atomism, nothing is immortal but the atoms, and even their immortality it is impossible to understand" (*Ibid.*, pp. 24, 25).

Atomistic logic, therefore, can never interpret an organic reality, though organic logic may, and must, be tested by its capacity to interpret experience. This bifurcation between what might be called the reductionism of analysis and the constructionism of synopsis is illustrated in a statement of Schopenhauer that human love exists only that there may be next generations. To this Brightman replies, "There are next generations in order that love may be preserved" (*Ibid.*, p. 33).

Idealism is forever on the side of organic as opposed to atomistic logic, and therefore asserts the objective reality of value in our experienced world. Brightman lists Fichte's three arguments for immortality: (1) The self's possibility of growth is infinite. (2) The moral law commands endless activity for good, for the development of holiness. (3) No really developed individual can ever perish. Hegel, in Brightman's view, was ambiguous: on the one hand, his thought implies that the absolute swallows persons; on the other hand, he spoke of the immortality of self-conscious spirit. In any case, "the organic logic of idealism is the only fruitful instrument for the interpretation of personality" (*Ibid.,* p. 52).

Brightman repeatedly asserted that he was under no illusion of infallibility. Nonetheless, along with the rest of us, he defended his right to think. Not label or fad, but rational thought is the sole arbiter of truth. Philosophy, in his view, may be defined as the attempt to think truly about human experience as a whole, to make the whole of our experience intelligible. As he puts it: "Philosophy, like woman's work, is never done. If philosophy is difficult, it is not wholly the philosopher's fault. We live in a difficult universe" (*An Introduction to Philosophy*). No one, Brightman admits, can draw a mathematically straight line; nonetheless, we cannot afford to give up the effort to draw lines as straight as possible. In his words, "There is a great gulf fixed between the holding of philosophical opinions and the genuine philosophical spirit which holds no opinion that it has not earned the right to hold by intellectual work" (*Ibid.,* p. 6).

Since science is analytic, and philosophy is synoptic, the criterion by which to distinguish truth from error is comprehensive coherence — not instinct, custom, tradition, the *consensus gentium,* feeling, sense experience, intuition, correspondence alone nor practical consequences. Indeed, "pragmatism fails because of its ambiguity in defining the end relative to which true ideas are practical" (*Ibid.,* p. 58). Coherence simply means that wherever there is inconsistency there must be error. In other words, coherence, which is systematic consistency, means literally "sticking together." Therefore, any judgment is true, if it is both self-consistent and coherently connected with our system of judgments as a whole. The coherence criterion cannot be denied without being affirmed. Skepticism, as a system of thought, is self-defeating; if nothing can be known, skepticism cannot be known. All genuine self-knowledge, in Brightman's view, is dualistic: that is, I know, and I am known. The idea and the object are not each other.

There seems a basic contradiction between Brightman's view that evil is not objective, and therefore in some sense pedagogical, and his final view that the objective reality of evil is a Given, which God did not create, and which he must try to overcome. Note these words: "Evil is essentially incoherent, both within itself, and with fundamental aspects of truth; it is contradictory and negative, not positive and coherent. Hence the presence of evil in the universe does not prove the objectivity of evil" (*Ibid.*, p. 162). If evil is not objective, it is something other than a Given limitation upon God, and must therefore be accounted for as a reality of pedagogical experience, itself included within the purposive universe.

In any case, on Brightman's terms, thought drives us in the direction of the hypothesis of a supreme Mind or person as the ultimate reality of the universe and the home of values. The hypothesis, known as personalistic idealism or personalism, is true if it be, as it appears to be, the only thoroughly coherent solution of the antinomy. "Things . . . are activities of a supreme mind; universals are the thought-stuff of a supreme mind; values, the normative appreciations of a supreme mind that ought to be known and appreciated by human minds. All roads lead to mind" (*Ibid.*, p. 165).

To Brightman, idealism does not mean that everything exists only in and for the individual or social human mind, and does not deny that physical things, universals, and values exist. It does, however, assert that the existence of nature and of all validity and value can be maintained reasonably and without contradiction only on the hypothesis that there is a supreme or divine Mind, for and through whom the universal order exists, who is being gradually apprehended by finite minds as knowledge increases and experience deepens. Personalistic idealism is opposed to absolute idealism, because, in Brightman's view, monism cannot squeeze the many persons into one. Personalism is simply the view that interprets reality as a society of persons; there is one supreme Person, in and for whose thought and will all physical things exist, so that they are nothing apart from him. Human persons, nonetheless, in their possession of freedom, are no part of him. Purpose in the universe explains mechanism, while mechanism cannot explain purpose. The laws of mechanism are the principles of co-operative procedure for the realization of values.

Brightman seems never to perceive the possible purposiveness of man's experience of evil. In his words, " To say that this is a universe of purpose means that everything that is is in some sense a manifestation of purpose; that nothing is real save purposive beings, namely, persons " (*Ibid.*, p. 309). Elsewhere he discovers evil that has no (apparent) purpose, and therefore classifies it as the Given which resists God.

As Brightman sees it, actual religion is the total attitude of man toward what he considers to be superhuman and worthy of worship, or devotion, or propitiation, or at least of reverence. His definition of normative religion involves an " ought ": religion ought to be characterized by the feeling of dependence on a personal God and dominated by the will to co-operate with God in the conservation and increase of values. Where reason is analysis, synthesis, and synopsis, faith is trust, confidence, and devotion — and immortality may well be the goal of evolution. In Brightman's words:

" The final, and, in the writer's opinion, most fundamental argument for immortality is the character of God. If God be good, then somehow human persons must be immortal. To promise so much, only to destroy us; to raise such hopes, and then to frustrate them; to endow us with such capacities that are never to be fully used; to instill in us a love for others, all of whom are to be annihilated, is unworthy of God. Faith in immortality thus rests on faith in God. If there be a God, man's immortality is certain; if not, immortality would not be worth having " (*Ibid.*, p. 349).

Always Brightman ends, as he begins, with the attempt to interpret religious experience, and he is convinced that his views are not absolute truth, rather aids to thought. He considers theology committed thinking, philosophy uncommitted thinking, and thereby too simply disjoins the two necessary activities of thinking itself — criticism and commitment. Indeed, his own philosophy turns out to be committed thinking, after all, and therefore a theology, for he is committed to personalism and to theistic finitism as the answer.

Religion differs from science, in Brightman's view, in being concerned about values, while science ignores the value of its facts and confines itself to objective description. And there is no such thing as a religion without a set of beliefs. Brightman finds five types of religion: primitive, tribal, national, universal, and living. In all alike he discovers eight chief beliefs: (1) There are experiences of great and permanent value. (2) There are gods or God. (3) There is evil as well as value. (4) Man is a soul or spiritual being, not merely a physical organism. (5) There is purpose in human existence. (6) The human soul is immortal. (7) Religious experience is valid. (8) Religious action is valid also. The central philosophical problem is not, Is religion true? but rather, Are any religious beliefs true? The consistency of our beliefs with each other and with experience is the test of their truth. No certainty is possible to man, yet man may unite relativism in knowledge with a practical absolutism, a certainty " pending further developments " (*A Philosophy of Religion,* p. 131. Prentice-Hall, Inc., 1945).

To Brightman, God is always beyond the present achievement of man and is objective, either as a reality to be known and appropriated or as a goal to be sought. God is never used as a name for man as he now is. God means that toward which man moves when he rises in the scale of value, viewed as a source of that movement. Brightman thus discovers the objective reality of God, but at the end of his thought, not at its beginning. The priority of God to all human knowledge and action is not perceived.

Polytheism, in Brightman's view, personifies a particular value; henotheism personifies the national spirit; monotheism recognizes a supreme personal Creator; pantheism identifies God as the whole of reality; agnostic realism considers the source of all being unknowable; humanism stresses human aspiration for ideal values; deistic supernaturalism believes in a superhuman and supernatural revealer of values; impersonal idealism focuses its attention upon a system of ideal values; religious naturalism perceives a tendency in nature to support or produce values. Against Barth's God as revolutionary, Brightman asserts his faith in God as evolutionary — a conscious mind immanent in nature and values. " The object of worship is a cosmic experiencer and continuer of ideal values " (*Ibid.,* p. 162). Again it is clear that Barth begins with the priority of God, Brightman with the priority of human consciousness. This either/or is not irreconcilable: revolution is a stage in evolution, and the actual priority of God does not cancel the psychological priority of human experience. To Brightman, " the one essential factor in personal theism is that the ultimate creative energy of the cosmos is personal will. If the objective source of all value experience is a personal God, the datum self is rationally explained " (*Ibid.,* pp. 226, 227).

Further, on Brightman's terms, if impersonalistic naturalism be regarded as the chief alternative to personalistic theism or personalism, the rational superiority of personalism may be shown by its more inclusive coherence. The evidence for God consists of empirical facts which survive all disbelief. The only empirical argument against a personal God, Brightman believes, is the fact of evil. The criterion of comprehensive coherence, however, could be pressed farther than Brightman presses it. Put it this way: It is more, rather than less, comprehensively coherent to perceive the priority of God to the human experience of evil, to perceive therefore the priority of Purpose to the fact of evil, than to consider, as Brightman does, the independent priority of evil as the Given with which God must wrestle.

In any case, on Brightman's terms, any belief in the unconscious superpersonal is at best but a label for the unknown, and not a definable hypothesis. Brightman therefore finds himself driven to a trilemma: agnostic humanism, theistic absolutism, or theistic finitism. He explains that he was forced by the fact of evil to the development of the idea of a personal finite God, whose finiteness consists in his own internal structure: an eternal, unitary, personal consciousness whose creative will is limited both by eternal necessities of reason and by eternal experiences of brute fact. Correctly or not, Brightman lists among his fellow believers in theistic finitism John C. Bennett, Robert L. Calhoun, Henry Nelson Wieman, and Georgia E. Harkness. He simply dismisses Barth as an exponent of antifinitism.

Brightman finds six beliefs that finitists share with absolutists: (1) God is a Person. (2) Ideals are objective. (3) God is worthy of worship. (4) God is responsive to man. (5) God is in control of the universe (on Brightman's view of the independence of evil, this statement is simple fideism). (6) God is limited by reason and by his creation of free beings.

Something very like Christian hope in sufficient grace, in omnipotent good, breathes through Brightman's pages. In his words:

" If at times the outlook appears gloomy, there is nevertheless profound reason for hope. Religion is rooted in the very nature of man, his instincts, his mind, his needs. The hectic abuses of present-day life are on the surface. Either our material civilization will collapse of its own weight, through war or other internal dissensions, or it will be spiritually renewed from within. In either case the essential office of religion will continue. Indeed, as knowledge and progress advance, the need for a unifying spiritual force, to keep our inner life from collapse and society from disintegration, becomes more and more acute. Human ideals are part of the universe and will thrive only when fed from their source in divine reality. It is unthinkable that the purpose of the universe should fail. Religion will survive " (*An Introduction to Philosophy*, pp. 350, 351).

Brightman concludes that God is perfect in purpose but not in power. The universe, however, is perfectible. Real change, real improvement, is the purpose of life. In Brightman's definitive words:

" Personalism . . . is not too delicate and beautiful to face the facts. It too sees life as a tragedy; there is the shadow of a cross on the face of the personalistic universe. Humanity suffers and dies. Many fail to see the suffering in the light of ideal values. The world is tragic enough still, although all that personalism teaches be true. The secret of the practical significance of personalism is that it faces the tragedy and sees that it is not all. There is tragedy, but there is also meaning, and the meaning includes and transforms the tragedy " (*Ibid.*, p. 364).

Conclusion:

A GLANCE AT THE FUTURE

We are half-finished men in a half-finished world. Our theology is similarly incomplete. No worship of the *status quo* is Christian. The full truth is ahead of us, not presently possessed. Every generation has to fight its own theological battles; when a battle is won, it turns out to have been only a single engagement in a larger war. The work of theology, especially in America, is still in the future.

This volume has attempted to analyze the life and work of eleven contemporory Americans. The preceding volume, *Major Voices in American Theology,* presented in fuller detail the life and work of six leaders. The seventeen together provide a motion picture of theology at work in our land. The two volumes are more suggestive than exhaustive. Much important work could not be described in so limited a space; even more, much valuable work, now unfinished, will bear fruit in decades to come.

It is my purpose in this conclusion to outline theology's two unfinished tasks, and to list the names of additional workers in the field. The builders of tomorrow, in the long run, may, and should, erect a nobler temple than the pioneers of today.

This preview of the theology of tomorrow can be no more than a sketch, yet its broad outlines may be more or less accurate. Time will tell. The two unfinished tasks are: theology in itself, its own dynamic and structural development; and theology in relation, the study of the depth dimension in every area of knowledge. The second task is the more neglected. It is here that theology comes to grips with the historical process. Without a growing grasp of the

218

dimension of depth in every technical discipline, our society must become increasingly schizophrenic — split between meaning and mechanism. The separation of meaning from mechanism means the end of creativity. The separation of Purpose from process is final frustration. The creative society of the future will be delayed or prevented as long as Purpose and process are held apart.

The second task seems to this writer the all-important necessity of the future. "One world" is a political cry in our time; even more, it is the theological alternative to futility. Relational theology has barely opened its eyes. Little work has related theology to contemporary political economy; this is the more grotesque when you consider that the modern social gospel is now seventy-five years old. Here and there theologians are aware of the problem; that is all you can say for our present achievement.

Similarly, insufficient work has related theology to the physical and biological sciences — in an age devoted to scientific discovery. Little work has related theology to sociology, to history, to psychology. Some work has related theology to literature and the fine arts, but current production is small. We are entering the Age of Relation, when the attempt will again be made to see life steadily and see it whole.

The question will be asked, Why has so little been done to relate individual sciences to depth and transcendence? Specialization is both virtuous and vicious. An increase in knowledge is accompanied by a decrease in relation. To understand theology is a lifetime occupation; to understand psychology is similarly a lifetime pursuit. To grasp their deep, dynamic, creative relation is a third lifework. How can any man do the work of three? It is clear why relational theology has made so little headway; the task is beyond the scope of a single life — even when attention is centered upon one technical discipline and its depth. To put it simply, there is work to be done — both in theology and the theology of relation. Perhaps time will show that the third lifework — the study of relation — must be undertaken from the beginning, even to the neglect or oversimplification of the fields to be related. The only other answer is this: with men relational theology is impossible, but with God all things are possible. To put it differently, the third lifework is impossible but imperative. The work must be done, whether or not it can be; it therefore will be done — by men not content to do less. It is obvious that it will not be done by any one man, though certainly not without him. Relational theology is clearly a relational task — a community enterprise. The Revised Standard Version of the Bible illustrates the method: 92 scholars from 42 denominations labored together with God, labored together with love, to make it available. They constituted a true, if miniature, communion of saints. The infinitely larger enterprise of relating theology to each technical discipline and to the total of modern life will require the mobilization of thousands of dedicated workers across all denominational divisions. Contributory work will undoubtedly be done by non-Christians — both theologians and technical scientists.

One can only shout, " On with the task! " That the task is understood and undertaken is itself a hopeful fact. Among men now laboring to relate theology on its own terms to psychology on its own terms are: David E. Roberts, Anton T. Boisen, Albert C. Outler, and, with greater attention to pastoral mechanics, Seward Hiltner and Russell Dicks. Where five are mentioned, a hundred are at work, and a thousand are needed.

Younger men who are grappling heroically with the relation of theology to history are Roger L. Shinn and Arthur M. Munk.

The relation of theology to modern education (the primary mission field in America) is dealt with by Bernard E. Meland, Bernard Iddings Bell, J. A. Martin, Jr., John A. Hutchison, and Cornelius Jaarsma. A nation of one hundred and fifty million ought to produce more explorers in the dark continent of public education than these heroic pioneers.

Among many who are probing the relation between theology and secular culture are: Emile Cailliet, Bernard Iddings Bell, Edwin E. Aubrey, and Chad Walsh. This enterprise is worthy of a Legion of Honor.

Following the lead of the father of the faithful, Lynn Harold Hough, two others are relating theology to " the best that has been thought and said ": Amos N. Wilder and Stanley Romaine Hopper.

May their tribe increase! It ought to be impossible for literary folk to consider themselves prepared for their work without careful attention to modern theology. Literature is the field of the idea; it *is* therefore theology, whether for good or ill. Not three but three thousand dedicated men are needed on this front.

The relation between theology and philosophy is as old as Plato, yet, strangely enough, only a few American theologians are engaged in this " third lifework ": Julian Victor Langmead Casserley, Charles Hartshorne, Edward J. Jurji, Theodore Greene, and William H. Bernhardt. Other forms of relational theology impinge on this field, but for each one now dedicated to theology's philosophical task a thousand are required.

The vital relation between theology and prayer calls for mass production, yet in addition to the labor of Nels F. S. Ferré, Douglas V. Steere, and Georgia E. Harkness, only Thomas S. Kepler is making the devotional method and meaning available for moderns.

One might take for granted the relation between theology and Protestant Confessional history, yet here also too little has been done. Important study is in process by Edward A. Dowey, Jr., Willard Dow Allbeck, Jaroslav Pelikan, and Abdel Ross Wentz. Obviously, the transcultural theological analysis of Hinduism, Mahayana and Hinayana Buddhism, and Islam, and of Greek, Russian, Roman, Lutheran, Calvinist, and Anglican Christian fragments, is still in the future.

The broad field between theology and missions is white unto the harvest, but the laborers are few: Henry P. Van Dusen, Edward J. Jurji, Edmund Davison Soper, William Owen Carver, Charles S. Braden, and Albertus Pieters.

Innumerable pastors and thinking laymen are relating popular theology to the American mind. This important undertaking is primarily a job of translation. C. S. Lewis at Oxford is making theology speak English; D. Elton Trueblood, Elmer G. Homrighausen, and Harry Emerson Fosdick, with distinct styles and motifs, are attempting the same task in America. The public relations department of theology is never adequately staffed.

One writer with breadth of vision and boundless optimism is

exploring the relation between theology and the long evolutionary future: E. Burdette Backus. Though a pantheist, praying to the fathomless universe, he is aware of the historical objective as few theists understand it. There is both charm and force in his work.

These names represent the active and significant labor now under way in the vast and neglected continent of relational theology. All together constitute no more than scattered light rays in the colossal darkness still to be invaded. Modern mechanisms of every sort, whether religious or secular, will add good works to faith — if faith can be found.

Where the task of relational theology is colorful and immediate, the work of theology-in-itself is quiet and permanent. Here also the harvest is plentiful but the laborers are few.

Strange that few Americans are specifically dedicated to the study of Christology. The subject is treated, of course, in many studies, but often as a tangent interest. Conrad J. I. Bergendoff, William R. Cannon, and Albert C. Knudson seem to have this field to themselves.

The specialized study of Christian ethics, including the domain of Christian political theory, has in the main been left to Paul Ramsay and Albert C. Knudson. This is clearly an undernourished enterprise in our time. The internal threat of American fascism and the external threat of Russian Communism now necessitate greater exertion toward ethical maturity — to advance the preaching and practice of democracy in the service of the human race.

The theological concept of the Kingdom of God has focused the attention of John Bright. However, the subject, in both present and eschatological dimensions, is worthy of an army of scholars.

Contemporary Americans seem largely allergic to the careful science of systematics. The comprehensive labor of L. Harold DeWolf is a long stride toward the future; the probing work of Richard Kroner, Joseph Haroutunian, and Hugh T. Kerr, Jr., is of help. Much more must be done in this area; in my view, systematic theology needs increasingly to become *humane* — to think exactly in terms relevant to history and available to the man in the street.

A wholly neglected study is the doctrine of the Holy Spirit. At the moment, only Nels F. S. Ferré seems engaged in this significant task — central to the self-understanding of the Christian community.

Theology's own self-examination is provided in the patient and rewarding work of Daniel Day Williams, Robert McAfee Brown, and Arthur C. Cochrane. To take stock of the best of theological self-criticism is to stimuate new venture on all fronts.

The study of theism, of theology proper, is ably advanced by Roger Hazelton, John Dillenberger, and Claude Welch. Clearly this constant task of the Church needs many dedicated minds — more than are now available.

The Bible itself, its critical sifting and creative use, always receives some attention, but never enough; usually the Bible is examined without skepticism or without faith, when both at their best are minimum necessities. The host of stout defenders of plenary and verbal inspiration suggests that America is especially susceptible to literalism: Louis Berkhof, Carl F. Henry, Cornelius Van Til, William Childs Robinson, Theodore Engelder, Wilbur M. Smith, Edward J. Young, Paul Jewett, Edward John Carnell, Bernard Ramm, Merrill Tenney, Merrill F. Unger, John R. Rice, and Oswald T. Allis.

Two younger theologians demonstrate the creative break-through to the Word of God in the words of Scripture: Joseph Sittler and Paul S. Minear. To rethink Paul and John and Luke and the greater prophets in terms of history and the future is the greatest need of our time. Where one labors, a thousand would be too few.

Others working at important tasks in the growing theological harvest are William T. Conner, Paul Lehmann, Carl Michaelson, Paul M. Robinson, Donovan Smucker, Kenneth Patton, and George F. Thomas.

The greatest hope in contemporary American theology lies not in particular achievements; our achievements are preliminary, preparatory, and premature. The real and wonderful hope is this: American theology has discovered its provincial and fragmentary character, has heard the call of God to hard work, the divine summons to patience, persistence, and perspiration; further, it has understood that theology is, and must be, a communal enterprise —